Media Literacy in Schools

Media Literacy in Schools

Practice, Production and Progression

Andrew Burn and James Durran

Paul Chapman Publishing

First published 2007

Paul Chapman Publishing
A SAGE Publications Company
1 Oliver's Yard
55 City Road
London EC1Y 1SP

SAGE Publications Inc
2455 Teller Road
Thousand Oaks, California 91320

SAGE Publications India Pvt Ltd
B 1/11 Mohan Cooperative Industrial Area
Mathara Road, Post Bag 7
New Delhi 110 044

SAGE Publications Asia – Pacific Pte Ltd
33 Pekin Street #02-01
Far East Street
Singapore 048763

Library of Congress Control Number: 2006940463

A catalogue record for this book is available from the British Library

ISBN-978-1-4129-2215-9
ISBN-978-1-4129-2216-6 (pbk)

Typeset by Pantek Arts Ltd, Maidstone, Kent
Printed in Great Britain by Athenaeum Press Ltd, Gateshead
Printed on paper from sustainable resources

CONTENTS

ACKNOWLEDGEMENTS

We are grateful to the students of Parkside Community College, Cambridge, and the teachers and support staff whose work is represented in this book, especially Jacqueline Billing, Emma Bull, Natalie Demain, Andrew Fisher, Jenny Griffiths, Craig Morrison, Kate Reed, Elaine Turnbull, Anne Spink, Fran Wilson, and Angela Webster. Also the students and teachers of Claydon Primary School, Ipswich, and colleagues in the primary Animation Project: Trish Sheil, Louise Spraggon, Lizzie Hobbs, and Andrew Lovett.

We would like to thank those who have read drafts of the book and given valuable advice: David Buckingham, Mark Reid, Jim Stewart, Steve Connolly, Kai Zhang, and Helen Fairlie, our editor at Paul Chapman.

We acknowledge with thanks the work of colleagues in the various research projects which inform the book, especially Diane Carr, Caroline Pelletier, Donna Burton-Wilcock, Jeff Woyda, Mark Reid, David Buckingham, David Parker, Sue Cranmer, Rebekah Willett, Shaku Banaji, Julian Sefton-Green, Barney Oram. In this respect, we also wish to acknowledge the support of the Arts and Humanities Research Council ('Textuality in Videogames'), the Economic and Social Research Council ('Making Games', RES-328-25-0001), the Department for Education and Skills (Best Practice Research Scholarships), the English and Media Centre (the 'Dubble' project), BECTa (Evaluation of the Digital Video Pilot Project), Creative Partnerships (Rhetorics of Creativity), and the Cambridge Film Consortium and Screen East (Evaluation of the Primary Animation Project).

We dedicate the book to the memory of our good friend and colleague Angela Webster, whose work was an inspiration to teachers and students, and whose support of the media specialism at Parkside was unstinting.

INTRODUCTION TO THE DVD

The DVD which accompanies this book contains films, animations and computer games made by students at Parkside Community College and partner schools between 1997 and 2006, as well as other resources useful to teachers in particular. It represents varied aspects of media production work since the school's designation as the first Media Arts specialist school in the UK in 1997.

The DVD is organised into chapters which follow the chapters of the book. Each chapter (except Chapters 1 and 9) contains the student work described and analysed in the book, as well as illustrations from the chapter, so that these can be viewed in colour. In addition, some chapters contain schemes of work showing how the various courses are planned; and also additional pieces of work where these might be interesting and relevant.

CHAPTER 2: SUPERHEROES

PICTURES
These are images of the comics designed by Year 8 students in the Superheroes course, so readers can see them in colour.
Figure 2.2, Super-Ellen, is the photo-story made by one group during the course.

SCHEME
Scheme of work for the Year 8 Comicstrip Superheroes course.

CHAPTER 3: ANIMATION

PRIMARY STOP-MOTION PACK
The Primary Stop-Motion Pack is a set of resources for primary school teachers to help make their own stop-motion animations. The ideas can easily be adapted to apply to the lower years of secondary school also. The sample films made by primary school children include those referred to in Chapter 3.

Flight to Freedom is the computer animation made by Year 6 students at Claydon Primary School, and described in detail in Chapter 3. The video file contains a documentary made by the class, describing how they made the film, as well as their completed animation.

PICTURES
These are images from Chapter 3: the storyboard from the Red Riding Hood animation; photos of the plasticine stop-motion animation; and stills from Claydon Primary School's film *Flight to Freedom*.

CHAPTER 4: HOSPITAL DRAMAS

PICTURES
Illustrations from Chapter 4, showing frames from Year 8 students' hospital dramas.

SCHEME
Scheme of work for the Year 8 Hospital Drama course.

VIDEOS
Example films by Year 8 students showing their hospital drama extracts.

CHAPTER 5: TEACHING HORROR

SCHEME
Scheme of work for Year 9 Horror Films course

ROBERT AND FAIZA PRESENTATION
Short film of a Powerpoint presentation about Psycho by two Year 9 students.

'GRABBING THE WEREWOLF: digital freezeframes, the cinematic still and technologies of the social'
An academic article by Andrew Burn, discussing young people's readings of digital images from horror films.

CHAPTER 6: SELLING CHOCOLATE

KIKA DUBBLE BRIEF
A brief for making an advert for the Fairtrade chocolate bar Dubble, by Kika Dixon, the product champion for Dubble. The full teaching pack for this project can be found in *The Media Pack: Units for GCSE English and Media*, published by the English and Media Centre, 2002.

SAMPLE STUDENT ADS
Examples of GCSE students' adverts for the Dubble chocolate bar.

CHAPTER 7: GAME-LITERACY

SCHEME
Scheme of work for the Year 8 computer games course.

PICTURES
Screen-grabs from Year 8 games analysed in Chapter 7, and made using the games authoring software *Missionmaker*.

CASTLE-QUEST
A game for English, based on Robert Browning's poem 'My Last Duchess'. The game was made by James, using Immersive Education's games authoring

software *Missionmaker*, and illustrates how the software can be used by teachers to construct game-based learning experiences. Download the Player application in order to open the Castle-Quest mission file. The pictures and PDFs in this folder show how the game was constructed.

STUDENT GAMES

Level 6 of Jimmie DeMora is the game level made by a pair of Year 8 students as part of the computer games course described in Chapter 7.

PLAYER APPLICATION

Download this piece of software in order to view the student games.

CHAPTER 8: THE HORIZONTAL ANGLE: MEDIA LITERACY ACROSS THE CURRICULUM

DANCE

Example films made by GCSE Dance students (described in detail in Chapter 8)

GEOGRAPHY

- Stop-frame animation of volcanoes made by Year 7 students (described in detail in Chapter 8)
- 'Defending the Coast': documentary about coastal erosion in North Norfolk made by GCSE students.

MATHS

Example animations made by Year 9 students using Macromedia's Flash, demonstrating mathematical concepts.

SCIENCE

Short films by students of scientific experiments (described in detail in Chapter 8)

ENGLISH

- Films of their own bilingual poems, by GCSE students
- Animated film of a scene from Macbeth, made by Year 10 GCSE students using *The Complete Animator*.

MODERN LANGUAGES

Animated film of 'meetings and greetings' in French, made using Kar2ouche, by Immersive Education.

EXTRA-CURRICULAR

- The Bare Blob Project – animated film based on the Garden of Eden, by an after-school animation club
- Duke of Edinburgh – a documentary made by students about a Duke of Edinburgh excursion
- School Song 2001 – winning entry for an annual college anthem competition, by Year 7 band Mundane Threat.

CHAPTER 10: BACK TO THE FUTURE: POSSIBILITIES AND PITFALLS FOR MEDIA LITERACY

PICTURES

Images of Babbage's Analytical Engine, Daguerre's Daguerrotype, and an Acorn Archimedes, illustrating Manovich's thesis of the histories of technologies of representation and of information-processing, converging in the multimedia computer.

School Song: RIDE. Video of a winning entry for the college anthem competition in 2000, edited by the band's drummer, whose work is referred to at the end of Chapter 10.

PREFACE

We write this book from the context of a school in which we have both worked: Parkside Community College in Cambridge, which was the first school in the UK to be designated a Media Arts College under the UK government's specialist schools programme, in 1997. Parkside, which has a history of generously accommodating reform and change, and has been in its time an Edwardian Central School for Boys and Girls, a girls' grammar school and a comprehensive school (since 1974), has been an exhilarating context in which to work. In socioeconomic terms, the student intake has a substantial proportion of middle-class students, although the proportion of children with special educational needs is 'broadly in line with the national average' (OFSTED, 2000). In addition, about 7% of students are from minority ethnic backgrounds, and up to twenty languages are spoken.

Since designation as a Media Arts College, we have explored with students a wide rage of media forms: comics, music videos, films, hospital dramas, horror films, computer games, sports TV programmes, news television, to name some. A sample of these different forms, and the literacies associated with them, form the subject of most of this book. We have also worked with colleagues in other subject areas to see how media forms and genres could be used in Music, Maths, Geography, History, Science, Modern Foreign Languages, Dance and Art; and we will describe and discuss in Chapter 8 how media literacy might operate in these subjects. Finally, we have evolved some idea of how media literacy in schools might develop through the five years of compulsory secondary schooling, the subject of Chapter 9.

Media Arts Colleges in the UK need, perhaps, further comment. The government's use, in this designation, of the word *Arts* indicates an emphasis on a desired trajectory from education into the creative industries, seen by New Labour in particular as a key element in the UK economy (Buckingham and Jones, 2001). In this respect, the initiative belongs to a rhetoric running through the era of New Labour in which creativity is defined as a regenerative force, with the ability to promote values of community and inclusiveness, develop collaborative, problem-solving approaches in the workplace and to create a workforce equipped for the creative industries and the hi-tech sector (Seltzer and Bentley, 1999).

We do not dissent entirely from this vision, except when it becomes a constraint. As we will explain later, our conception of creativity allows for a wider set of social and artistic purposes, including dissent, critique, subversion and self-representation, none of which obviously fit within the doggedly pro-social policy rhetorics of the New Labour policy formulation.

Similarly, the development of a group of Media Arts Colleges in the UK has had its own momentum, its own imperatives, its own interpretations of media education, media literacy and media arts, which, naturally, vary from school to school. It is fair to make one general point, however: the Arts emphasis has tended to shift the centre of gravity of media education in these schools away from its traditional home in English, towards the other Arts subjects. While it remains true that most media teachers in the UK are English teachers (QCA, 2005b), these schools have been active in promoting cross-curricular media work, especially in the Arts; and in synthesising media work, especially creative production, with the traditional pedagogies of Art, Music, Dance and Drama.

This emphasis may also explain some apparent gaps in our account. We do not, for instance, include any account of work on the news media, which we do not see as related to the media arts. Similarly, it is not yet clear to us that the Internet, whose primary importance for children and young people is communicative, is a distinct component of the media arts. While the authoring of web-pages does involve the aesthetic and compositional work we see as typical of media arts work, its primary significance in relation to the media arts is as a medium of exhibition (which we consider in relation to the distribution of student work). However, much of this may change in the future, and we consider possible developments, especially in relation to new media, in the concluding chapter.

Nevertheless, we are both English teachers by training. In this respect, we have always been close to the details of print literacy, and the cultural interests of the literature curriculum, though we would locate ourselves closer to the 'cultural analysis' model identified originally in the Cox report (DES, 1988) than any of the other models. However, the emphasis on a semiotic approach in this book can be traced back to our interest as English teachers in systems of signification: how they are used by children, and how they can be understood by them. No doubt this background will colour our account. However, we do not pretend to paint any kind of ideal, general picture of what media education *should* look like. On the contrary, we expect it to be richly diverse.

The account we give of our work represents an interrelation between research and practice. James still teaches at Parkside as an Advanced Skills teacher; Andrew lectures and researches at the Institute of Education in London, but worked as a teacher for 23 years before that, 17 of them at Parkside. While our current jobs produce inevitably different emphases, we have both always been involved in writing and research as well as teaching. Also, while our work has sometimes been focused inwards on the classroom, it has at other times been directed outwards, in dialogue with colleagues in the

UK, Europe, Australia, the United States, Korea, China, New Zealand. While this is inevitably a very local account of the learning and teaching of media literacy, we hope it will bear some traces of this wider dialogue.

This book, then, emerges from researched accounts of our work. Every chapter has involved some kind of reflective analysis, whether as part of large, funded research projects, or small, informal action research efforts. While the accounts of media literacy work here may serve as examples other teachers might want to explore in their own classrooms, they are also intended to show how practice and research intermingle. We hope, then, that they will suggest ways for teachers to think beyond instrumental models of the curriculum. For these purposes, we are not offering detailed templates, but rather suggestive accounts of what can be achieved and, as importantly, how we might think about what students get out of it. All the projects described here are, in principle, replicable without any need for expensive equipment or special resources.

The book is also intended to indicate to researchers how the daily detail of work in the classroom over long periods of time can feed into the analytical and theoretical processes of research.

We hope that our account will complement other books about media education which currently address important needs in this field. David Buckingham's *Media Education* (2003) gives a valuable overview of both the history and the current debates in this field. Julian McDougall's *The Media Teacher's Book* (2006) gives practical advice about how to develop programmes of media education. Our book, by contrast, gives an account of research and practice in one school over ten years or so. While it is a book about media education, its focus is on media literacy. We are looking through the lens of what the student is doing, making and learning, rather than the lens of what the teacher is doing. In practical terms, this means that most chapters in this book provide a descriptive account of the processes students go through in various projects, followed by an analysis of selections of their work. The final three chapters consider how media literacy can be addressed across the curriculum, how it can develop as students move up through secondary education, and what it might look like in the future.

We imagine that the readers of this book may be quite diverse. Among them will be teachers of specialist media courses, teachers of media within English and perhaps teachers of other subjects who use, or would like to use, the media and its associated technologies in the kinds of ways we describe. We have worked with many teachers in many different subject areas over the years, and hope that we can offer something of interest across many different contexts. We have also worked with teachers at many different stages of their careers. Some readers of this book may be newly qualified, or still in training, with elements of textual, cultural and media theory fresh in their minds from university courses, but keen to know how such knowledge can be mediated for the classroom. Others may be experienced teachers, with a wealth of class-room practice, interested in reflecting on the implications for schools of new media and the cultural practices associated with them.

Similarly, readers who work in academic research will, we know, have a range of different backgrounds and interests. Some may research the cultural lives of young people; some may be interested specifically in how young people engage with the media; others may be interested in the practice of media, literacy, ICT or arts education. We have tried to give some sense for this audience of the analytical and theoretical backgrounds which lie behind our accounts. We have also given ample references to more detailed or more technical accounts of the projects which have been the subject of specific research projects.

Finally, we know from experience that descriptions in words, even with illustrations, never do justice to the variety and inventiveness of media pro-duction work by young people. For this reason, the book is accompanied by a CD-ROM, which contains the pieces of work by students which Chapters 2 to 9 focus on. It also contains additional examples where appropriate, and other information, such as schemes of work.

WHAT IS MEDIA LITERACY?

IONA: If he killed spiders in the movie everybody wouldn't like him because he'd be a coldblooded killer. You have to keep Harry Potter as nice as possible.

OGEDEI: Yeah but Harry Potter's like sad, he's just like such a little, um, um, he's like a teacher's pet, he's just running around doing this stuff. ... I'd like it if he could get better spells –

IONA: Like Avadakedavra, the killing spell?

OGEDEI: No, like flame, like a flamethrower [*laughs*]

These two 13-year-olds are talking about Harry Potter in a research session which invited ten children to participate on the basis that they were familiar with the book (Rowling, 1998), film (Columbus, 2002) and computer game (Electronic Arts, 2002) of *Harry Potter and the Chamber of Secrets*. The conversation raises a number of issues about literacy generally, and media literacy specifically.

Literacy is *cultural*: these children are all involved, in different ways, with the cultural phenomenon of Harry Potter. They are intimately acquainted with the popular myth of Harry Potter, have invested time and energy in it, owe it various kinds of allegiance, see it as representative of values and ideas they find important.

Literacy is *critical*: it is about taste and pleasure, and the kinds of judgements these involve. For Iona, Harry's 'niceness' is appealing, and she sees him as an admirable figure, heroic and courageous. For Ogedei, 'he's like a teacher's pet', too good, too complicit with adult authority, too much like the kind of boy Ogedei increasingly doesn't want to be. This suggests that critical judgement, pleasure and taste are often intricately bound up with identity: our judgements and tastes are public expressions of the kind of person we are, we are becoming, we hope to be. There is also a conceptual grasp of how the text works: Iona's argument that Harry has to be 'as nice as possible' shows an understanding of his narrative role as hero, and how it connects with its audience, how they need sympathy for a protagonist. The understandings and judgements at work here roam across three media forms, finding both commonalities across them and critical differences between them.

Literacy is transformative and *creative*. It does not simply involve understanding a text – it involves, to different degrees – remaking that text. This always involves internal mental operations, to which teachers, psychologists, academics and literacy experts have no direct access. Their job begins the moment the transformative work becomes externalised, most immediately as speech, but later as writing, drama, visual design and so on. In this interview, though it appears to be about what we traditionally think of as response. Ogedei's last remarks give us a clue about the transformative process. He imagines Harry Potter with a flamethrower, a proper action hero instead of the lame substitute he perceives.

We have highlighted these features – *cultural, critical* and *creative* – because they are common to many emerging definitions of media literacy at the time we write this book and because, for that reason, we have adopted them within our own model of media literacy, which we outline in Table 1.1. Nevertheless, any attempt to clarify and simplify such a complex set of practices must also recognise how contested all definitions are, and how the various interests and perspectives of teachers, researchers and policymakers can pull in different directions.

What are teachers to make of this complex, shifting world of warring definitions, half-realised policies and widely divergent practices? We have taught, over the past ten years, many young people whose differing interests and needs make such abstract notions even more complex. Megan, who loved the textuality of the media, and at 15 showed around the vice-chancellor of a local university, explaining to him what film semiotics meant. Sam, who hated reading and writing, and was even bored and disillusioned by the challenges of digital video editing, but who knew the script of *Robocop* so well he could mouth the lines a split second before the onscreen characters uttered them. Alex, for whom the creative endeavour of digital video production was a passion, and who, at the time of writing, is studying for a degree in Media Studies at the University of Westminster.

Teaching is an oscillation between the complicated, lived experience of working with teenagers like these, and the distanced, reflective exploration of the principles that underlie how we work with them. We hope to throw some light on this oscillation as we work through the examples of media literacy represented in this book, emerging from our work with children and young people over the past ten years. We will present, in this chapter, a summative outline of our working model of media literacy. This provisional model incorporates many elements others have proposed, but with some changes of emphasis and some re-combination of different schema. For the sake of clarity, we make no attempt to include every possible element here, but select those which are most pertinent to our own work – media education in schools.

The term *media literacy* is in many ways unsatisfactory. As both Kress (2003) and Buckingham (2003) have pointed out, it is irrevocably related to language, it becomes something more metaphorical when applied to other media and it doesn't make sense in languages where the term used is even more literally print-related, as in the French term *alphabétisme*. Indeed, it simply does not translate into some other languages, so that educators outside the Anglophone world who wish to employ the concept sometimes use the phrase 'media literacy' in English.

However, we believe that the term is useful for three reasons. First, it is not easy to think of another term which would serve a similar purpose and be somehow more accurate. Such expressions as 'communicative competence' (Germany and Austria also have the term *Medienkompetenz*, for instance) emphasise functional skills at the expense of cultural factors. 'Literacy' implies cultural competence. It is something we use to claim membership of particular social groups, whether these be players of the online roleplaying game *World of Warcraft*, afficionados of the films of Ken Loach or the Harry Potter fan club. These kinds of affiliations may be rooted in claims of cultural value or in common experiences of pleasure, but they are all connected to social identities, and part of our efforts to be a particular kind of person moving in a particular kind of social world.

Secondly, media literacy is not simply (or not only) a metaphor, but draws attention to important connections between print literacy and the way people engage with the media. These connections are present at all points of the three-part conceptual structure media education is often seen to operate: *institution, text, audience*. Institutions imply the study of how media texts are produced, the political and economic contexts from which they emerge, the messages their producers intend them to convey. Texts suggest the 'languages' of the media: how they represent the world, how they use particular structures or grammars to form these representations, how they are composed. Audiences are, of course, the counterparts of producers, traditionally seen as consumers of media texts, and can be studied in terms of their social uses of the media, their tastes and pleasures and their interpretive strategies. This is a simple explanation of this three-part structure; needless to say, life is more complicated than this, and we will return to these ideas later. Institutions and audiences are typically not attended to by traditional literary studies in schools, but there is every reason to argue that they should be. Literature is produced by commercial publishing houses as well as authors, after all, and marketed in similar ways to films or computer games – indeed, as the Harry Potter example shows, such marketing may extend across a corporate franchise. Similarly, of course, literature addresses audiences, who make particular social uses of their reading, develop allegiances, even fan cultures, and build what reader-response theory calls 'interpretive communities'. In respect of the 'text' part of this structure, there are also important, literal, connections between print and other media. The conversation about Harry Potter, for instance, included a discussion of the system of 'person' in book, game and film. The point here is not to flatten out the different modes in question, but to explore how they all deal with the choices texts have between looking *at* a character in the fictional world, or looking at this world *through* that character's eyes. This involves seeing the common features here: books, games and films all have some equivalent of 'first-person' and 'third-person'. But it also involves seeing what is specific to each medium: a 'third-person' game, for instance, still involves being close to, and controlling, the protagonist, and so it has some 'first-person' characteristics. To be literate, then, involves understanding the grammar of a text, at least implicitly. It is interesting here that the Slovakian term for media literacy is *mediálna gramotnosť*, a term in which 'grammar' combines the idea of language structures with a broader concept of 'educatedness'.

Finally, 'media literacy' is a useful general shorthand for a complex set of phenomena which would otherwise be very difficult to talk about in the policy arena, which we must constantly keep in mind. Media literacy means something in the UK in the contexts of the National Curriculum, the BBC and OFCOM, the media super-regulator. Of course, it means something slightly different in all these cases, and something different again to media teachers; but the debate about what it means for children to learn about books, films, comics and computer games can at least take place under the general umbrella of media literacy. Beyond the UK, there is a long history of campaigning in Europe for recognition of the importance of media literacy by the member states of the European Union, while in the Anglophone world media literacy is a banner for campaigns for media education in Australia, New Zealand, Canada and (though rather differently inflected) the United States.

For all these reasons, we prefer, with the obvious qualifications, to keep the term *media literacy*, and this book is our way of elaborating how it can be made to mean something in practice and in research.

However, before moving on to look at more specific questions related to media literacy, some additional points need to be made. First, the notion of expanding the concept of literacy to apply to other modes of communication has been well rehearsed over the past ten years or so. In some ways this debate has been parallel to the debate about media literacy, linked with it but distinct.

It is best represented, perhaps, by the notion of *multiliteracies* (Cope and Kalantzis, 2000), which poses a notion of literacy broader than media literacy, in that it encompasses all semiotic modes; and also in that it relates literacy to new technologies, a point we will discuss in more detail in Chapter 10.

Media literacy, then, may be best conceived as a subset of multiliteracy, applicable to mass media forms in particular. Within media literacy, it is also possible to conceive of even more specific forms of literacy. There is a well-established notion of *moving image literacy* (Burn and Leach, 2004), as well as its variant, *cine-literacy*, proposed by the Film Education Working Group, and emphasising the cultural value of film (FEWG, 1999). By contrast, Buckingham proposed some time ago a notion of *television literacy*, encompassing the forms of critical 'reading' young people display in viewing television (Buckingham, 1993). Similarly, we have been engaged for three years in a research project one of whose aims is to develop a model of *game literacy* (Burn, forthcoming,). These 'literacies' can be seen as subsets of media literacy, just as media literacy can be seen as a subset of multiliteracy, or simply of 'literacy' more generally, in its expanded form.

These models are by no means straightforward or uncontested and we will explore some of them further in the course of this book. However, one final point about the adequacy of the literacy metaphor remains to be made. The idea of literacy persists partly because it often seems appropriate. Media forms often behave in ways comparable to print texts: marks are arranged on paper, or on timelines in editing software; the principles and processes by which these signs are selected and combined often look like a kind of writing. These forms of composition seem to require certain skills, and they result in the making of meaning through practices of inscription, like writing. Similarly, they can be 'read' – the signs can be decoded, the texts can be analysed, the forms of representation can be understood, engaged with, enjoyed in ways analogous to the reading of print in general and literature more specifically.

However, there are times when the literacy metaphor seems less appropriate. Sometimes the process of meaning-making and composition does not obviously resemble the fixity of print. While editing digital video can feel like making a filmic 'sentence', using a camera to film the footage in the first place can feel much more fluid, much more improvisatory, much more like taking part in a performance. Making a media text often literally involves performance. Young people play dramatic roles in the videos they make; they use dramatic voices for animated and computer game characters; they play roles using game avatars.

These forms of communication and representation resemble print literacy less than they resemble traditions of oral composition and performance. The scholar of language, literacy and literature, Walter Ong, laments the demise of oral traditions as print literacy comes to dominate the cultures of developed societies; but he also argues that residues of oral culture persist, and even transmute into new forms through new technologies of communication, a phenomenon he terms 'secondary orality' (Ong, 1982). This notion has been developed to account for forms of speechlike writing in new media, characterised again by improvisation, immediacy and ephemerality (Lanham, 1993). The differences between written and oral modes of communication are memorably represented by the linguist M.A.K. Halliday:

> The complexity of the written language is its density of substance, solid like that of a diamond formed under pressure. By contrast, the complexity of spoken language is its intricacy of movement, liquid like that of a rapidly running river. To use a behavioural analogy, the structure of spoken language is of a choreographic kind. (1989: 87)

We aim to keep Halliday's metaphor firmly in view. Where the literacy metaphor is most apt, whether at a general or a specific level, we will develop it. However, where the engagement with, or making of, a media text seems better described in terms of dramatic performance, roleplay, improvisation and dialogue, we will invoke the idea of orality.

EVOLVING MODELS OF MEDIA LITERACY

Notions of media literacy, and the processes of media education that aim to develop such literacy, are well-developed, not least in Buckingham's comprehensive account *Media Education* (2003). In the UK, the British Film Institute has also been influential in developing models of media literacy, and more specifically a subset that focuses on film, which they have termed cine-literacy (FEWG, 1999). We will explore this subset more closely in Chapter 5.

However, the notion of media literacy exists beyond the world of media studies and media education. In recent years it has developed a high profile in policy arenas around the world, essentially in response to the growth of new media. In many parts of the Anglophone world, ideas of media literacy are often well-established in school curricula, and typically located in English, literacy or language arts sections of the curriculum. In Europe, the idea of media literacy is receiving unprecedented attention as we write, reflected in the establishment of a media literacy initiative by the European Commission. The consultant group supporting this move emerges from many different national contexts. In some cases, Italy and France, for instance, these began with national traditions of film culture. They are all moving, however, at different rates, towards a recognition of the need for children to learn about all media, of children's immersion in media cultures and of the growth of new media, especially computer games and the Internet. In our view, there is a danger that the prime function of media education – learning *about* the media – becomes confused with the new possibilities of e-learning, which is something quite different – learning *through* the media (Buckingham, 2003). We will return to this question in the final chapter. Nevertheless, this new urgency for the development of Europe-wide common approaches to media literacy is obviously welcome.

In the UK, the new super-regulator OFCOM has a remit to develop media literacy. Shortly after its formation in 2004, it published a consultation paper with a draft definition of media literacy, and subsequently decided on a three-part working definition, derived from earlier models (e.g. Aufderheide, 1997): *Access, Understand, Create* (OFCOM, 2005). In many respects this is a positive development for media educators in the UK. It represents the first solid policy commitment to the importance of media literacy, indicated in advance of a seminar in London by the words of then Culture Secretary Tessa Jowell:

> I believe that in the modern world media literacy will become as important a skill as maths or science. Decoding our media will be as important to our lives as citizens as understanding great literature is to our cultural lives. (UK Film Council press release, January 2004)

Furthermore, the inclusion in OFCOM's model of the 'create' element shows a welcome recognition of creative production as part of media literacy, which is a central theme of this book.

There are, however, some criticisms to be made of the OFCOM model. In their policy paper on media literacy (OFCOM, 2005) there is a recurrent emphasis on the function of digital media to provide information, and a corresponding neglect of functions such as narrative, fantasy, roleplay, social networking, which are arguably the functions most important to young people, and the functions we emphasise in this book. By the same token, the emphasis on information erodes the cultural aspects of media literacy: the word 'culture' appears nowhere in this paper. By contrast, we see media literacy as invariably culturally located. In some ways these restrictions are consequent upon OFCOM's general brief, which does not include all media: print media, film and computer games (except, perhaps, as online activities) are beyond its remit.

Debates about media literacy, then, reveal both consensus and division. On the one hand, there is a wide degree of consensus about what media literacy is at a general level, in particular that it involves both a critical understanding of media texts as well as a creative ability to produce them. This consensus is now well-established in the UK, and to some extent in Europe.

On the other hand, there is considerable debate about more specific aspects of what media literacy might be. Its cultural dimension means for some countries a promotion of heritage film culture, for others a commitment to popular culture across different media. The nature of 'critical understanding' varies between a suspicious, critical reading of information media to a more appreciative reading of the aesthetic properties of audiovisual texts. The emphasis on production is stronger in some versions, weaker in others; and the nature and purpose of this kind of 'creativity' differs widely from one interpretation to another. The relative importance of different media forms varies between stakeholders: for policymakers at the present time, the perceived opportunities and threats of the Internet are central; for advocates of particular media, such as the BFI, their institutional commitment to moving image culture is crucial; for representatives of media industries, whether print media or computer games, their commercial imperative provides the focus.

What we hope to achieve with our model (Table 1.1) is, first, an accommodation with the most popular current approaches. The central 'trunk' which we identified at the beginning of this chapter – cultural, creative, critical – is deliberately aligned with an emerging consensus in Europe about the key features of media literacy (these features are emphasised in Table 1.1). However, we want to elaborate this model in certain ways. The cultural contexts on the left are drawn from the academic tradition of Cultural Studies, which has been influential in the UK in explaining how people engage with the media, and, indeed, on how the function of media education in schools has been understood. On the right, what we have called semiotic processes are largely derived from the tradition of social semiotics which has influenced thinking about language and literacy in the Anglophone world.

Needless to say, this model looks a lot neater than the ragged messiness of actual practice. It does not represent a rigid orthodoxy we have enacted over the past ten years. Rather, it is an analytical tool, an attempt to pull together, describe and explain what we have tried to do in teaching and research, and what the children we have taught have produced and learnt. Its neatness belies persistent uncertainties, continuing aspirations, risky improvisations and the ever-present unpredictability of how teenagers use and engage with the media.

In this spirit, we will move on to explain our thinking behind this model, around which the rest of the book is structured.

TABLE 1.1 Media literacy: a cultural-semiotic model

Cultural contexts	Social functions	Semiotic processes
Lived	**Cultural**	Discourse
Selective	**Creative**	Design/Production
Recorded	**Critical**	Distribution
		Interpretation

Cultural contexts

Thirteen years ago, in *Cultural Studies Goes to School* (1994), David Buckingham and Julian Sefton-Green argued that the insights of Cultural Studies needed to be applied to the purpose and practice of media education, and gave examples of how this might work.

In many ways our book is a successor to Buckingham and Sefton-Green's. Like theirs, it is written by a teacher and an academic, working for a synthesis of practice and research (but also productively confusing the two categories). Like theirs, it argues the case for popular culture as a legitimate field of study. Like theirs, it exemplifies a model of media education which now attracts a wide international consensus. And, like theirs, it recognises the contribution made by the Cultural Studies tradition to our understanding of the ways in which people engage with the media, and the significance of the texts they themselves make. Cultural Studies here refers generally to the academic discipline usually seen as beginning in Britain with the establishment in the 1970s of the Centre for Contemporary Cultural Studies (CCCS) at Birmingham University.

Culture is a paradoxical idea in education. On the one hand, schools are full of it. Parkside, like many schools, abounds in music, from madrigal groups to rock bands; it holds art shows in local pubs, dance and drama shows, school plays and talent shows, which showcase the widest variety of creative forms imaginable, from rap to piano compositions based on the computer game *Final Fantasy 10*. In addition, it promotes the media arts, through animation, film-making, computer game authoring and a variety of multimedia work.

On the other hand, the idea of culture is curiously absent in the documents of the UK's National Curriculum. In the provision for the 14–16 age group, for example, culture in Art and English seems to mean, effectively, what has in the past been called multiculturalism: attention to 'different cultures and traditions' (QCA, National Curriculum programme of study for EN2, Reading). There is no sense of the pervasiveness of popular culture in the lives of young people, and no sense of all art, language and literature as cultural.

So it is still an urgent task for media education to argue for the place of popular culture in schools. Cultural Studies has been, in its short life, preoccupied with the politics of popular culture, presenting it as the culture of an oppressed working class, at one moment a consolation in the leisure breaks of industrial labour, at another a transformative force in which people can use its symbolic resources to make a better life. Its classical studies of the so-called 'spectacular' youth subcultures of postwar Britain, from Teddy boys to punk (Clarke et al., 1976), have more recently given way to less deterministic theories of youth culture, which pay attention to its fragmentary, fluid nature and to the relationship between global and local cultures (Thornton, 1995; Bennett, 2000). We will revisit these later formulations in subsequent chapters. However, in our model of media literacy we want to return to first principles, and one of the founding thinkers of Cultural Studies, the cultural and literary theorist Raymond Williams.

Williams proposed a three-part view of culture which we consider appropriate for media education, and which forms the first part of our model. Williams was one of the first thinkers in the tradition of English literary studies to take a largely positive view of popular culture, from comics to television. He conceived of this in the context of a 'lived culture', a social definition of culture 'in which culture is a description of a particular way of life, which expresses certain meanings and values not only in art and learning but also in institutions and ordinary behaviour' (Williams, 1961: 41). It is this which has led to the close attention to popular culture in the Cultural Studies tradition, which in turn has informed the practices of media education.

Alongside the lived culture, Williams identified two other levels: the culture of the 'selective tradition' and the 'recorded culture'. The first of these he saw as the product of a gradual process to build ideal and universal cultural values. The second, he proposed, was the process by which the study of culture attempted to reconstruct a partial picture of the lived culture of a former society through the documentary record.

The culture of the selective tradition poses problems, of course, in the light of long battles in recent years over canonicity in the English curriculum in particular: the resistance by many teachers to imposed canons of literary texts which are often traced back to the 'Great Tradition' promoted by F.R. Leavis and his associates (Leavis, 1948), whose stance Williams was firmly opposing. Traditionally, both media education and Cultural Studies have dismissed the selective tradition, identifying it with elite culture, and with the oppressive function of dominant social groups. For us, however, the selective tradition needs to be considered by teachers and students, though not because it represents 'certain absolute or universal values', as Williams argued. Rather, we adopt the account of Hodge and Kress (1988), who argue that culturally valued texts become so through a historical accretion of competing commentary. It is this continuing process which, we believe, students can benefit from taking part in. In the context of media education, the 'selective tradition' can be seen over a relatively short timescale. For instance, in Chapter 5 we will look at what it means for students now to work on Hitchcock's *Psycho*, once a popular shocker, now a revered cult classic.

The notion of the recorded culture offers the possibility of cultural history as an approach to be used in media education. Media literacy is sometimes presented as if it only applies to the contemporary moment, and is apparently a-historical; the OFCOM document, for instance, contains only references to the electronic media of its particular historical moment. However, media literacy is, for us, inconceivable without history. And the personal history of an individual merges indistinctly into the history of a decade, a half-century; and by extension into family history, a century. The Masters' students we teach at the Institute of Education are sometimes asked to construct a 'media autobiography', which throws up personal involvement in the history of punk music, Gothic lifestyle, French ska, 80s New Romantic music and so on. Similarly, in our work at Parkside we have encountered young people who have learned from their grandparents how to use a Playstation, who have re-discovered the music of Jimi Hendrix, or who have developed an interest in the 1930s horror films of Universal studios. All of these examples show how the 'recorded culture' of the past can be rediscovered, revalued, profitably researched, even reintegrated in 'retro-cultural' elements of the 'lived culture'. In our view, then, the recorded culture is not necessarily the desiccated record of vanished communities (though the greater the distance in time, the more it becomes so). Rather, the recorded culture is intimately related to the contemporary moment: it is the history out of which the lived culture emerges.

These, then, are the cultural contexts we borrow from Williams – the landscapes, backdrops, broad accounts of different approaches to culture we consider important and legitimate. The question of *why* these cultures are important and *what* people do with them in the context of media literacy forms part of our next category: social functions.

Social functions

What we have called social functions, which we want to see as central to our model, echoes the '3-Cs' model of media literacy we have referred to above, and which is gaining popularity as we write. For instance, a Charter for Media Literacy produced by a Media Literacy Task Force in the UK (representing broadcasters and relevant agencies, including the BFI and the UK Film Council) presents an outline of media literacy which emphasises cultural, critical and creative functions. A version of this charter is currently being distributed by a Europe-wide campaign. In the field of academic literacy studies, there is a long tradition in Australia of similar models, such as Green (1988), which argues for a three-part model: operational, cultural and critical.

Media literacy, then, has a *cultural function*: it is about the cultural practices in which we engage. These are too various to rehearse here: the academic tradition of Cultural Studies has focused on media cultures such as those we look at in this book, but also on cultural practices as diverse as clothing, body-piercing and skateboarding. Media cultures, in this sense, are only a part of a much wider cultural landscape.

The cultural practices of media literacy also have a wide range of purposes and we will explore these in subsequent chapters as they apply to students and teachers working together. Here, we will emphasise one, because it is so pervasive and so important in the contexts of young people and learning: the development of identity. Buckingham and Sefton-Green relate the interpretation and making of texts to cultural contexts in which the tastes, pleasures and critical opinions of young people are developed, and along with them, their sense of self, which Buckingham and Sefton-Green theorise in characteristically post-structuralist terms as multiple and shifting, diverse and contradictory (1994: 30). In the same kind of way, we will see engagement with the media as part of wider cultural complexes of taste, pleasure and critical engagement, in which social identities are built and negotiated. A conception of selfhood useful in relation to media literacy is the one proposed by Jerome Bruner. Bruner's position, from the perspective of what he describes as 'cultural psychology', is that we need to pay attention to two central aspects of selfhood. First, 'the meanings in terms of which Self is defined both by the individual and by the culture in which he or she participates'. Second, 'the practices in which "the meanings of Self" are achieved and put to use' (Bruner, 1990: 116). This allows for a conception and study of identities which are *negotiated* (between the individual and the culture) and *distributed* (throughout the individual's cultural world and its other inhabitants). An apt metaphor for media educators might be the UK television gameshow *Who Wants to be a Millionaire?* Success here depends not on knowledge as a hermetically sealed repository inside the skull of the individual contestant. Rather, memory, guesswork and informed hunches are integrated with dialogue with others in the show's 'lifelines': 'Ask the Audience', and 'Phone a Friend'.

The examples we use in later chapters of media production work by young people can be seen in terms of Bruner's negotiated and distributed selfhood. Sometimes they are obvious 'practices of self', such as Sophie's comicstrip superheroine in Chapter 3, which experiments with fantasy projections of self. At other times they represent the tastes, interests, pleasures, knowledge and expertise which contribute to selfhood and the social identities which, in adolescence, are such malleable constructions, like items in a drama wardrobe, tried on for size. While literate practices, even broadly defined as work with image as well as text, game as well as video, multimedia as well as print, are obvious tools for the construction of such experimental identities, the wardrobe metaphor reminds us again that literacy is not always the best image. In many ways this kind of self-representation is more like the kind of dramatic performance proposed by Erving Goffman (1959).

Bruner raises another question in his consideration of self: the question of *agentivity*, or agency: the extent to which the individual has control over his or her identity, cultural circumstances, forms of social action, ideas and beliefs. The idea of agency leads easily enough into the second of our social functions of media literacy: *creative functions*. An essential element of our idea of creativity is the capacity of the creative act to transform the creator. In making something valuable, worthwhile, new, we change our sense of ourselves, whether through representing some aspect of ourselves in what we have made, or in our altered sense of what we can do. We want to indicate a change of priorities in placing the creative function of media literacy before the critical function. Traditionally, it has always seemed the other way round: we read the media before we make the media; we develop a critical understanding which we then consolidate by making our own texts. Indeed, media education historically develops from literary studies, which is a purely analytical discipline with no interest in creative production.

However, in recent years there has been a marked shift in emphasis from *critique* to *production*. Influential research in the practice of media education has reflected this, including *Cultural Studies Goes to School* and later work by the same authors (Buckingham et al., 1995; Sefton-Green 1999; Buckingham, 2003), as well as by others, such as McDougall's account of media education practice (McDougall, 2006), a series of BFI studies in production work (Parker, 1999; Sefton-Green and Parker, 2000) and our own work (Burn and Reed, 1999; Burn et al., 2001; Burn and Durran, 2006). This shift is influenced by many factors, most importantly changing attitudes to the relations between production work and analytical work, the advent of accessible and affordable digital authoring tools (which we explore in following chapters and a closer association between media education and the Arts, especially in the context, in the UK, of Media Arts specialist schools like Parkside. In this book, then, the emphasis is strongly on creative production, out of which different forms of critical understanding can emerge.

From the semiotic viewpoint we will explore in relation to the third component of our model, creativity is about the three overarching functions of all forms of cultural production: representation, communication and the composition of coherent texts. However, it also relates to current debates about the nature of the creative act in relation to education. In this respect, creativity is a vague and confused term, variously appearing as post-Romantic conceptions of artistic genius (Scruton, 1987), psychological accounts of the cognitive mechanisms of creative thought (Boden, 1990), cultural notions of 'grounded aesthetic work' (Willis, 1990), or policy notions of the collaborative problem-solving skills necessary for new kinds of workforce (Leadbeater, 2000). Our approach to creativity draws on the work of the Russian psychologist, Lev Vygotsky, for whom the creativity of children was closely related to play (Vygotsky, [1931] 1978, 1998). In playful activity, children learn the meaning of symbolic substitution through the manipulation of physical objects: so a broomstick becomes a horse, to use Vygotsky's example. These symbolic understandings become internalised and develop into the mental processes which generate creative work. We will explore (particularly in Chapter 2, in the context of children's animation work) how such creative work draws on children's cultural resources, how it depends on social forms of learning, and how creativity is linked to intellectual development, rather than being something mysteriously separate from it.

Bruner's notion of agency also leads into the third of our social functions: the *critical functions* of media literacy. A greater degree of agency would seem to depend on a greater ability to read texts critically. Like Bruner, Buckingham and Sefton-Green tread a careful path in their consideration of the autonomy of young readers. They point to the dangers of one tendency of Cultural Studies, to celebrate the power of readers to turn media texts to their purposes. This kind of cultural populism paralyses any form of cultural politics – if all readers are automatically capable of critical and transformative reading there is no further debate to be had about the power of media messages and the media industries. Similarly, there is no further role for education.

However, while recognising this danger, it is important not to lose one of the central benefits of the Cultural Studies tradition, which is to focus attention on the real audiences of soap operas, disco music, horror comics, punk, hip-hop and other popular forms, demonstrating empirically that these audiences are far from the 'passive dupes' of the media assumed by earlier thinkers and educators.

This debate is still with us. Buckingham and Sefton-Green have more recently presented an account of how children engage with the media, in which they frame the question in terms of the classical sociological opposition between structure and agency (Buckingham and Sefton-Green, 2004). Drawing on the outcomes of an international research project looking at how children engaged with the cross-media craze of Pokémon, they argue that neither structure nor agency should be emphasised. Children's identities, beliefs and behaviour are not automatically determined by structures of political and economic power, ideology, language or history. On the other hand, neither can we assume that they have complete control over the influences all these forces exert. The project produced evidence of children's critical and purposeful interpretations and transformations of Pokémon texts; but it also recognised that children do not always 'read through' the persuasive sales techniques built into this franchise, or its representations of childhood, culture and ethnicity.

We believe this middle path is the only sensible one. All children are different, and their experience of media cultures varies considerably, as do the processes of mentoring and informal pedagogy they have received from peers and parents. In some cases, the structures of textual messages may affect what they think and believe; in others, they may not. The kind of critical reading Buckingham and Sefton-Green are aiming for remains the kind we want: it allows for pleasure, for contingency, for negotiation of meanings in social groups and in classrooms, for diversity of taste and experience. It does not seek to police meaning or taste, but rather to open them to debate.

Critical literacy is usually seen as opposing and supplanting the critical practice of literary studies in the first half of the twentieth century, and in
particular the work of Leavis, which is seen to emphasise a select canon of
culturally valued works, refined processes of cultural distinction and
approaches to texts which largely ignored their social and political circumstances. By contrast, notions of critical literacy arising from philosophical and
sociolinguistic approaches to language, discourse and power (Foucault, 1976;
Fairclough, 1989) have rejected the focus on aesthetic qualities, substituting the
need for critical questioning of 'who constructs the texts whose representations
are dominant in a particular culture at a particular time; how readers come to
be complicit with the persuasive ideologies of texts; whose interests would be
served by such representations and such readings ...' (Morgan, 1997).

These kinds of critical practice see texts and those who produce and receive
them as rhetorical systems, a stance which can be traced back to the Greek
philosopher Aristotle. Aristotle's *Rhetoric* lays the foundations of many of the
practices which critical literacy proposes today. It suggests that rhetoric has
ethos (how believable its speaker is), *pathos* (how moved the audience feels)
and *logos* (the structures and meanings of the words themselves). This tripar-
tite structure is remarkably similar to modern notions of media literacy and
critical literacy such as the one described by Morgan; and indeed, modern
notions of institutional context and the importance of audience can be found
in current models of rhetorical studies (Bigum et al., 1998; Andrews and
Haythornthwaite, 2007).

On the other hand, the emphasis in literary studies on aesthetic form and
effect can be seen as deriving from Aristotle's *Poetics*. It proposes notions of
genre, form, performance and audience engagement which can still be dis-
cerned in recent debates on these topics. Most importantly, however, it
proposes the category of the *aesthetic* – though very differently to the modern
understanding. For Aristotle, *aisthesis* meant the sensory perception of a work
of art – almost the opposite of the rarefied, refined, chilly kind of appreciation
we more usually associate with 'high art'. This curious reversal is well represented by the German philosopher Immanuel Kant, whose *Critique of
Judgement* saw aesthetic distinction as a refined faculty in which one could be
educated. This form of judgement has been roundly critiqued by the sociologist Pierre Bourdieu (1984), who accuses Kant of disguising the exclusive
cultural tastes of his own (bourgeois) social class as a universal form of aesthetic judgement. Bourdieu opposes this aesthetic of the 'pure gaze' to the
visceral vitality of popular cultural tastes, legitimising the latter in terms
which have been highly influential in the study of popular culture and its audiences. Needless to say, in rejecting the universality of cultural judgement
proposed by Kant, Bourdieu emphasises how cultural taste is determined by
specific social and historical conditions, such as our family, education and,
above all, our social class.

But what might these rather elevated and abstract ideas mean in the context of young people and the media? A good example is popular horror. In Chapter 5 we give an account of a course based on horror films, in which, like Bourdieu, we aim to take this disreputable popular genre seriously, to explore young people's interest in it, and to recognise its appeal to the senses (Aristotle's *aisthesis*) as well as the intellect. A few years ago, we used an episode of the popular teenage horror series *Buffy the Vampire Slayer* with Year 8. This provoked a complaint from two parents, who said that their son was being corrupted by this experience. When we asked them to be more specific about their objection, they argued that the episode contained supernatural elements and was morally ambiguous. When we pointed out that, in the following year, their son would be studying Shakespeare's Macbeth, of which the same arguments could be made, it became clear that their arguments were in fact a rationale for a much less rational judgement: one of cultural taste. Our view, then, was that Buffy represented the vitality and immediacy of popular culture, which Bourdieu celebrates as dynamic and energetic. However, we also believe that the apparent opposition here between Shakespeare and Buffy is a sterile one: we do not need to choose, but can have both.

We propose, then, that media literacy requires something of both these approaches. It needs the 'suspicious' critical reading of the *Rhetoric*, but also the 'appreciative' reading of the *Poetics*. The two, of course, are connected. The exercise of aesthetic judgement, linked in Bourdieu's account to the distribution of power through social class and education, is never a neutral affair. On the other hand, the exploration of cultural taste and judgement in the classroom may seem less like class warfare than it once might have done. The inclusion of comicstrips, computer games and horror films as legitimate content for the curriculum, alongside Shakespeare, Dickens and Milton, sounds like a classic confrontation between elite and popular art. However, these old binary oppositions have lost at least some of their force, not least in what Connor calls the 'pick 'n' mix aesthetic' of the postmodern era (Connor, 1990). Baz Luhrmann's *Romeo + Juliet* successfully replaces 'bardolatry' with the MTV aesthetic; Dickens can be viewed through the medium of popular musical and film; Milton's epic themes are rehearsed in contemporary children's literature such as Philip Pullman's *His Dark Materials* trilogy (1995–2000). Meanwhile, popular art forms – even computer games! – are increasingly well represented in the 'respectable' critical discourses of journalistic review and the academy.

Semiotic processes

The third segment of our model takes us into the nuts and bolts. If media literacy allows us to engage in cultural practices through which we make sense of and take control of our world and ourselves, in expressive practices in which we represent ourselves and our ideas, and in critical practices in which we interpret what we read, view, play, then the final question is *how* does all this take place?

The tools which make our cultural, expressive, interpretive work possible are *semiotic* tools. Media literacy operates through systems of signification, or sign systems. This is, of course, indisputable – it is clear that the words of language, or the moving images of film, television and games, belong to different signifying systems. The problem arises when we try to find a coherent system which will somehow account for all the media we might want to include in our notion of media literacy.

To return again to the example at the beginning of this chapter, if we want a model of media literacy which can somehow account for how children engage with the Harry Potter story across book, game and film, we need something beyond language. The study of sign systems, as is well known, begins with (amongst others) the Swiss linguist Ferdinand de Saussure (1983), who forecast a general science of semiology, in which language would become merely one among many systems of signification. Over the twentieth century many attempts were made to apply the systems of de Saussure and others to a variety of media, especially to the moving image. Some of the more productive of these attempts are still widely used by media studies teachers today.

However, the picture is patchy, to say the least. We do not believe that a coherent idea of what media texts are or how they might be interpreted exists in the tradition of media education, although all influential models of media education require an understanding of the 'languages' of the media. In our view, these 'languages' consist at present of a confused bundle of interpretive practices, mostly from the structuralist semiotics of the sixties and seventies. In our view, a semiotic approach is needed, but it needs to be rationalised, to be extended to cater for new media and to be integrated with the emphasis of Cultural Studies on real audiences and the cultural contexts in which they live.

The approach represented in our model is derived from the tradition of *social semiotics* (Hodge and Kress, 1988; van Leeuwen, 2005). This tradition emerges partly from earlier semiotics, especially that of Barthes; but also from traditions of sociolinguistics, which have been particularly influential in the study of literacy, especially in Australia, New Zealand and the UK (Halliday, 1985). Social semiotics proposes a functional view of all acts of signification. All texts are seen to fulfil three social functions: *representational, interactive, organisational* (there are various versions of this triad; this is our own 'remix'). These overarching functions mean, in the case of our concern with media, that all media texts will: *represent* the world in some way; *communicate* with audiences; and be *organised* in systematic ways as coherent and cohesive messages. The function of the last is primarily to serve the other two.

To return again to Harry Potter, then, to be fully literate across these three media, we might want this group of teenagers to:

- Understand how Harry *represents* certain ideas and values, through a system of narrative; and how narrative actions are differently possible in a book, a film and a computer game
- Engage with these media, and understand how they differently locate and address their audiences, what different possibilities there are for *interaction* with the world of the text, and how these kinds of engagement might work for other audiences
- Understand how these texts are *organised* to present coherent meanings, through different 'grammatical' systems, but with certain common principles.

However, the means by which these kinds of understanding can be explored is not necessarily (or only) through abstract analytical approaches. It might be, as we have argued above, by making their own text: writing the first chapter of a new Harry Potter novel; storyboarding or filming a scene from a new film; designing a new Harry Potter computer game.

This example also makes clear that our experience of media texts, whether 'reading' them or making them, is not by any means a simple, one-off event. Rather, it is a series of processes, which a social semiotic approach encourages us to unpack. This unpacking is valuable, not only for analytical reasons – it reveals buried layers of meaning and motivation behind the meaning – but also because of learning, which takes place, sometimes slowly and gradually, throughout these processes.

Our image of the semiotic process is borrowed again from a social semiotic model. Kress and van Leeuwen propose a scheme of four strata: *discourse, design, production, distribution*. To these, we have added *interpretation*, which forms the subject of another part of their book (Kress and van Leeuwen, 2001). These strata are offered by Kress and van Leeuwen as a model of *multimodal* communication: that is, they are intended to apply across all semiotic modes (such as visual design, language, music, the moving image). The development of multimodality theory is in one sense an attempt to realise Saussure's original vision of a general science 'which studies the role of signs as a part of social life', and within which language would merely be one among many signifying systems (Saussure, 1983: 15). From another point of view, however, it is the logical counterpart of the 'multiliteracies' approach referred to above. If we are to be seen as 'literate' in different modes and media, then we need some kind of analytical approach to understand what kinds of text such literacies engage with.

We will explore how these strata might work in relation to children's anima-tion work in Chapter 3. For the moment, the following brief account is enough.

Discourse: Kress and van Leeuwen define discourse as 'knowledge of (some aspect of) reality'. We can see discourses as related to genres, so that human knowledge of some aspect of reality, whether large and grand (such as warfare, or the Gothic imagination) or small and domestic (such as domestic chores or homework) will always be coded in particular communicative patterns. We see discourse, not just as the precursor to any act of meaning-making (though it is always that), but also as a pervasive medium which completely surrounds it; all aspects of the making of a text are discursively situated and informed.

Design: Design is the choice of mode. To tell a story you need to decide whether it will be told orally, or in writing, or perhaps as a visual narrative. Mode here means an individual signifying system. Multimodality theory, however, proposes that particular media forms integrate different modes: film integrates language, the moving image, music, visual design, dramatic action; comics integrate visual design and written language; and so on.

Production: Production involves the choice of medium. Modes are always realised through material media – once we have decided to tell a story in words we have to decide whose voice will tell it; if we write it, we have to decide on the material tools for the writing (fountain pen or word processor), the visual design of the writing, the paper on which it will be printed, and so on. These choices are not insignificant afterthoughts, but part of what makes the text mean what it does, and can affect the process of textual production significantly. The introduction of electronic media goes much further, not simply adding another set of material resources, but changing the nature of representation in profound ways, a question we will return to in Chapter 10.

Distribution: Texts can be distributed in many ways, sometimes through complex technologies, which can reproduce, disseminate, re-design, transform in many different ways. In the case of commercial media texts, how they are distributed forms part of the conceptual framework of media literacy, in which we might feel it important for students to understand how TV scheduling works, or how films are distributed to different kinds of cinema which affect how they are presented and viewed. In the case of students' own media texts, a rather different set of questions apply: what kinds of distribution, publication, exhibition are possible? Again, the arrival of digital media opens up a wider range of possibilities here, in which teenagers might exhibit their work on *YouTube* or *MySpace*, on their school website or on portable formats and platforms.

Interpretation: Interpretation is a *dialogic* process – it faces two ways. It is the process through which we understand the media texts we encounter, from an informal chat with friends as we emerge from the cinema to more formal kinds of analytical work. However, it then faces in the other direction – towards our own production of texts, and our future audiences. As we will see in subsequent chapters, a student's film, comic, computer game is always an act of interpretation as well as production; it grows out of interpretations of texts already encountered.

This, then, forms the backbone of our semiotic model of the processes through which media literacy is made possible.

One final – but important – observation remains. We are proposing this model for two rather different reasons. One reason is to *understand* how young people develop media literacy, just as literacy researchers and educators will use linguistic theory to analyse and explain what children are able to do with reading and writing. This purpose does not suppose that children necessarily acquire this analytical framework. If, in a study of print literacy, we discover that 11-year-olds use subordinate clauses successfully in their creative writing, this by no means requires us to argue that they know what a subordinate clause is, or that such knowledge would improve their ability to produce one. Indeed, a recent review suggests that there is no good evidence that grammar teaching improves the writing of young people (Andrews et al., 2004). However, this review does suggest that there might be other good reasons for teaching grammar, especially to provide a better understanding of how language works.

In much the same way, our argument here is that, when children arrive at school, they bring with them highly developed forms of media literacy already. They have extensive *implicit* knowledge of how media texts work; and the semiotic approach we describe here can be used to analyse *what they are already able to do*. As importantly, however, it can be used to outline what we want them to be able to do in addition. We might find, for instance, that they are instinctively able to *represent* characters and landscapes in their animation, but not so able to manage *interactive* aspects of their texts: to design their images in ways which indicate how the spectator is positioned (Chapter 3 will explore this area in more detail).

Our second reason for proposing a semiotic model, then, is that, in common with all specialist media educators, we also wish to help students to develop a conception of the semiotic workings of media texts. Such an understanding of the 'languages, codes and conventions' of the media is, indeed, a core component of the conceptual framework of media education. We will return in Chapter 5 to what we mean by a 'concept' in this respect, but we want to emphasise here that a concept, in our model, is also a semiotic entity: it is developed by using 'semiotic tools', as Vygotsky argued (1978), and it cannot be separated from semiotic expression, whether in language or in some other mode. The degree of complexity, sophistication and technical detail we might aim for in students' understanding will be dependent on their age (we may feel this is more appropriate for older students), or on the particular critical focus of a specific course. However, it will also depend on the development in future years of suitable frameworks of the kind we describe here, adaptable for use with young people. We do not expect English teachers to be professional linguists, but rather to have some informed grasp of how language works, at a level appropriate for their students. The same applies with semiotics and media literacy. We have made a tentative start towards such practice at Parkside, but we will return to this question in subsequent chapters, as we consider how such practice might develop in the future.

CONCLUSION: TOWARDS THE SPECTATORIUM

Our focus in this book is on media literacy, though also on media education. Buckingham (2003) sees the former as the product of the latter, and we agree with him. The examples we give in this book will give some idea of the processes of teaching and learning in which we hope to develop media literacy along the lines we have proposed in this chapter. Our aim has not been, of course, to produce a cast-iron model in which every gap is plugged, every question answered, every uncertainty resolved. Many of these questions will always remain open to different views, depending on the variety of purposes informing media education; and some of them are genuinely difficult questions to answer from a theoretical point of view. Our work will reflect a take on media literacy which we hope can be useful to others in our situation: working with primary and secondary school students, both in specialist media programmes and in other areas of the curriculum where media literacy has something to offer. A century ago classrooms were modelled on the mediaeval monastic scriptorium: a place of work where written language was the way to represent and understand the world. Half a century ago, tape-recorders and record-players introduced recorded archives of sound: folksong, popular music, the plays of Shakespeare, poets reading their own work, radio programmes in all genres. The scriptorium had given way in some respects to the auditorium (though the primacy of print literacy persisted). In the last decades of the twentieth century, visual media in the form of television, film, projected images, video and eventually digital audiovisual media grew in importance. The classroom was slowly becoming a spectatorium, where the persistent reign of print was at least complemented by the still and moving image. These developments were largely confined to pedagogies of display: children listened and watched, rather than making. In this book, we focus especially on the meaning-making by students made possible by digital authoring technologies, the functions of the different forms of signification involved in such authoring, and the cultural value of what can be said that could not be said before in quite the same way.

DESIGNING SUPERHEROES: CULTURAL FUNCTIONS OF COMICSTRIP LITERACY

In this chapter we will propose some of our reasons for teaching comics and superheroes. We want to look at them through three stages of the Year 8 (12–13 year-olds) comics course at Parkside, reflecting on three examples of work by students. In the course of this, we want to consider the cultural value of comics and their place in the literacy curriculum; the nature of the literacies involved in understanding and making texts which employ the superhero metaphor; and the way this kind of media production can allow for playful experimentation with social identities.

First, however, we will describe the course at Parkside.

SUPERHEROES IN YEAR 8

The course at Parkside has been running for well over a decade. In the current version of the course, Year 8 students work on superheroes for a number of weeks. The course begins with watching and discussing the animated film *Batman and the Mask of the Phantasm* (Radomski and Timm, 1993). The film is presented to students as imitating quite closely the visual style and spirit of the original DC Comics Batman cartoons: it derives from a TV series which consciously resurrected the 'Dark Knight' and Art Deco detail of Bob Kane's design in the 1940s.

As students watch the film, they make notes on four aspects of *representation*:

- how criminals are represented
- how women are represented
- how the city environment is represented
- the character of Bruce Wayne/Batman.

Before watching, they are introduced to the idea of representation. We draw a figure on the board and ask the students what it is, teasing out the point that this is not a person, but a representation of a person.

By adding and changing details in the drawing, ideas about representation can be elicited: representations can be stereotypical or differentiated, positive or negative, realistic or unrealistic; they may be encoded in clothing, or words and actions, or physical arrangements. With this conceptual equipment, students are asked to comment on representations in the film. Criminals are stereotyped as broad-hatted, cigarette-smoking gangsters, or – in the figure of the Joker – made exciting and extraordinary. Women are either shallow and weak, or secretly dynamic and physically powerful. These representations are related in discussion to what students know or can be told of the cultural values and concerns of 1940s America.

This discussion is the groundwork for a close reading of the film, through the analysis of still images. Students are presented with specific stills, chosen for their relevance to the four areas students have been looking at in the film. So, for example, there are two stills in which women are represented, and two in which criminals are represented, and so on. Students discuss the images in groups and present their ideas to the rest of the class. To help them, they have some prompt questions, and the teacher also models ways of reading the images. Students are shown how to read meaning into details; they are also introduced to some conventions of filmic images: aspects of shot construction such as lighting, camera angle and shot distance.

The film provides an immediate frame of reference for discussing some of the 'ingredients' of a superhero: an alter-ego, powers, gadgets, masks, motivation, the nemesis, exotic imagery and so on. Students then research and compare heroes from myth and legend – Hercules, Robin Hood, Anansi, Mwimbo, William Wallace. The emphasis in subsequent discussion is on how this twentieth-century popular–cultural phenomenon might be part of a continuity across history and cultures. What is the universal appeal of such narratives? The question of the representation of gender is also raised: why have superheroes and action heroes been so overwhelmingly male in the past? How are the new wave of female action heroes (Xena, Warrior Princess, Buffy the Vampire Slayer, Lara Croft) different? As we will see, one aspect of these fantasy characters which appeals to young people can be the symbolic resources they offer to reflect on their own identities: their 'real' selves as well as aspirational versions of themselves which they can construct and experiment with through the making of their own media texts.

Discussion then focuses on the idea of the mask. Students make their own superhero or villain masks, for invented characters. But first, they watch clips about masks from a range of films: *The Mask* (Chuck Russell, 1994), *Gladiator* (Ridley Scott, 2000), *Batman* (Tim Burton, 1990) and *Spiderman* (Sam Raimi, 2002). They discuss the significance and function of masks, worn by both heroes and villains. Here, there is an emphasis on the relevance to the students' own lives and to their observations of the 'real' world. When do they and others wear different kinds of 'masks', and why? How do people conceal or alter their identities in everyday life?

While in an obvious sense such work is rooted in contemporary popular culture, it also raises questions about what exactly such culture might mean; where it comes from, and what history of cultural practices it might derive from. The iconography of comicstrips, as is well known, borrows heavily from classical myth (Wonderwoman's Amazon heritage), Norse myth (The Mighty Thor), and folktale and romance; as well as from the symbolic resources of the nuclear age and the tropes of sci fi and modern horror. While there is something specifically anchored in the modern moment in children's engagement with contemporary superheroes, the social significance of spectacular figures who offer magical solutions to impossible social problems is providing something of the kind that the legend of Robin Hood must have held for the mediaeval English peasant. Similarly, the formal properties of comicstrip superheroes can be seen as similar in certain ways to those of the heroes of oral narratives of the past, as we will suggest also in Chapter 3 in relation to popular animation. The scholar of oral narrative Walter Ong lists what he calls its 'psychodynamics', which include 'heavy heroes': larger-than-life figures, characterised by one or two memorable features, who address the problems of the world 'agonistically', through physical action rather than internal angst (Ong, 1982).

We can see the culture of comicstrip heroes in this tradition, then, to a certain extent: this is a kind of continuation of the values of oral narrative, characterised by fluid, improvisatory, performative kinds of text. In this respect, as we have suggested in Chapter 1, 'oracy' may be a better metaphor than 'literacy', with its associations of the fixity of print and the primacy of language. While on the one hand, they belong to the immediate 'lived culture' of young people, superheroes also belong to a cultural history which can be seen as the 'recorded culture' of the past, in the model of media literacy we outlined in Chapter 1.

Of course, essential to all of this discussion is a consideration of audience – of what superheroes mean to people, at various levels. In the next activity students are focused on the centrally important idea of 'audience pleasure', through close-reading of the covers of some superhero comics. Details in the covers promise cathartic action and excitement, ideals of protective power and fantasies of transformation. They offer dystopian reflections of urban menace and they promise the utopian triumph of good over evil. Students are encouraged to consider the needs of particular audiences: perhaps the strong but feminine 'Miss Fury', sending a group of suited men flying with well-aimed kicks and punches, provided a fantasy of liberation for young girls in 1950s America; perhaps an image of Batman confronting a top-hatted, cigar-smoking capitalist was an inspiration to post-Depression workers. In this kind of work, our aim is to encourage the kind of *rhetorical* critical reading we out-lined in Chapter 1, in this case in relation to how texts address readers in specific social contexts.

Students also look at the 'comic cover' as a genre of its own, finding patterns and listing conventions in the layout and the imagery. This prompts a further development of students' understanding of visual grammar; and the framework we use is borrowed from Kress and van Leeuwen's *Reading Images: The Grammar of Visual Design* (1996). Students then design a cover for an invented superhero comic, and – if there is time in the course – they design a page of the comic too. We will analyse two examples of comic covers by students in the final section of this chapter, exploring the aspects of literacy and creativity at stake in such work, and providing a more detailed account of the aspects of visual grammar taught in this section of the course. Here, the emphasis is on the semiotic construction of media texts, and especially on the mode of visual design.

THE VALUE OF COMICSTRIP CULTURE

Comicstrips have been seen in the past as trash culture by conventional standards of cultural value. They were exactly the kind of text demonised by F.R. Leavis and Denys Thompson, in what is often seen as the first version of media education (1933). Its aim was to teach children to resist the malign influence of the media – what became known as the 'inoculation' approach. Behind this apparently enlightened exercise in critical reading was a set of assumptions about cultural value. The perceived worthlessness of mass popular culture was opposed to the value of a select canon of texts famously dubbed by Leavis 'The Great Tradition' (1948). A follower of Leavis, David Holbrook, was even more specific about what he saw as the debased nature of visual popular texts in particular, as if the visual image somehow threatened the sanctity of the word, in which the values of English teaching are so enmeshed:

> ... the word is out of date. It is a visual age, so we must have strip cartoons, films, filmstrips, charts, visual aids. Language is superannuated. ...
>
> Some teachers fall for the argument. ...
>
> We must never give way: we are teachers of the responsiveness of the word. ... The new illiteracy of the cinema, television, comic strip, film-strip and popular picture paper they accept as the dawn of a new era. (Holbrook, 1961/1967: 36–37)

This argument was never tenable, of course. If the image so violently undermined the word, what would we make of other combinations of word and image more conventionally valued in Western culture: the paintings and poems of Blake? Doré's illustrations for *The Ancient Mariner*? Tenniel's illustrations of *Alice*? These examples make it clear that the wholesale assault on the image here is actually an attack on something different: popular culture.

Since this period, of course, popular culture has become very differently understood by academics and teachers, to such an extent that we would see ourselves as polar opposites of Holbrook's anguished defence of language against image. Comics are taken seriously as a vibrant and important popular cultural legacy of the twentieth century, and the superhero genre in particular has straddled the popular media of Japan and America, has been transformed from the print medium into hugely successful film franchises, and shows no sign of losing its energy. In recent years, Stan Lee's *Spiderman* has developed into two imaginative feature films by Sam Raimi, *The Incredible Hulk* has been transformed into an intelligent, brooding film by Ang Lee, while new transformations of the genre are evident in animated films like *The Incredibles*. At the same time, the aesthetic of the comicstrip hero has been revived in a series of television franchises, the most influential being Sam Raimi's *Xena, Warrior Princess* and Joss Whedon's *Buffy the Vampire Slayer*. The course we describe here invokes this cultural context, using a film derived from the animated TV series of *Batman* (Altieri, 1992–95).

Meanwhile, studies of how children and teenagers engage with comics and magazines have indicated how they might be important in the cultural lives of young people. The academic field of Cultural Studies has paid most serious attention to comicstrip culture as an element of broader youth culture. At the risk of generalisation, this tradition of research has shifted from a pessimistic view in the 1970s of, for instance, the ideological effects of comics on girls, locking them into oppressively stereotypical social roles (McRobbie, 1978) to later arguments that girls' readings of magazines and comics are more negotiated, allowing them space to pleasurably explore representations of girlhood, and initiating them into aspects of womanhood (McRobbie, 1991; Gibson, 2000). Perhaps the best-developed account of comics, the social anxieties they represent and provoke, and their importance in the cultural lives of their fans, is given by Martin Barker (1984). This shift is consonant with a general move in Cultural Studies towards a view of active readership, in which readers are more autonomous, more able to interpret, transform and use texts for their own purposes. However, within this more optimistic turn, there remain concerns about the social meanings of popular culture, and how the contradictory nature of gender identity, especially, is negotiated with difficulty through the mediating function of popular cultural texts (Walkerdine, 1997). We will explore this theme in relation to a comicstrip design by a girl in this course, later in this chapter.

In relation to education, views of comics as appropriate texts for literacy courses have also changed considerably since Leavis, Thompson and Holbrook. Anne Haas Dyson (1997) demonstrates that superheroes are valuable symbolic resources to be appropriated by children for the exploration of identity, a theme we will also further develop later in this chapter. Styles and Watson (1996) emphasise the value of comics as powerful, motivating texts for classroom work; though they also express concerns about the negative attitudes of teachers to the cultural values of such texts. Millard (1997) gives an unequivocal endorsement to comics as suitable classroom fare, however, arguing that the cultural values they represent should be respected, and they should be included in literacy programmes as worthwhile objects of study, especially at a time of decline in boys' motivation to read.

These arguments about the cultural importance of the comicstrip for teenagers, the value of its narratives and metaphors for the exploration of identity, and the benefits it offers for literacy programmes, we consider sufficient justification for the devotion of curriculum time to such texts. However, such arguments are not to be confused with the difficult question of cultural value, which we have briefly considered in Chapter 1. One criterion sometimes proposed for culturally valuable texts is difficulty, and our view is that this is a wholly spurious criterion intended to discriminate in favour of 'high' art, especially literature, and against popular texts. A recent example can be found in a report from the UK Qualifications and Curriculum Authority, purporting to convey views of English teachers on the relative merits of media texts as against literary texts:

> Alongside views that media and screen-based texts [can] have their place in English 21 there is the caveat that these should never be at the expense of our rich book-based literary heritage – a point more fully elaborated in terms of the purpose and value of engaging with verbal language: *the study of literature has one conspicuous advantage over the study of film and television media, in that it develops the skills of analysis, argument and discourse alongside language skills.* (QCA, 2005a; emphasis added)

This kind of argument can be seen as a diluted residue of the Leavis and Holbrook attack on popular culture. The authors of the curriculum here display a softened stance on the teaching of texts such as comics, films and television, allowing them a place as part of a wider cultural landscape: but there remains the firm belief that they need to be treated suspiciously, and to be seen as somehow thinner, more insubstantial, less nourishing than literature. Our intention here is to oppose this view, by argument and example. The argument is that there is no logical reason why the study of comicstrip and animated film should not develop 'the skills of analysis, argument and discourse alongside language skills' just as effectively as the study of literature.

The first part of the superheroes course, involving close study of still images from *Batman and the Mask of the Phantasm* (Radomski and Timm, 1993), allows students to consider not only the formal composition of these images, but to engage with them and the narrative to which they belong, in an affective way as well. The following piece of writing by a Year 8 boy, John, follows a discussion of an image of Bruce Wayne standing looking up at a painting of his dead parents. This piece of writing is by a particularly able student – but that is exactly our point, that media texts do provide sufficiently rich cultural resources to stretch any children. It demonstrates by example that the perception of media studies as an option for 'less able' students, a regrettable practice in some schools, is completely misconceived.

It is also suggestive of the pleasure which students can find in such analytic work. Far from being at all dry or mechanistic, John's reading of the image is imaginative, and is conducted in a rich, emotive language; and he is clearly enjoying breaking ground intellectually, as he subjects familiar material to a new way of seeing.

> This Image appears about halfway through the film, and it comes at a time when Bruce has become uncertain about his future. He must decide whether Batman takes precedence over Bruce Wayne, or whether the time has come to desert his quest for justice and break through the isolation and solitude that it has created in him.
>
> The room he stands in, and its features, symbolises where he stands in life. This huge empty room, devoid of any homely touches or comfortable furniture, despite being in his very own house, represents how, even within himself he cannot seem to unearth the part of Bruce Wayne that will let him conquer the loneliness and isolation that Batman has breathed into him.
>
> In this shot Bruce is indeed just a sad, lonely and vulnerable human being but the fact that he cannot communicate with anyone means that he cannot lead a normal life, because he would have to maintain the secret of his second existence whether from his lover or from a friend.
>
> He stands in this room, a reflection of his life, faced with two options. The portrait of his parents that he is gazing at represents a route to the past and the open window lying behind him is the path to his future: Batman. At this point the past seems a better option and this is shown to us by the colour in his mum's dress – it is red while everything else is blue. A dark blue, nearly engulfed [*sic*] him, shrouds much of the room, but it is just being held off by the light from the window. This may perhaps represent how, although he longs to be back in happier times, the Batman side of Bruce is the only thing keeping him from being swallowed up by the

turmoil within. And yet, as the picture shows, it is also the only thing that makes him long for the past (as the window sheds light on the portrait letting him see it). The fireplace below the portrait is empty and this adds buckets to the cold inhospitable atmosphere of the room. It also represents for me what will happen to him if he tries to grasp out for the past. The way Bruce must crane his neck to look up at his parents and the way that they look down on him, implies that they are just out of his reach. If he tries to haul himself up to them he will slip and be swallowed by the huge gaping mouth of the fireplace.

Another thing that makes the past a predominant feature in our minds as well as Bruce's, is that it is on the left side of the picture so we come across it first and only later do we realise the presence of the open window. This again implies the current importance of the past to Bruce, and the desperation to turn away from the remaining possibilities.

If the image is flipped, it reads as 'The open window sheds light on Bruce looking at the portrait', rather than 'The portrait is being looked at by Bruce as the open window sheds light upon them'. Indeed, because the light is now coming from the left and we see it first, the picture seems brighter. The light has been placed so that it comes from the right because subconsciously our mind treats it as a secondary feature, and this reflects Bruce's mood. However, I believe that the light coming from the open window is the most important part of the picture; it shows strongly the influence of Batman on Bruce Wayne, and that for me is the main thing about this character.

This example speaks for itself: there is clearly nothing in the text which inhibits complexity of interpretation and response; on the contrary, the text provides rich and ample resources for such engagement. The writing balances personal response with more objective analysis – each supporting the other; in order to be precise, he uses higher order abstract terms ('predominant', 'subconsciously', 'secondary') and composes complex sentences; he places ideas in context, explaining how details relate to the whole; he handles difficult psychological ideas; and he manages to articulate the complex relationship between reader and text.

Finally, this work is an example of what we called the 'semiotic' dimension of media literacy in Chapter 1. While it does not grapple with formal semiotics, it is in fact a systematic reading of what Hodge and Tripp call the *synchronic syntagm*: a spatial composition which is organised as a kind of visual sentence within the flow of the moving image (Hodge and Tripp, 1986). This rather technical term means that the image is representing one moment in time (*synchronic*) rather than a sequence of events over time (*diachronic*). Syntagm is the technical term in semiotics for a combination of signifiers (as opposed to *paradigm*, which is the class or category from which they are drawn). Paradigm is, then, the plane of selection, so here we could say that the author of the image has chosen Bruce Wayne from various possible categories (male rather than female, superhero rather than villain, protagonist rather than other character types); and combined him with other elements in the image – the location, the view through the window, and so on – each of these also drawn from larger categories. This compositional act is the syntagm, or plane of combination.

While the example of John's writing does not use these particular terms, this is nevertheless a systematic reading of the compositional features of the text (what we have called the 'organisational function' in Chapter 1). This can be seen most clearly in the last paragraph, in which John considers the meaning contributed by the left–right organisation within the image.

COMIC MASKS AND PLAY

Superheroes inspire the childhood impulse to dress up. Their costumes, so outrageously at odds with the grey banality of everyday clothing, suggest fantasy, fancy dress and carnival. The merchandise which surrounds the release of films in particular provides ready-made elements of superhero costumes for children to wear: Batman's full outfit, complete with moulded musculature; Harry Potter's gown, scar and glasses; Luke Skywalker's light sabre; Zorro's cape, mask, hat and sword.

This kind of dressing up can be seen as a feature of committed fan behaviour, a form of textual appropriation, of the kind Henry Jenkins describes (Jenkins, 1992). It is a use of dramatic form to make meaning: the costume carries its own set of symbolic properties, whether ready-made or home-made; but the meaning is not realised until the costume merges with the body of the wearer, and with whatever repertoire of movement, dramatic action and improvised speech is deployed. This kind of roleplay is often regarded as essentially trivial: quite different from the roleplay of educational drama, or of adult theatre. It is certainly true that superhero dressing-up among young children is likely to be light-hearted, accompanied by laughter, and not a form of the extended or developed roleplay which more formal theatrical modes expect. But this does not mean it is trivial, nor that the meanings it conveys are worthless. Anne Haas Dyson (1997) demonstrates how dramatic activity based around superheroes can allow children to explore questions of social identity and power. Similarly, in the Parkside course, students are asked to make their own superhero masks and develop simple dramatic 'still images', or frozen tableaux, which correspond to frames of the comicstrip, and are then photographed and composed into a kind of photo-story (Figure 2.1).

FIGURE 2.1 *Student superhero photostrip*

This kind of activity is an example of how closely the creative function of media literacy is related to play and to dramatic expression. For the Russian psychologist Lev Vygotsky, play allows young children to learn to manipulate symbolic objects (a broom used as a horse is one of his examples) in ways which later become internalised as imaginative thought. By the age of the children in our comics course (12–13), creativity can function as internalised play (Vygotsky, [1931] 1998); so it is worth asking why a secondary teacher would employ methods apparently more suited to the developmental stage of much younger children?

Two points need to be made. First, this is not entirely like the roleplay of young children's dressing-up – it is certainly the external manipulation of symbolic objects, but it is also the conscious connection of those objects with higher-order conceptual thought, in this case related to the representation of gender in media texts. This connection between concept and imaginative thought is, for Vygotsky, a feature of adolescent creativity. We will explore the links between play, imagination, creativity and concept development further in Chapter 3.

Secondly, our view is that the development of creative work with teenagers is best seen as an oscillation between internal and external creative work. The development of new ideas builds on earlier ideas; but the provision of external objects – 'semiotic tools' in Vygotsky's terminology – offers concrete representation of new ideas and the space for learners to play with these. This allows them to extend their thinking in a social space with others, testing it out through exaggeration, parody and other kinds of transformation; and finally to be able to create in their own minds new representations which draw on these resources.

In this page, *The Adventures of Super-Ellen*, the resources of body, mask and cardboard speech bubbles are used in a collaborative social process to produce a humorous but effective critique of the male dominance of the genre, with ironic references to the 'damsel in distress', and gestures that indicate flying, punching, kicking and strength. At the same time, this hybrid of drama and print employs key conventions of comicstrip composition: speech bubbles, action bubbles of the kind used in the 60s TV series of Batman, and the comicstrip representation of profanity, termed a *grawlix* by the cartoonist Mort Walker in his not-entirely-serious *Lexicon of Comicana* (Walker, 1980).

From this highly collaborative, playful exploration of the iconography of superhero comics, we turn to individual productions, which form the final part of the course.

THE VISUAL GRAMMAR OF COMICS: ANALYSIS AND PRODUCTION

The final section of the course returns to a focus on the comic as print medium, as students analyse comic-book front covers and design their own. This kind of work allows the teaching and learning of conventions of visual design in a framework which derives from the social semiotic approach we described in Chapter 1. In particular, we draw on Kress and van Leeuwen's *Reading Images: The Grammar of Visual Design* (1996), which argues that the visual image does have a kind of grammar which can be systematically described and analysed. Images *represent* the world in various ways – for instance, as visual narratives (a superhero fighting a supervillain), or as conceptual structures in, say, diagrammatic form (a diagram of the circulation of the blood). They also work *interactively*, to position the viewer in certain ways – looking up or down at the image, directly at, from the side and so on. Finally, they use specific elements of composition to indicate what is important (which might be larger, more central, more densely coloured), or how they want the viewer to read the image (in what order, what to prioritise, how to make connections between the elements). They also use physical subsections of the image to suggest particular meanings – top and bottom, left and right, foreground and background. What these might mean in any given image will change, but the meanings will not be random or accidental, as John's analysis of the Batman still showed above.

In the course we use a projected image of a superhero comic cover to teach key conventions by demonstrating an analysis, encouraging students to attend to specific details of the image. We look at narrative, at the grammatical function of the characters and objects represented on the page and the suggestions of movement and intention associated with them; at the locative functions of background; at genre, and how it is suggested by the image. In particular, there is an emphasis on the process represented in the image – the system of meaning described in linguistics as transitivity. In this kind of narrative image, the process will usually be *actional* – representing some kind of narrative action – or *presentational*, representing a key character, in this case the superhero.

The students are taught terms to describe the elements in the 'visual sentence' – 'actor', 'vector' and 'goal'. In some ways, this corresponds to the well-known grammatical pattern of the typical sentence in English of subject–verb–object, though the terms here are those Kress and van Leeuwen draw from functional linguistics. In terms of the narrative, though, the question is reasonably straightforward: *who is doing what to whom?* In addition, the characters have 'attributes' (such as superhero costumes, masks, weapons) and are placed against 'circumstances' (of location).

This kind of analysis, and the terminologies it uses, raises a number of questions we have explored in Chapter 1. Our argument is that social semiotic and multimodal theories of textuality offer a coherence which is lacking in the approach to texts within the conventional conceptual framework of media education. This approach encourages students to see connections between language grammar and the semiotic structures of texts in other media: these connections are strong in this model because social semiotics draws a substantial part of its framework from functional linguistics (Halliday, 1985). Thus, the idea of *Actor* here (a functional linguistic term) opens up the possibility of discussion with children of grammatical categories on the one hand (the subject of a sentence, for instance); and narrative, dramatic and social ideas of agency on the other: Who is acting? Who has agency? Who has power? Similarly, the notion of *Vector* here (a line of intention signalling an action) can lead to discussions of the significance of *action* in the world and in fiction, as well as the way such action is represented in texts in formal structures like verbs in language, vectors in still images, dramatic movement in film, or player interaction in computer games. Meanwhile, the notion of *attributes* (often realised as adjectives or as adjectival phrases in language) helps students to analyse details of the characters' costumes and other characteristics; while *circumstances* leads to discussion of setting and location.

After presenting their own analyses, also using projected images, students go on to design their own superhero. The idea is that they use this to work on the metaphorical significance of the superhero as explored earlier in the course, but this time attributing their own meanings to the figures they invent; but also to practise the visual grammar of comicstrip design. At one level, this work can be seen as a form of consolidation, an opportunity to internalise the conceptual learning about textual structures explored through the reading of film and print images, talk with peers and teachers, dramatic action and photography. At another level, however, as with all the media production work examined in this book, we expect the students' work to exceed the predictable and limited objectives of the course. In particular, we expect it to engage with the cultural and critical functions we outlined in Chapter 1. Because superheroes provide such rich raw material for the representation of identity, this function is one we would expect, though exactly how different students might exercise such a function, how seriously they might take it, how important it is to them, are all matters that cannot and should not be controlled or policed by us.

The following analysis considers two products of the course, one by a girl, one by a boy. As well as evidence of their control of the semiotic resources of comicstrip design, these pieces of work are evidence of the motivation of their makers to represent ideas, aspects of identity and forms of cultural commentary which are significant to them.

Sarah's comic-book cover: Tiger Woman Sarah's comic-book (Figure 2.2) reveals a complex understanding of narrative conventions. Like any form of language, her work shows an extensive implicit understanding, increasingly made more explicit by the processes of articulation and reflection invited by the course. Most of our analysis of her work centres on her construction of narrative, within a particular set of genre conventions; and how this operates as a version of the real and imagined world. We also briefly consider how she constructs the imaginary relationship between author, represented participant and audience.

The central element is the figure of Tiger Woman herself, Sarah's invented superheroine, related to contemporary images and icons of exotic female power: Scary Spice, Madonna, Catwoman, Xena, Warrior Princess. This is not entirely a narrative image, however: Tiger Woman is not actually doing anything, but rather presenting herself, in a stance typical of many superhero comic covers. It is a *presentational* image: its function is to classify and categorise, to elaborate an idea. As with SuperEllen (Figure 2.1), one idea represented here is a challenge to a male-dominated genre. However, this is just a starting-point for Sarah. What it means to be female, to be a girl moving into womanhood, is a concrete, personal affair as well as a generalised political statement. The signifiers of femininity most salient to 12-year-old girls, at the upper-end of the 'tween' age-bracket, are faithfully reconstructed by Sarah here as *attributes* of the character: painted nails, exposed midriffs, eye makeup, tight clothes, dramatic decoration. These are aspects of tweenhood that she, in fact, has not experimented with, but must be aware of as a world of tantalising possibility, laden with moral and sexual ambivalence, opening up a route to adulthood, but also to risk and name-calling. Furthermore, comics and magazines are traditional repositories for such concerns, arguably fulfilling an educational function for girls; while more recently, 'tween'

FIGURE 2.3 *The front cover design for 'Tiger Woman'*

websites similarly construct their audiences as 'vulnerable, sexual, potentially powerful, curious, in need of guidance and having their own valid popular culture' (Willett, 2006).

The exaggerated perspective on the hands is another genre convention, associated with superhero power and the projection of that power towards the reader. The nails dominate the image, and all other elements are subordinate to them. In a way they are more threatening than anything else: it is a convention of the genre that the hero should be frightening – part of the ambiguity of the form. The nails also relate to the glamour of the character: they are talons, but they are also erotic accessories. As with the figure of Tiger Woman generally, Sarah has constructed the organisational aspects of this visual text to emphasise the meanings she wants to convey: the central positioning of the character, the size of Tiger Woman and her hands; these all lend salience to the important elements of the image.

The complex of ideas that Tiger Woman represents is further developed in the piece of writing which accompanies her comicstrip, an explanatory commentary that forms part of the assignment. Here, she explains:

> Tiger Woman is not real, she is in a dream. The girl that dreams about her is disabled and has spent all her life in a wheelchair. She is like Tiger Woman's alter ego, and can escape her disabilities to become an athletic heroine.

If Tiger Woman can be interpreted as an image of tween-girl fantasies of sexual confidence, then it seems reasonable to interpret her wheelchair-bound alter ego as a metaphor for the constraints of shyness, lack of confidence, uncertainty and moral regulation that lie on the other side of the tightrope that girls of this age are obliged to walk.

However, the relationship between Tiger Woman and Fang can also be seen as a finer set of distinctions in this representational field of girlhood and sexuality. Fang has an exposed midriff and short skirt; Tiger Woman is fully covered. The masked Fang conforms to the genre convention of the sexually provocative female villain; standing triumphant before the threatened city, she echoes the image of a supervillainess on a comic cover that the class had analysed earlier, who postures victoriously before an already burning cityscape. In the conventions of comic covers, as opposed to comicstrips, speech is replaced by gesture. Fang's raised hand is an utterance of defiance, threat and conventionally premature celebration: according to narrative convention, she must be foiled. The attractiveness of the villain is another genre convention. The evil character must be attractive – funny, or clever, or witty, and always appealingly amoral. Here, Fang's clothes and catwalk posturing might be seen as a typical projection of a teenage girl's experimentation with fantasy identities. The excitement represented by the villain character reflects a fascination with what is forbidden.

The background images are no less significant, and serve a locative, descriptive and affective function. The enlarged moon works as a genre signifier, a piece of iconography which Sarah had observed and commented on in actual comic front covers she had studied, such as an image of the Marvel superhero Daredevil, outlined against an enormous moon. In Sarah's design, the moon has a temporal function, signalling time of day and a mood function, signalling mystery and femininity – one of her main intentions was to explore the representation of gender. In terms of the visual composition of the page, it has a framing function, highlighting the hand of the villainess holding the explosive trigger, emphasising a central image of the narrative which signifies threat, conflict, challenge (to Tiger Woman), the immediate future.

The cityscape is another typical genre icon, signifying urban threat, insecurity, alienation, in all the same ways that it does in the traditions of the DC and Marvel comics in which the superhero narratives have been played out since the 1920s. The lit windows complicate the contribution this image makes to the affective quality of the image and the narrative – they suggest human warmth in contrast to the blackness of the towerblocks, and make the threat of the dynamite all the more powerful.

The relationship between the image and the reader (what Kress and van Leeuwen call the *interactive* function of the text) is dominated by the gaze of the central figure. The eye vector straight out of the picture is involving and inclusive of the reader in the narrative. It positions the reader as an object of Tiger Woman's power, subject to the threat of her nails. This kind of image act is described by Kress and van Leeuwen as a 'demand act': it demands particular kinds of response from the reader. It is the equivalent of the imperative mood in the grammar of verbal language. As the villainess, Fang, is also looking directly at the reader, the central demand here may be to respect the power of the dominant female, and all the suggestion of risk, as well as enticement, offered by both heroine and villainess.

The form of the comicstrip, then, and the symbolic figure of the superhero and her dual identity, offer ways for Sarah to explore the contradictions of sexual identity as experienced by girls between childhood and adolescence. These issues, and representations of them in the media, are of concern to children, but their concerns are often swamped by adult fears and paranoias, constructed as the destruction of childhood innocence. Valerie Walkerdine sees education as particularly prone to this anxiety; and the figure of the working-class girl as the most significant threat:

> The little working-class girl presents, especially to education, an image which threatens the safety of the discourse of the innocent and natural child. She is too precocious, too sexual. While she gyrates to the music of sexually explicit popular songs, she is deeply threatening to a civilizing process understood in terms of the production and achievement of natural rationality and nurturant femininity. (1997: 4)

By contrast with the 'little working-class girl', it may be that the middle-class world of Sarah's childhood has 'protected' her from such precocity, and that her experimentation with these images draws on more adventurous performances of female sexuality she sees around her, both in her peer group and in media images. Social class may, then, be one of the variables in the cultural mix which surrounds her, though binary oppositions are perhaps not helpful here, and certainly not easy to distinguish. The important thing, from our point of view, is that this kind of activity allows the child to produce the imagery: she has, if temporarily, some control over how these contradictions can be represented, in a world where such aspects of childhood are almost exclusively controlled by adults. In this respect, this kind of identity play corresponds to Bruner's notion of the development of selfhood we referred to in

Chapter 1. It is negotiated – experimental, non-committal, playful; and distributed: produced as shared text for peer and adult response.

Chris's comic-book cover: The Toaster Chris's invented superhero is called The Toaster (Figure 2.3). His 'myth of origin', tells the story of a hapless café chef whose hands become merged with two toasters, transforming him into The Toaster. Needless to say, the intended meanings here are much more light-hearted than Sarah's: Chris's explicit intention is an ironic parody of the genre. His design can be seen as a form of visual play; indeed, this kind of play is much closer to adult play forms than children's. Parodic texts are subversive, offer opaque meanings, challenging more straightforward representations.

FIGURE 2.3 The front cover design for 'The Toaster'

They hold us at arm's length, refusing simple interpretation, refusing serious-ness. Anne Haas Dyson sees her children's superhero play in terms of the notion of carnival developed by the Russian literary theorist Mikhail Bakhtin. For Bakhtin, carnival referred to mediaeval rituals in which ordinary people were able, if only temporarily, to upset the usual relations of power exerted over them by church or state (Bakhtin, 1968). In a modest kind of way, this in some ways is an apt metaphor too for Chris's text. It is playful in a carniva-lesque sense in that it refuses the seriousness of schoolwork, of the 'official' curriculum, testing its values by developing a sophisticated kind of silliness.

While it refuses straightforward reading of the kind possible with Sarah's comic, it does indicate a wide range of textual literacies. To begin with, it draws much less on the content of the course than Sarah's comic, and much more on a range of influences Chris brings with him. The Toaster is not, prop-erly speaking, a superhero, but much more like the anti-heroes produced by Marvel comics in the 1960s: reluctant, tortured monsters like the Incredible Hulk or the Thing. These characters are much more anarchic than the conven-tional superheroes, as likely to do harm as good, victims of the tragic consequences of human scientific hubris, like Frankenstein's monster before them. In this respect, then, Chris's Toaster belongs to a form of play which Brian Sutton-Smith characterises as the rhetoric of Fate: chaotic, even danger-ous forms of adult play (2001).

The visual style of Chris's design both exemplifies this and contradicts it. He skilfully employs a range of features typical of post-1960s comics: the departure from conventional rectangular panels; the dramatic exploding shapes; the delineated musculature of the superhero; the forbidding silhouette in the doorway. However, these conventions are wittily combined with a quite different tradition of funny comics, ranging from those for children such as *Dandy* and *Beano* to adult comics such as the British comic *Viz*, which spe-cialises in politically incorrect and scatological humour. Visual elements which recall these influences are comically exaggerated bodies, shiny, bulging eyes, steam-clouds bursting from the ears and huge teeth. The use of this visual style produces the parody, refuses seriousness and introduces a note of anar-chic humour which oddly complements the urban pessimism of the Marvel anti-hero tradition.

Chris's stance in this course is a familiar one, adopted particularly by boys on finding the material of their popular cultural experience suddenly at the forefront of school work. Unsurprisingly, the reaction is to grasp the opportu-nity for a pleasurable exploration of these familiar texts on the one hand, while developing mildly provocative variants of the task on the other. Chris's intention here is to send up the whole superhero genre and the seriousness with which it takes itself: Superman's dull civic mission; the inflated language of the Marvel characters; the general melodrama of the genre. The most explicit sign of this critique is The Toaster's mortal enemy – Really Quite Strong Man, a conventional but dull American hero, horrified by The Toaster's arbitrary acts of violence.

In respect of media literacy, Sarah's and Chris's comics represent different kinds of purpose, then. For Sarah, the exploration of the imagery of teenage girlhood, and its relation to conflicting social identities, is the point. Her interest is primarily in aspects of representation which test out, explore and extend through playful fantasy some of the dilemmas faced by girls on the brink of adolescence. For Chris, there is also a pleasure to be had in the playful exploration of gender stereotypes, in this case the gleeful exercise of fantasy violence to break through the boring prohibitions of conventional adult morality.

Both their productions display projections of identity: guises of girlhood in one case, and the performance of pop-culture savviness in the other. At the same time, they can both be seen as examples of critical literacy. Sarah's comic develops a sustained critique of male imagery and values in this genre. Chris's develops a critique of the conventional morality of the superhero genre. At the same time, they display a grasp of the textual conventions of the genre: its iconography, its compositional features, its narrative types, its social preoccupations.

CONCLUSION

The examples drawn from this course suggest a number of aspects of the cultural function of media literacy.

First, there is a consonance between the textual material chosen for work in the classroom and the cultural experience of the students. They are experts in the history and iconography of superhero narratives; though it is important not to homogenise their experience, which is very varied. Some (like Chris) are passionate and knowledgeable *aficionados* of comicstrip culture; others may not read comicstrips at all (girls' magazines, for example, have all but lost the element of comicstrip which was so important in mid-twentieth-century publications). Most know something about superhero franchises on TV or film; the Batman animated series was regularly watched by children on this course when we began it in the mid-1990s. This consonance, then, can be seen as a form of what the sociologist Pierre Bourdieu called *cultural capital* (1984): cultural knowledge from school and home overlaps, combines, extends, mutually reinforces; informal knowledge becomes legitimated by official educational processes of formal recognition and assessment.

Secondly, media texts like comics (though this will also be the case with other kinds of media texts, especially games) are playful texts, and encourage playful representations in children's own productions. Playful here means, on the one hand, dramatic, physical, concrete manipulation of symbolic resources which recalls Vygotsky's models of both play and creativity. On the other hand, it also recalls the different rhetorics of play described by Sutton-Smith; so that while students' work can be seen as progressively playful in some respects (enacting positive challenges to the representation of gender in comics, for instance), it can also be seen as sometimes exploring irrational themes better described by Sutton-Smith's rhetorics of Fate or Phantasmagoria. As teachers, we need to welcome and understand these kinds of contradictions and ambiguities, not suppress them or iron them out.

Thirdly, the cultural function connects with the critical function. For Sarah, possible fantasy identities are both a form of pleasurable aspiration and a critique of the roles really available to her in the world. For Chris, a sophisticated parody of mainstream comicstrips is an assertion of his cultural credentials, his artistic prowess, his ironic stance: these may be critical faculties, but they are also part of the person he wants to be. The pedagogic stance of the teacher needs to be open to such varied and unpredictable representations of self and forms of critical judgement, and find ways to give them room to develop.

These kinds of literacy can flourish, as long as our approach to forms of popular culture such as the comicstrip can finally shake off the shadows of Leavisism still lurking in the beliefs and actions of curriculum policymakers. The wide consensus among teachers and academics is that comics have value as complex, pleasurable, powerful narratives, entirely capable of inspiring sophisticated and sensitive analysis. And through their own productions, children can enter, passionately or ironically, wittily, exuberantly, into the ways in which comics explore the nature of human identity, employ central symbolic images of our culture, provoke the intense pleasures of the unofficial culture we too often undervalue in our classrooms.

ANIMATION, MOVING IMAGE LITERACY
AND CREATIVITY

The projects described in this chapter are examples of collaborative production work between Parkside and local primary schools. The making of these short animated films raises the question of media-specific literacies, in the sense used in Chapter 1: in this case, moving image literacy. It also raises the question of creativity, especially as they are constructed in many ways as media arts projects.

We have worked with animation in many ways: computer animation in the context of Art, literacy, Maths and ICT; stop-frame animation in Design and Technology, in Geography and in the context of after-school clubs. We will return to some of these uses in Chapter 8. Here we will explore the making of two films, both of which can be seen on the accompanying CD-ROM. One, based on the story of Red Riding Hood, is a stop-frame animation made with Year 3 and 4 children (7–9 years old), as part of a series of projects with primary schools, aiming to provide the primary teachers with the knowledge and resources to repeat or adapt the projects themselves. The other is a film called *Flight to Freedom*, made by Year 6 children (10–11 years old), a computer animation made during a series of more elaborate animation projects involving local cinemas and artists-in-residence.

Before looking more closely at the projects, we will briefly consider the question of creativity: what is it, and how does it relate to the model of media literacy we are developing in this book?

The word 'creativity' is used with many different meanings in different contexts, as we argued in Chapter 1. In particular, it carries rather different meanings in art education and media education, and in many ways animation projects cross the boundary between these territories.

In arts education, the notion of creativity is inevitably associated with artistic intentionality, and the aesthetic properties of the work of art. In media education, on the other hand, creativity is often simply a more interesting word for 'production': the making of media texts rather than the analysis of them. Such production may be undertaken to help students grasp new concepts, to expose ideological meanings, to prepare students for work in the media industries: Buckingham et al. list a number of rationales commonly used for production work in media education, among which the expressive purpose of such work is only one (1995).

Moreover, it is common among media educators to mistrust certain notions of creativity, as Buckingham (2003) explains. In particular, Romantic notions of creativity as a form of divine inspiration, mystically conferred upon a small number of individuals and denied everyone else, clearly conflict with democratic impulses in arts education (Robinson, 1999), and with the aspirations of education generally, which must develop rational notions of the skills it aims to impart.

However, attempts to redefine creativity for democratic and educational purposes have often produced further problems. If creativity is associated with development (as all other skills acquired by children are), how does it develop, and how can such development be evaluated by teachers (Sefton-Green and Sinker, 2000)? If creativity is in fact a glorified form of problem-solving, a desirable social and professional quality for workers in the new economy (Seltzer and Bentley, 1999), how do we account for creative acts which seem to be subversive, anarchic, even destructive? And if creativity is some spark of originality which happens in the mind, how is it connected with culture? If creativity has to be original, does that mean it cannot involve imitation? If creativity is about cultural *production*, how is it connected with cultural *consumption*? (see Banaji, S. and Burn, A. 2006)

We will return to some of these questions as we discuss the implications of the animation projects in the final section of this chapter.

ANIMATION AS SEMIOTIC PROCESS

The sequence of making an animated film can be seen in terms of the semiotic processes in our model of media literacy, derived, as we explained in Chapter 1, from the semiotic strata proposed by Kress and van Leeuwen (2001): *interpretation, discourse, design, production, distribution.*

It sounds a little odd to include interpretation in a project where the emphasis is so firmly on the production of children's own texts. However, textual production always involves some kind of response to texts previously encountered by the author. In the case of this project, while on the one hand children may be quite literally interpreting literary texts such as Red Riding Hood, transforming them into audiovisual form, they are also, as we shall see, incorporating elements of visual design from the discourses of popular animation.

The *discourses* which form the cultural contexts in which these films are made come, in effect, from two sources: the literacy curriculum and children's media cultures. While there is some cultural dissonance between the two, as we shall see, this also allows for ironic, subversive work by the children. Discourse here can be seen, as we suggested in Chapter 1, as knowledge of some aspect of the world: so in this case, the teachers and the children both have certain kinds of knowledge about fairytales and about popular animation, but this knowledge is differently weighted, valued and used. Discourse is often seen also as the negotiation of unequal relations of power (Tyner, 1998). In relation to this project, the visual discourses of popular cinema and television may be less well regarded by, say, artists working in the project than by some of the children; so as narratives and images are chosen and designed, these different emphases will be negotiated.

The processes of design and production form a kind of sequence as we tell the story of the making of these two films. Stories, images, dialogue, music, sound effects are all designed in turn and feed into the later processes of editing. The *design* modes are various: visual design to make the artwork of the animation and to draw the storyboards; written language to design the dialogue and write the script; music to compose the sound track. Meanwhile, the physical media used for *production* are various. The first film uses plasticine, plastic models, digital film and digital editing software. The second uses drawing, painting, collage, computer animation, musical instruments, vocal performance and digital editing software. In many cases, these media contribute to the meanings created by the children. In particular, the affordances of digital media allow for certain processes of design and production which were not possible with older analogue technology. These features are summed up in our previous work (Burn, 2007) as iteration, feedback, convergence and distribution.

These categories are adapted from earlier work, such as Reid et al. (2002), who considered the advantages of digital video editing, adapting their categories in turn from Moseley et al. (1999).

- *Iteration* refers to the ability constantly to change the digital work, to keep improving it through the sort of 'editing' which has long been a feature of effective writing work in English.
- *Feedback* is the capacity of authoring tools to show the edited work in real time as it is changed by the author, thus feeding into the cycle of improvement.
- *Convergence* is the ability of authoring packages to handle different modes (such as moving image, graphic design, music, speech) all within one software, either by importing material made in other digital composition packages, or the creation and editing of such material within one multipurpose package.
- *Distribution* represents the capacity of digital media to be output in different formats, and displayed on different platforms. So the animated films we describe in this chapter were shown on TV screens from DVDs, on

computer screens from hard drives, projected in cinemas and exhibited on the Internet as multimedia files.

This last affordance relates to the final stratum in our semiotic framework, of course. *Distribution* is, in the case of these films, determined by the opportunities offered by digital display, exhibition and publication possibilities. These are not merely technical, but confer different kinds of cultural recognition on the children's films, as well as taking them to wider audiences. In this project, as we shall see, the ability to screen the films in a cinema, or take them home on DVD for parents, makes real differences to all participants in the project. This kind of exhibition moves their work beyond the context of simulation which so much school work is often constrained by. The films become 'real' by their screening in a real cinema.

TRANSFORMING RED RIDING HOOD

In this primary outreach project, Year 3 and 4 children make simple stop-motion animations, using the software Stop Motion Pro, running with ordinary webcams. The software allows them to capture single frames, fifteen per second; to review captured frames running as a film, at any point; and to delete unwanted frames as often as necessary.

To simplify the process, rather than animating drawings on a computer, they animate toys, such as small plastic figures with movable limbs and heads, or homemade clay models. The webcams have a very flexible focal length, and can focus closely enough to take full-screen close-ups of heads a centimetre across.

The films are based on well-known tales chosen by the primary teachers, who often select stories which more or less fit the conventional canon of the primary literacy curriculum: folktales and fairytales such as The Boy Who Cried Wolf, The Gingerbread Man and Little Red Riding Hood, either in a traditional form or retold subversively, as in Roald Dahl's *Revolting Rhymes*. These kinds of story belong to discursive worlds that many children are familiar with from an early age: they pervade the language and imagery of picture-book genres, school reading and storytelling sessions, and in some cases, parental reading-aloud cultures. Though folktale and fairytale have become part of the world of print literacy, and grist to the mill of Early Years literacy teaching, they retain qualities of the oral narrative cultures from which they derive: they are often read aloud, often improvised upon, often transformed in a dizzying variety of versions: see Jack Zipes's excellent *Trials and Tribulations of Red Riding Hood* for a documentation of that particular set of transformations (Zipes, 1982).

However, connecting computer animation to the discourses of folktale and fairytale is only half the story. For many children, the story chosen by the teachers is only a part of the cultural resources available to draw on. The children, unsurprisingly, draw on the visual discourses of popular culture, especially forms of animation which they have enjoyed, as we shall see.

The children first discuss the meaning of 'animation'. They watch a short animated film, and then look at how a series of still frames from the film can be run together to create the illusion of movement. They are then introduced to the software and the webcams, and they practise animating toys or other objects as smoothly as possible. At this age, they need very clear reinforcement of essential concepts and of routines for animating, and there is a need for more demonstration than with older children. However, children as young as 7 find the process accessible and enjoyable. This process appears to put production before design: but the advantage of using the production technology first is that the children have a clear idea from practical experience of what this medium can do as they undertake *design* processes such as storyboarding.

The children storyboard the film carefully, working first as a whole class. At this point, they are introduced to notions of moving image 'grammar', deciding whether portions of the script demand long shots or close-ups, cut-aways or reaction shots, and so on. Each shot is given a defined length, which is converted into a number of frames. The storyboard is created on A4 sheets, each containing one shot. After the process and the outcomes have been modelled, the class divides into small groups to continue planning the film. Each small group is responsible for designing and animating a small portion of the overall work.

As the project is constructed, the whole process may take just three or four hours. The software is very easy to learn and to use, and there is very little post-production work to do. In this respect, the project is easily replicable by any school wishing to begin work with animation.

The explicit learning objectives of the activity are to do with moving image literacy. On the table-top, the children are able to construct a range of camera shots, and they quickly and easily acquire a vocabulary with which to describe and analyse these, as they storyboard and as they translate their ideas into animation:

> 'The [shots] I found most useful were two shots (with two people), over sholder shots (Looking over a figures sholder at other figiurs) close-ups and one shots (one person)'. (Layla)
> 'First before you make the animation you need to plan it because if you don't it wont work and you wont know what sholder shots are or Birds eye view'. (Victor)

There is a continual emphasis in discussion on how moving pictures can tell stories, and how the images which the children are creating can best do that.

Children are therefore learning about the narrative affordances of different kinds of shot, steered away from simply drawing long shots in storyboard frames to represent action, towards designing shots to tell the story of what a character is looking at, or of what is most important, or of the emotion of a moment.

Much of this discussion takes place at the storyboarding stage. The emphasis here is on how pictures tell stories. This example is the beginning of a storyboard, designed in discussion with a class to model the process and outcome (Figure 3.1). It illustrates how the process can draw on children's understanding of both verbal and visual grammar.

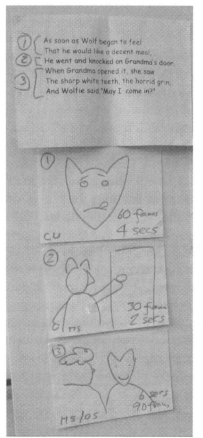

The script divides naturally into three sections, each of which is then represented by a camera shot. The choice of shot type reflects the way agency operates in the script, as represented by verbs.

In the first section, the main verbs are 'feel' and 'like'. The 'actor' is the wolf, and his 'actions' are internal – to do with his feelings. The shot type suggested is therefore a close-up of the wolf, taking the audience close to this inner experience.

In the next section, the main verbs are 'went' and 'knocked'. The wolf's actions are now physical, and involve interaction with the external world ('Grandma's door'). The cut to a medium shot reflects this shift, while the view over the wolf's shoulder maintains his viewpoint.

In the third section, Grandma is the actor ('opened') and the point of view changes ('and saw'), so the view changes to a shot over her shoulder. This shot allows the audience to share her view of Wolf's 'horrid grin', and to see him speak: 'May I come in?'

FIGURE 3.1

The *production* of the shot represented in Figure 3.1 involved the use of models and Plasticine™, moving them by tiny degrees and filming each stage as a still image using the webcams, capturing the sequence of images directly into the Stop-Motion Pro software (Figure 3.2).

FIGURE 3.2 *Animating Red Riding Hood*

However, production is never simply the translation of careful designs into material form. It always involves further kinds of meaning-making; but since the attention of the teacher is likely to be on the practical production process, it is here that unexpected, improvisatory meanings may appear. In making the animation, then, the children decided to rotate the wolf's head 360 degrees, reflecting the playfulness of the poem and successfully suggesting his danger-ousness; and to make his Plasticine stomach visibly rumble (Figure 3.3). Both devices indicate the children's understanding of how animation can convey meaning through filmic codes typical of popular animation and, in the case of the revolving head, the horror genre. The important features of the act of pro-duction are that these ideas of how cartoon animals might behave are made possible by the physical medium, the Plasticine, which contributes to the semi-otic work. Its physical nature – its lumpiness and malleability – are part of this contribution; but also it is already endowed with prior meanings, through the history of claymation, and especially the Aardman studios' *Wallace and Gromit* films. Production here, then, continues the design process, but begins to exceed the rather neat constraints of the storyboarded planning conducted with the teacher, and to improvise new kinds of meaning.

Similarly, in one of the stop-frame animations (The Boy Who Cried Wolf, by Year 3 children at Newnham Croft Primary School), the children impro-vised a quite different scene from the one planned on the storyboard. The villagers in the story, ignoring the boy who cried wolf, were supposed to be lying around peacefully, but the children made them rush about playing a bizarre and manic game of 'duck under the cross-bow'. This was a much more pleasurable way to manipulate the toys they were using for the animation, and produced a more dynamic film. As we shall see, creativity, play and media lit-eracy are all facets of the same social process of making a media text.

FIGURE 3.3 *Animating the wolf*

As the animation is created, children are continually editing – deleting frames to correct errors or to refine the effect. The construction of meaning here continued a process of thinking and invention from the earlier design stages. Primary teachers comment on how cognitively challenging the work is for young children, requiring the planning of whole texts (the film) and component parts of texts (scenes and shots), which must be visualised, represented in quite abstract ways on a storyboard and then interpreted with models and camera positions. The children have to think in complex ways about both the spatial and the temporal nature of the moving image: the film, its scenes and individual shots have to last a particular number of seconds, and therefore a particular number of frames, to fit the script and to pace the narrative.

Interestingly, a lot of the challenge derives from various kinds of limitation. First, there are the technical and practical limitations of the technology of the medium, which determines what is possible, and therefore what can be planned. These have to be considered at every stage: a dragon cannot realistically fly; people cannot easily be made to jump; and too many characters in a shot take too long to move. These constraints demand thoughtful planning; they also promote problem-solving thinking and talk.

Secondly, there are creative constraints, necessary for continuity: every background must have the same colour of grass or sky and be painted in the same style; the action of each scene must be congruent with that of the ones before and after it; there must be consistency of tone. Teachers have mentioned how such 'purposeful constraints' – practical, aesthetic and imaginative – actually fuel learning, rather than inhibit it.

The conceptual challenges of the medium are accompanied by the physical and social demands of the process: children are engaged in difficult group work, and continual problem-solving; moving the 'actors' requires fine motor skills; and the whole process requires a considerable degree of patience. It is the latter which is commented on most of all by both the primary teachers and the children, when asked about learning in the project.

> '[I have learned] to be kind and cooperate but to be very patient and to move the characters carefully and slowly.' (Kerry)

THE FANTASY OF FLIGHT

The second film, *Flight to Freedom*, made by Year 6 children at Claydon Primary School in Suffolk, arises from a more complex arts project, involving local cinemas and artists-in-residence in making computer animations of narratives based on a variety of ideas and sources with 10- and 11-year-olds in Year 6 of primary school. It ran over five years (2000 to 2005), expanding to work with six local schools as well as other primary schools in the east of England, in a development of the project funded by the regional screen agency, Screen East. Although Parkside conceived the project, and remained central to it, it became a collaborative venture of the Cambridge Film Consortium, involving Parkside, Anglia Ruskin University and City Screen, an arts cinema chain who own the Arts Picturehouse, an arts cinema in Cambridge.

The part played by the cinema was important. The children were able, at the beginning of the project, to spend a day there watching a special screening of animated film, and taking part in workshops that demonstrated key aspects of animation, the importance of music and the processes of design, scripting, storyboarding, sound work, filming and editing. At the end of the project, the children returned to the cinema for a screening of their own films.

The next stage of the project involved the choice of a story or theme with the primary school class teachers, scripting a story, storyboarding it and making the artwork for the animation. The processes involved media specialists from Parkside team-teaching with primary class teachers; but also the involvement of a professional animator-in-residence throughout the project.

The final stages included making the animation itself, using a cheap digital animation software tool called The Complete Animator; composing the music and recording the music, sound effects and dialogue with the composer-in-residence.

The discursive landscapes which fed into the children's work were very varied, incorporating traditions of independent cinema, their own experiences of popular animation and examples of both popular and fine arts animation shown to the children at the beginning of the project. In the case of *Flight to Freedom*, the base text was not a literary narrative as it had been in previous years, but a documentary theme of 'Flight', prompted by the centenary of the Wright Brothers' first flight, and its connection to an air museum in Cambridgeshire, a regional centre of the Imperial War Museum. For the children, however, this rather worthy aim was simply a springboard for an inventive, anarchic fantasy, emerging from the audiovisual landscape of children's TV animation. The respectable theme of flight soon metamorphosed into the development of a zany tale of the luckless Captain Hudson, kidnapped by evil aliens while flying over the Bermuda Triangle, and his girlfriend, the heroic Phoebe, who rescues him from the aliens' wicked leader Ursula with the help of a Marmite sandwich.

Similarly, in an earlier year of the computer animation project, in a film also based on Red Riding Hood (not to be confused with the Year 3 film described above), two of the children's designs for the characters of Red Riding Hood and the Woodcutter closely resembled Britney Spears and Arnold Schwarzenegger respectively. These representations evoked qualities of fantasy sexuality and aggression pertinent to these children's experimentations with gendered identity. At the same time, the image of Red Riding Hood operated as a kind of refusal of the anodyne and powerless character bequeathed to us by the dominant version of the Red Riding Hood story – Charles Perrault's eighteenth century French version, which transforms the strong peasant girl of earlier versions, who outwits the wolf, into a powerless victim of the wolf's jaws (Zipes, 1983; Carter, 1991; Perrault, 1991).

In the last two years of this project (during which *Flight to Freedom* was made) we made more conscious attempts to encourage students to explore different styles of animation. The launch event constructed a deliberate mix of popular animation (*Wallace and Gromit, A Bug's Life, Shrek*) and arthouse animation by independent animators, including the artists-in-residence. In practice, these various styles and genres seem to have mixed without any problem. One of the primary teachers whose class made *Flight to Freedom* notes how James drew on the children's knowledge of animation, and how this knowledge influenced their work:

> James brought a lot out of it. He was asking them questions about what was happening in the Simpsons, and how things were animated, expressions and things like that. And they knew ... they went away – Those who didn't ... who couldn't say off the top of their head were able to go and watch things and pick things out. Such as, like, blinks and things to show characters. And you could see it in their work. They'd put blinks in and things. And things going on in the background so things weren't so static. They had the goons banging away in the background and things, and then something going on in the front. So, yeah, they definitely ... I mean, they all watch animations. A lot of them love the Disney films.

Specific aspects of moving image literacy were first foregrounded in the story-boarding process. It had become clear during the first two years of the project that many of the children, left to their own devices, would produce a kind of default view of each shot in their storyboards: they would present everything in long shot, wanting to include the whole bodies of all the characters in each case. The project developed, then, a wide range of activities through which the children could learn through practical activities the importance of framing and shot types. These included looking at frames from popular animated film, and the making of brief live action films, as well as the idea of storyboarding a nursery-rhyme (first introduced by a resident animator, Louise Spraggon). Trish Sheil, the Film Education Officer at the cinema, describes a moment in one of these sessions, in which one child's difficulty with the idea of close-up becomes dramatically apparent:

> ... they'd have a big sheet of paper, and they'd do the full body of Georgie-Porgie running round, and then, because we were saying, oh maybe try it with a close-up, you know, what they did was, the hand was the same size, but just in the page, so it was like a little hand in the middle of a big sheet of paper.

It would seem that the ability to imagine and produce different shot distances is not something which children necessarily learn from prior experience of moving image media, although they obviously have learned in some ways to read such shots. This implicit knowledge needs to be made explicit if they are to apply it in their own work. This aspect of media literacy needs to be modelled for children, and cannot be taken for granted. By extension, the whole system of what has come to be known in the industry (and the academy) as 'continuity editing' (Bordwell and Thompson, 2003) might be assumed to be invisible to children. Indeed, this is of course its intention: to fragment its representation of the world between different viewpoints, but stitch these fragments together so that the meanings they construct are taken by the spectator as natural and seamless. In classic 'suture' theory, this process 'stitches' the spectator into the ideological world of the film.

Our view of children's engagement with film and television is much less deterministic: earlier studies have shown that children do develop critical capacities in their readings of television and film, and can make complex judgements about how the world is being represented (Buckingham, 1993, 1996). However, such critical readings vary from child to child, and they also vary in their certainty and their level of articulation. The intervention media education can make is to render completely explicit how the grammar of the moving image works, and how it conveys narrative and social meanings.

The children we interviewed in the final year of the project had gained this kind of explicit understanding of how the storyboard designs aspects of moving image grammar. These two girls, when asked about the differences between different shots on their storyboard, had a very clear idea of shot distance:

> INTERVIEWER: What's the difference between this kind of picture [on your storyboard] and this kind of picture, would you say?
> PUPIL 1: That's a far, that's a long shot, kind of thing, and that's a close-up –
> PUPIL 2: – that's a close-up. And that – was not done with care!
> INTERVIEWER: Did you just automatically think of doing long shots and close-ups?
> PUPIL 1: No, well, they kind of said think about long shots and close-ups and …

Meanwhile, two boys from another school were able to reel off seven different shot types they were using:

> PUPIL 1: Wide shot, over-the-shoulder, bird's-eye view, worm's-eye view – looking up –
> PUPIL 2: – medium shot, close-up, extreme close-up.

One of them goes further, making a more abstracted observation, perhaps of his own accord, that this aspect of the moving image is general to all films, and finding an example from his favourite animation (this group cited *The Simpsons* and *The Incredibles* as their favourite animations):

> But obviously you've got the same views because every film has like, well similar views. *The Simpsons* doesn't have like over-the-shoulder views that much, but it's got a lot of views like we have.

The storyboarding, then, helped students to learn, quite formally, but also through the creative act of drawing, the 'grammar' of the moving image in terms of framing and shot distance (Figure 3.4). The subsequent artwork developed this further. The drawing, painting and collage work involved not only realising landscapes and characters planned in the script and the story-board. It also involved imagining what kinds of movement would be needed, and catering for this by producing different views of characters so they could be seen from different angles, and making separate pieces of artwork for objects that would need to be moved independently, like eyelids, limbs or vehi-cles such as planes and spaceships.

However, the artwork was also the mode through which the children were able to connect the bare bones of the narrative with detailed aspects of their cultural lives. Just as the image of Red Riding Hood, three years earlier, drew on the children's experience of images of popular cultural icons such as Christina Aguilera or Britney Spears, so the image of Phoebe, the plucky hero-ine of *Flight to Freedom*, recalls images of femininity of interest to tween girls

(Figure 3.5). She has yellow bunches, big shoes, bright red lipstick and (in the side view) a pronounced bust. This aspirational image of a femininity a few years beyond the grasp of its author belongs to a family of playful explorations of such images by young girls, which include narratives of risky behaviour with boyfriends in cars in playground clapping games (Opie and Opie, [1959]/2001), or girls' engagement with images of teenage femininity in animated film, as in Richards's account of how his daughter plays with the image of *The Little Mermaid* in Disney's film, appropriating features of an apparently precocious sexuality (Richards, 1995).

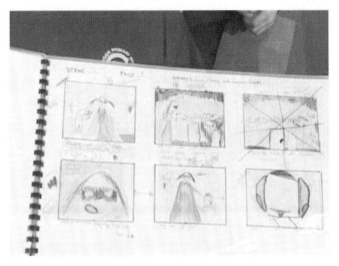

FIGURE 3.4 *A sample of the storyboard for* Flight to Freedom

FIGURE 3.5 *Phoebe, the heroine of* Flight to Freedom

Other images in *Flight to Freedom* recall the children's experience of popular animation. Captain Hudson wears a cap similar to those worn in Gerry Anderson's puppet animations of the 1970's, such as *Captain Scarlet* and *Thunderbirds*, recently re-released for this generation. The images of the alien creatures bear a striking resemblance to ET, still a point of reference for children's images of cinematic aliens through perennial Christmas television screenings of Spielberg's film.

The children also designed the sound for the film: sound effects, dialogue and music. These were made and recorded with the composer-in-residence, Andrew Lovett. For the music, Andrew worked with whatever instruments the children played or the school possessed. The learning process centred on the relation between the music and the film; on the creation of mood; on the kinds of narrative suggestion the music could make; on the possibilities of motifs related to characters. It is also clear that the music brings with it part of the 'cultural capital' that the children contribute to the film-making. Andrew gives some sense of how the music-making draws on popular cultural knowledge:

> ... they can be very resistant to someone coming in and saying, 'I'm a classical music composer.' ... But if you say, 'OK, who's been to the latest Harry Potter film? The music was by John Williams, let's talk about that for a moment.' Then you know, almost everyone in the class will respond to that and will have something to say about it.

The design process here is practical and improvisatory: the music is not formally notated or written down; rather, musical phrases are tried and adapted, instruments are explored and played with, and the pieces are refined by practice up to the point of recording. Design here blurs into production. In *Flight to Freedom*, for instance, there is a repeated motif consisting of a militaristic drum rattle followed by a discordant five-note sequence in a minor key, the two together representing Captain Hudson's professional role and the sinister events to come. The multimodal combination of music and image here, then, is *complementary* and *anticipatory*: the music amplifies the meaning of the image on-screen, and also suggest something of what will happen next.

The children also play games with the music and the media conventions that usually apply. Music is extra-diegetic, that is, it is outside the world of the story, performing a separate function to suggest mood. However, as Captain Hudson flies over the Bermuda Triangle, a cheerful dance tune begins to play; and Hudson says 'I love this tune', breaking the rule that characters can't hear extra-diegetic music and sound. The tune then repeats under the credits at the end of the film.

In the case of the older children who made *Flight to Freedom*, the main production process was the use of the animating software. This allowed the still images made earlier to be realised as a moving image sequence. In addition, the animating was the equivalent of editing in the making of live film sequences. In this respect, it was a combination of design (the design of movement, duration, speed, rhythm, action) and production (the use of the digital medium and its affordances).

The animation was made with Iota Software's The Complete Animator, a cheap 'edutainment' package which allows the user to scan in images as 'stamps', which can then be further edited (scaled, rotated) before being placed within a frame and fixed with a mouse-click. Unlike more sophisticated animation softwares (such as Macromedia's Flash), Animator has only two layers – the foreground, in which the stamps are assembled, and the background, which can be imported as a single image which automatically runs through the whole film. The frames are made one by one, and the software allows 'ghosting' in which the previous frames show up faintly, so that the user can accurately position the next frame, making up the movement. This process emulates the physical process of cel animation, in which transparent cels reveal the previous drawings below the current one. The software requires every frame to be made manually; in other words, it does not provide, like Flash, automatic in-betweening, in which only the first and last frames of a sequence may be made manually, while the software creates the in-between frames automatically according to a route designated by the user.

However, the limitations of this program arguably make it very appropriate for this purpose. The two-layer provision allows younger children to learn the concept of layering without the danger of confusion from too many layers; while the need to manually construct each frame helps to develop a full understanding of the process of animation, as well as echoing the laborious work of animators and 'in-betweeners' in the earlier days of the industrial animation studio.

In the interviews with children and teachers, it was clear that a particular conceptual difficulty they had to grapple with was the notion of how a single frame represented only a fraction of a second (a twelfth, in the ratio used in this project, half of the more usual industrial standard of 24 frames per second); and how the degree of movement constructed from frame to frame determined the speed of that movement. These two girls indicate both the surprising nature of the number of frames needed, and also how they have taken this concept beyond the project, thinking about it as they watch animations on TV:

PUPIL 1: I was thinking because this morning, because I had a sleep over and we were watching a cartoon. And we were watching *Lilo and Stitch* and I was just wondering how many pictures for the whole film.
Interviewer: And how many frames.
PUPIL 1: Yeah, I mean it was how many frames.
PUPIL 2: And for how long it took them.
PUPIL 1: It was really long.

In *Flight to Freedom*, the children demonstrate in their 'making of' film (see CD-ROM) how the animation created motion, using the descent of a character's arm as an example, slowing it down so that the sequence of frames can be seen. In the film itself, animation is used, of course, to realise the narrative meanings devised in the storyboard, through a wide variety of moving image conventions. There is a variety of shot types and angles: a high-angle long shot to show Hudson's plane in flight; a big close-up to show his hand waving Phoebe goodbye; over-the-shoulder, frontal and profile shots of the characters.

The design of the sound also included scripted dialogue. The design mode here was, of course, written language in the form of a script; but as important was the move into production – the oral performance of the script. The meanings of the dialogue in *Flight to Freedom* are fully realised by the children's performance at the point of recording; and while this is explicitly encouraged by the adults, the nuances suggest complex influences at work. The girl who voices the evil Ursula, for instance, uses intonation, volume and pauses to create dramatic meaning. In the following line of dialogue, there is a rising–falling intonation on the second syllable ('ha'), and an ironic pause before 'enjoyed'; both vocal characteristics of comic-strip baddies, Bond villains and sci fi megalomaniacs:

> Ah ha, Captain Hudson – at last you've woken up! I hope you – enjoyed your flight!

We emphasise these details because it is all too easy for them to pass unnoticed. Teachers of language have a panoply of tools to develop aspects of writing which equate to these forms of oral emphasis: adverbs to describe tone of voice, punctuation to represent pause. But they are much less likely to be specific about features like intonation in spoken language. In the making of complex multimodal texts, formal attention to the different modes is uneven, depending on curricular legitimation, academic and professional training, and the degree to which different modes are formally fixed in 'grammatical' systems. In language, speaking and writing may receive quite different levels of explicit attention even by literacy specialists. The introduction of oracy as an assessed element of the English curriculum has shifted the emphasis here; but even so, it is more likely that explicit attention will be given to lexico-grammatical features of speech – vocabulary and grammar – than to the meaning of intonation, simply because the latter is not well-known, despite being systematic (Halliday, 1985).

The most important aspect of the *distribution* of *Flight to Freedom* was its screening at the Ipswich Film Theatre. The teachers argued that it made the films seem more 'real'; and that the audience in their case was wider than children and teachers, but involved parents, press and governors:

TEACHER 2: Well, they got a huge boost out of it, because it wasn't just watching it on a TV in the room, they got to see it at the cinema, which made it a film. It was a real film, it wasn't just a little thing we'd done on the computers.

TEACHER 1: And they got to invite their parents, and we invited … Although they didn't turn up! We invited local press and local education people, and our governors came as well.

TEACHER 2: So, yeah, we tried to make it a grand thing. My mum didn't show, I was quite disappointed about that.

TEACHER 1: But my dad did, and my husband. They took the afternoon off.

Children we interviewed across the project had not yet seen their films, but were aware that they would be screened, though they were a little uncertain of what this might entail. However, it is clear from their remarks that the screening provokes some complex thinking about the process of exhibition and the nature of audiences. In this extract, one of the boys interviewed also considers the possibility of exhibition on the Internet:

PUPIL 1: Well I know that they sit … Just about … But I know that we're gonna be the first people seeing it so I can see us. I can see it basically right now just us in a small cinema room just us. Maybe our parents and stuff that are just watching it and thinking I did that. And I did that and stuff. And thinking that it's gonna be so cool.

INTERVIEWER: Anyone else? Do you think anyone else will see it?

PUPIL 1: Well our parents will definitely see it because hopefully we're gonna get copies you know so each person's gonna get a copy so.

PUPIL 2: No way.

PUPIL 1: Probably the whole school will get one to copy.

INTERVIEWER: They will put it on a website in school I suppose.

PUPIL 1: Yeah and anybody can download it.

INTERVIEWER: What about . . . it's going to be shown in a cinema isn't it?

PUPIL 1: Yeah, it is.

PUPIL 2: Yeah.

INTERVIEWER: How many will see it then do you think?

PUPIL 1: Millions of people. Well loads of people really because we don't know. We don't know what people are looking forwards to it maybe.

Two issues are raised here. One is a question of authenticity, the chance to break out of the simulated world of school media production for once. The other is the related question of the children's perception of audience. The assumption behind making productions for real audiences is that students will anticipate audience interests, needs, desires; and will learn to conceptualise audiences as social groups, distinguishing them from the more immediate contexts of media consumption they are used to, in particular family and peers.

These interviews suggest that this assumption is partly true. Some of the children are mapping a continuum from their immediate family and peer group to wider audiences, first 'the whole school' and then the 'millions of people' on the Internet. However, this also suggests the problem of imagining a large, anonymous, unknown audience. As Buckingham et al. propose (1999), young film-makers may need the security of first being their own audience; and the specificity of this boy's image of himself in a 'small cinema room' seems to support this.

Finally, the distribution stratum has its own media, its own technologies. While the children have used paper and paint to storyboard and design, voice and instruments to make dialogue and music, and a multimedia package to animate, the media of distribution and exhibition are a cinema projector, the Internet and the portable storage medium of the CD-ROM. While we often take these for granted (with the exception of the cinema projector!), it is worth considering their particular affordances: the possibility of endless replay as opposed to single screening; different audiences, both specific to the time and space of a screening and not, in the case of the Internet; the forms of social control available to the children (high with the CD-ROM and Internet; low with the cinema); the forms of social esteem accorded to the different media – perhaps lower with the CD-ROM, higher with the Internet, highest with the cinema.

CONCLUSION: CREATIVE MEDIA

Some of the lessons about media literacy we can learn from these projects develop familiar themes, which will be repeated in different ways in following chapters. Children will draw on their own cultural experiences in making their own media, and we need to be aware of these influences and the significance of images, styles, sounds from popular cultural texts, genres and the discursive worlds which produce and shape them. Similarly, children will always have their own expressive purposes in making their own media; and we should be ready for these, able to accommodate them, open to subversive intentions, to unexpected twists of meaning, to anarchic humour. These transformations of the visual discourses of popular animation can be seen as simultaneously playful – learning to manipulate symbolic objects, and to explore the rules of the real world by inverting them – and creative, combining the imaginative work of new cultural representations with the intellectual effort of mastering new concepts.

But what exactly do we mean here by creative? In the context of media literacy, we need to consider how creativity is related to the media cultures which feed into production work like these animations; we need to consider how creativity is a semiotic process, about the production of new texts; and we need to consider how creativity is, like literacy, a developmental process.

The work of the Russian developmental psychologist Lev Vygotsky ([1931] 1998) is helpful in answering these quite specific questions. For Vygotsky, creativity is an indispensable element of growth and development, not just for children but for the whole of an individual's life. It begins with play, which Vygotsky sees as a precursor of creativity, as we noted in Chapter 2, in relation to students' superhero designs. In his essay on play (1978), children learn that a stick may represent a horse, and this grasp of symbolic substitution, mediated by semiotic tools (in this case, objects which act as signs), is eventually internalised as imagination.

Imagination, then, can be seen as play 'gone inside'. It is not, however, a completely self-generating impulse, but depends on cultural experience. For Vygotsky, imagination is partly an act of memory: the ability to recreate the past from cultural experience, and to imagine a new future by transforming memories of past perceptions. In early adolescence, he argues, imagination combines with the developing ability to think in abstract concepts, which also begin with play, where children experiment with the rules of the adult world, through trial and error, and through 'topsy-turvy worlds' in which they invent their own rule systems. Fully formed creativity is, then, both cultural and cognitive, both imaginative and rational.

As we have seen, the Red Riding Hood animation involved the playful transformation of signs from the children's media experience, from which they knew that a rotating head is a sign of monstrosity, and a visibly rumbling tummy a sign of comically exaggerated hunger. To combine these signs with one from another source, the fairytale wolf of Red Riding Hood, is an act of semiotic combination and of creative transformation. To imagine this new sign is of course a mental operation, but it is mediated by the physical objects – semiotic tools – the children can play with in this activity. However, other tools which mediate the acquisition of new concepts – the notions of shot types taught by the teacher – are much less securely deployed by this age group. Arguably this is a distinction, as Buckingham (2003) suggests, between what Vygotsky calls 'spontaneous' and 'scientific' concepts; the knowledge that monstrous heads rotate is a different kind of knowledge from the knowledge that a close-up can signify interiority, or an over-the-shoulder shot indicate point of view; the latter have the kind of abstraction and generality criterial to Vygotsky's scientific concept.

In the case of the older children who made *Flight to Freedom*, the concepts of shot type and the meanings it can construct are much more firmly grasped, and evident both in the act of making the visual resources and animating the film, and in the metalanguage the children use in interviews. However, both here and in other projects we describe in this book, the associated processes of creative imagination and concept development are by no means a simple linear progression from external semiotic tools to internal mental operations. Rather, they are characterised by an oscillation between external work with the semiotic tools of media production and the internal work of developing increasingly sophisticated and independent understandings of textual structures and the conscious construction of meanings for others. The transformative work of children's animations – Red Riding Hood as Britney Spears, a demonically possessed wolf, or aviation as alien invasion – can be seen as the dialectical process of creativity Vygotsky described, in which external cultural resources are internalised, creatively transformed through acts of imagination and intellect, and externally produced or 'crystallised', returned to the wider culture.

It is, however, important to realise that the semiotic resources for this cycle come from two places: from the wider media cultures the children inhabit, and also from the classroom. The ability to make new media texts depends on imaginative transformations of images and narratives; but also on increasingly explicit attention to new structures.

This approach to creativity allows us to navigate some of the more common confusions which persist in notions of creativity in education. Creativity is often seen as synonymous with free expression, yet it has often been noted that constraints can produce the best creative work, as in an evaluation of digital video work in 50 UK schools (Reid et al., 2002). Vygotsky's approach allows us to see that creative work does indeed need some freedom, apart from anything else, to play. It needs room for ideas to be experimented with through the external manipulation of physical media, and also through the forms of language which represent new concepts: close-up, narrative, camera angle, character, mood. But it also needs the discipline of these structures: a way for infinite possibilities to progressively narrow, a use of the scaffolding of existing genres, images, narrative forms on which to build new stories and messages.

Similarly, we can negotiate the pitfall posed by the notion of originality, which has some place in all definitions of creativity. Originality here can proceed from the imitation of existing forms, can indeed be seen as a kind of apprenticeship. In certain ways, the work of these animated films is deeply derivative: it borrows many details from popular cartoons, children's television, advertising and other sources. Originality is formed on what in semiotics would be called the plane of combination – the syntagm. We have already seen, in Chapter 2, how a syntagmatic structure – the visual composition of a still from a Batman animation – was analysed by a Year 8 student. Here, children make their own visual compositions by combining old ideas and images in new ways to make new meanings. By connecting the woodcutter's axe with a square jaw and a scar, the imaginative effort of these students produces the subversive and witty hybrid of Red Riding Hood's saviour and

Schwarzenegger's Terminator. By combining a spaceship and a Marmite sandwich, the new text, *Flight to Freedom,* bizarrely integrates the exotic imagery of sci fi with the intimately familiar imagery of the family breakfast and school lunchbox.

We can also see that creativity is distributed throughout the other elements of our model of media literacy. It draws on the cultural contexts we have emphasised: on past experiences, cultural history and the media cultures of the moment. It is only possible through the use of semiotic tools in the processes of design and production we have identified. And, finally, it relates to the other social functions we have included in our model. It makes new representations possible, not least representations and transformations of self. For Vygotsky, creativity also transforms the creator. As we have seen, many of the representations in these animations are explorations of images of gender pertinent to the growing social identities of their makers.

Creativity can also be seen, in certain ways, as critical. In the comicstrips of Chapter 2 and the animations of this chapter, creativity involves making judgements of taste, selecting styles which are valued by the children and their peers. In some cases, they also involve critiques of certain styles through parody and caricature. Finally, the conceptual grasp of form and structure which is, for Vygotsky, an indispensable part of the creative process, is by the same token a part of the critical apparatus which media education seeks to develop. In the next three chapters, we turn to aspects of this critical function.

HOSPITAL DRAMAS: CRITICAL CREATIVITY AND MOVING IMAGE LITERACY

This chapter will continue our exploration of moving image production. We want to ask how work with the moving image, in this case television, can be a subset of a more general media literacy. But also we want to ask how even this subset is made up of many different components. The project we describe here focuses very specifically on some of these components rather than others – on filming rather than editing. Like all the other projects described in this book, it involves media production: filming a short section of a new hospital drama devised by the students (examples of student films can be seen on the CD-ROM). However, we also look at ways in which moving image media are made up of forms of signification beyond filming and editing, which media education sometimes lacks an adequate language to describe – in particular, the work of dramatic action. Examples of completed pieces of student work, including films by students referred to in this chapter, are provided on the CD-ROM.

In terms of the social functions in the model of media literacy we have outlined in Chapter 1, this seems most obviously a creative project: to construct new narratives and representations. However, as in the comicstrip and animation projects described in Chapters 2 and 3, this project also involves certain kinds of critical understanding, as we shall see.

In Year 8 (12–13 years), students at Parkside study hospital dramas. The course aims to introduce students to some key ideas about television audiences and scheduling. In terms of the conceptual framework of media education, this requires them to think about both media institutions and media audiences and the relation between them.

The course also aims to develop students' understanding of genre and narrative structure, and – at a finer level – to develop their understanding of how camera shots are edited together to convey narrative. There is also a practical element: students use video cameras to create a short narrative sequence, learning to edit 'in-camera' and learning some disciplines of simple video production. Meanwhile, they further develop their ability to structure and sustain complex explanations and analyses in writing.

The course begins with a general discussion of the hospital drama genre. In groups, students make a list of TV programmes that they have watched over the past week, and then try to group them into 'categories'. They discuss how these categories might be identified, and they are introduced – or reintroduced – to the concept of 'genre'. They then use TV listings to identify various genres and subgenres of TV drama. It becomes clear at this point that genres are not simply innate properties of media texts, but are also constructed by media institutions such as production companies, broadcasters and TV listings magazines. Neale (1980, 2000) proposes this point in relation to film genres: that they are socially contested terms, with discontinuities between studio constructions of genre (which might see a film as a thriller), academic constructions (which could see the same film as 'film noir') and popular audiences (which might see it as 'action adventure').

Accordingly, students are given plenty of opportunity to discuss personal preferences and perspectives, recounting and arguing about viewing experiences of hospital dramas. As with any media topic, students' experience of the material varies considerably: teaching has to differentiate not only for ability, but for the implicit and explicit understandings that come from being an audience. Some children will know a range of hospital dramas well, and will be articulate about their differences; at the other extreme, there will be children for whom the genre is mysterious. This differential prior knowledge and understanding may well be an inversion of the situation in most English language and literature lessons, where children from more 'literary' homes are immediately advantaged. At Parkside, there are occasional children whose parents do not allow them access to television; while they may have an extensive knowledge of literature, popular media can be baffling to them. Often it can be the formal demands of media lessons, rather than the informal pressures of peer culture, which prompt such parents to reconsider whether this kind of 'protection' is really an advantage for children.

Introduced formally to the idea of 'genre elements', students brainstorm such elements of hospital dramas. Then they start to watch an episode of the UK hospital soap *Casualty*, identifying examples of iconography, typical characters, typical settings, typical narratives and typical themes. At a basic level, students simply understand that TV dramas can be categorised, and are able to describe these categories. However, they usually display a rich, implicit understanding of these elements, and enjoy categorising and naming them more formally. At a more extended level, students apply the concept of iconography more broadly, and they begin to understand the importance of recognition and expectation in audiences' relationship with genres.

At this early stage of the course students are introduced to the longer-term project of inventing a new hospital drama for children's TV and 'pitching' it to CBBC (one of the BBC's digital channels for children). They brainstorm ideas for what might make a good children's hospital drama, and what would appeal to a target audience of children. At age 12–13 they are still connected enough to this audience to enjoy the imaginative investment, yet their emerging self-image as teenagers gives them enough distance to discuss this audience with (equally pleasurable) objectivity. The discussion necessarily ranges over the 'genre' of children's dramas, such as the London school-based series *Grange Hill,* or the youth club-based *Byker Grove,* set in the northeast of England. In relation to the critical strand of our media literacy model, this work encourages students to consider the institutions which produce media texts, and the way they imagine their audiences.

To begin the creative process, they invent titles for their new dramas. First, they examine existing hospital drama titles. What makes them appealing? What linguistic tricks do they employ? What do they connote? In groups, they brainstorm ideas. Subgenres necessarily emerge – emergency-based dramas, ward-based dramas and so on. Students then fix on a title for their own series, and – for homework – begin to create characters and broad situations for them. Creativity here involves the invention of new media representations, but they are clearly linked to a critical exploration of existing representations.

The next stage of the course involves looking more closely at narrative structure. Students are introduced to the idea of three layers of narrative: 'serial' narratives, which carry over from episode to episode; 'episodic' narratives, which are contained within one viewing session; and 'incidental' narratives, which are contained in a short scene or sequence. Continuing to watch the episode of *Casualty,* they note and discuss examples of each. They discuss how each narrative is incorporated into the episode – the pacing of each, the signalling of each and so on. How important is each kind of narrative in the episode?

They are given a worksheet with an example of a narrative broken down into sections, to introduce a simple version of Todorov's model of narrative structure – *equilibrium, complication, development* and *resolution* (Todorov, 1981). Todorov's model has been extensively applied to film narrative, and is reasonably well known to specialist media and film studies teachers, though it may not be familiar to English teachers. However, this fairly straightforward, simplified view of his model can easily be used by non-specialist teachers, and understood even by younger students. Julian McDougall, with some justification, criticises certain uses of Todorov by Media Studies teachers as a lazy, reductive way of approaching narrative (2006). It is certainly true that media education needs new ways of thinking about narrative and textuality more generally. However, in this case, while this simple version of Todorov's model might limit discussion for older students at GCSE or A level, it provides new insights for younger students.

In this course, then, students go on to consider the function of each stage of the narrative, and then they invent similar narratives for their own invented dramas. For homework, they write up a detailed account of one of the episodic narratives from the lesson. At a basic level, they understand that narratives have a structure, and begin to learn a terminology to discuss this structure; at a more advanced level, they are able to articulate the importance of each stage of the narrative structure in engaging an audience, and also begin to cross-refer to other examples of narrative – in film, perhaps, and even in non-fiction narratives.

The course moves on to look at title sequences. Students consider their function and importance, and they discuss the concept of 'branding' a show within the genre. They watch the title sequences for the UK dramas *Casualty* and *Holby City*, and the US drama *ER*, and then work in groups to explore the way each uses sound and music, graphics, elements of narrative, and genre iconography. They discuss the way each differs stylistically, and what this could suggest about each programme and the way it is produced. They then storyboard title sequences for their own hospital dramas. For some students, this is a way to develop an understanding of some straightforward ways in which title sequences create mood. For others, it is an opportunity to develop their understanding of iconography, articulate subtle features of graphics sequences and argue evaluatively about their effectiveness.

From this point on, the students use spare lesson time and homework to develop their series ideas and their pitches. Meanwhile, the course focuses on a production activity, in which students make short video sequences, edited in camera. First, they study a 20-second sequence from *Casualty*, in which a false expectation of an accident is built up through the use of camera shots, and through play on genre expectations. In the sequence a boy ascends a climbing wall, goaded on by another boy, accompanied by a girl who 'can't watch'. First, students just listen to the sound track, speculate about what is happening and discuss how tension is developed just by the diegetic sound – in *Casualty* there is no helpful mood music. Students are then given the 13 camera shots from the sequence as still images on cards, which they attempt to arrange in order. This is an activity familiar to English teachers: students are often given poems, narratives or examples of specific types of non-literary texts to sequence, in order to explore features of textual organisation. This kind of activity derives from the DARTs (Directed Activities Related to Text) devised by the Schools Council research project *The Effective Use of Reading* (Lunzer and Gardner, 1979), which proposed active approaches to textual comprehension. Although in many ways the same principles apply to camera shots, the activity is surprisingly hard. Many of the shots are very similar – over-head shots of the climber, close-ups of a hand gripping the rock, a foot nearly slipping, and so on. Teacher interventions focus on how the spacing of such shots creates tension, and on the following of basic grammatical conventions of continuity editing – the avoidance of jump-cuts, for example. The aim is not to guess the original order of shots, so much as to create a sequence that makes sense as narrative.

Students then view the sequence through and, in discussion, begin to analyse the shots, making notes on the function of each one within the sequence, and on how it might be formally described. In this instructional part of the lesson, students are focused on moving image grammar. They are revising basic shot types, distances and angles, but the main emphasis is on how shots work in sequence to create the illusion of continuous action in contiguous spaces and time. Meanings are created by juxtapositions: a shot of a boy and girl looking up is 'explained' by a subsequent shot of the climber; a close-up of a hand gripping rock follows a high-angle shot of a climber's frightened face, meaning that he is struggling to hold on; a shot of the climber glancing down means that a subsequent swinging view down the rock-face is his point of view. They learn formal terms to describe grammatical relationships between shots: cut-aways, reaction shots and reverse angles. They also reflect on the significance of camera movement and on the pacing of shots. Students then write analytically about the sequence, rehearsing and consolidating their understanding. This quite specific conventional understanding of the moving image is essentially the continuity system of Hollywood cinema, described in detail in the widely used Film Studies textbook, Bordwell and Thompson's *Film Art* (2003). For many purposes, this kind of account is more than enough as a basis for what we might want students to know about the moving image as a signifying system. In some respects, however, it is inadequate, a point we will return to below.

At this point, it is worth exploring further the moving image literacy at play here. First, while in a simple way students make sense of visual images as self-explanatory, and analogous to the way they see the physical world, in the end such images do not replicate experience in any simple way, as is argued by Messaris (1994), who suggests that visual literacy is intuitive and derived from experience of seeing the world. Rather, the experience of this course is that many aspects of the moving image are quite counter-intuitive, such as the way they fragment the events they represent, reassembling them to create the illusion of continuous action, and to construct relations between characters, spaces and times. Children learn to view such constructions not through their similarity to life, which is not fragmented in such a way, but by their experience of media representations, which 'teach' the skills needed to understand them (Buckingham, 1993); and by building on this in more formal kinds of analysis such as those presented here.

To focus this discussion, students view the sequence as a 'moving storyboard', with each shot embedded in PowerPoint as a separate clip, displayed on an interactive whiteboard. As students develop and contribute ideas, these are written onto the storyboard by the teacher, and copied by the students onto a paper copy. This is an example of a presentational tool – PowerPoint – deployed in the classroom as an anatomising tool. Its ability to display 'movie files' as embedded clips – sized, positioned and contextualised on slides for teaching purposes – is effective in the teaching of the moving image, especially when coupled with interactive whiteboard technology.

All along, the students are aware that this is preparatory thinking, leading to a production exercise. They are now introduced to the concept of in-camera editing: constructing a film by taking shots in sequence, with no subsequent editing. Their first task is to talk about what this will demand of them: it is technically difficult, and requires disciplined teamwork. It also requires specific kinds of thinking, as we will illustrate.

The practice of in-camera editing needs some brief comment at this stage, however. It might be regarded as an oddly truncated exercise in television production at the present time, when schools are becoming increasingly interested in editing, with the advent of cheap, accessible video editing softwares. The rationale for the use of cameras only in this course is twofold. First, it allows space for the consideration of the important role of filming within the continuity system – its role in shot construction, framing and many aspects of the semiotics of the moving image. Secondly, it allows for a finer sense of the different elements of moving image semiotics, which we have referred to throughout this book as multimodal. Many modes that make up film, we argue, can be seen as 'pro-filmic' (Metz, 1974), such as drama, music, lighting, script. Students need to understand the different properties of these modes, as well as how they are integrated into the overall mode of the moving image, the *kineikonic* mode (Burn and Parker, 2003) through the modes of filming and editing, which assemble, combine, frame, sequence and organise all the modes they subsume.

At a more practical level, there is simply a danger that filming is neglected in the rush to editing software. An evaluation of 50 schools working with digital video found that, in many cases, camerawork was of poor quality and little consideration had been given to simple lighting principles, the use of a tripod, the basic operations of the camera and principles of shot construction (Reid et al., 2002).

A second point about filming is to consider the social roles students take on in this kind of collaborative work. Earlier studies (Buckingham *et al.*, 1995; Burn and Durran, 2006) have shown that collaborative work of this kind can promote important forms of social learning, in which abstract concepts are rehearsed and consolidated through talk, negotiation and practical application. However, it is easy to be over-optimistic about the roles students take on. Teachers need to be aware of which students are in control, whether anyone is being marginalised and whether different tasks are being fully valued. For instance, the important role of acting can sometimes become an under-valued function in media production work, and given to the students who are perceived to be less competent with media equipment. This obviously is critical in terms of the social cohesion of the group; but it is also a question of multimodality, and the need to recognise dramatic action as one of the modes contributing to the moving image work.

Before planning their own sequence, students view examples made by previous classes working collectively – very short tense sequences, of between 10 and 20 seconds, composed usually of between six and ten camera shots. Such brevity is an essential element of the exercise. Of course, it makes the process manageable, and containable within the curriculum. But more importantly it enforces a thoughtful distillation of genre and filming conventions. Paradoxically, the students find this liberating: 'The simpler the idea for your sequence, the more you can do with it' (Lisa).

The viewing of these examples is structured carefully. They notice how the sequences are typical of the hospital drama genre. They are asked to count and time shots. They look at how shots are composed and sequenced to create tension, and how expectations are created and significances signalled. They comment critically on the success of different examples, and speculate about what will have been hard or easy to achieve. They are then ready (and very eager) to make their own (Figure 4.1).

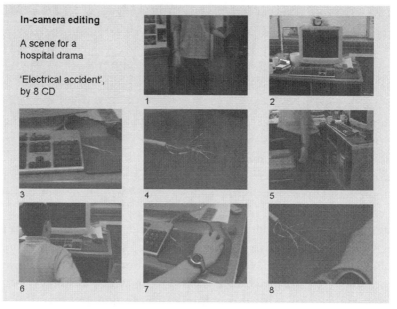

FIGURE 4.1 *In-camera editing: electrical accident*

Classrooms provide plenty of scenarios for accidents: *A student sits at a computer, unaware of the power lead which – the shots imply – is waiting to electrocute him.* Or: *A student ignores an injunction not to swing on a chair, and – a close up of the chair's feet suggests – will surely fall horribly.* And so on.

However, making a sequence with the whole class is not easy, and it is essential that the teacher has already practised. There are management challenges – keeping the whole class engaged (and quiet for shots) when only a few can be actively involved, for example. This difficulty is minimised if the camera is connected to a projector, or just to a TV screen, so that all of the class can 'share' the viewfinder. The student holding the camera is then just doing that – holding the camera. The whole class can join in and collectively own the directing of the shots. The composition of each can be discussed and revised, and it is through this that much of the explicit teaching of visual and moving image grammar can happen. The sequence is storyboarded very quickly – a series of very rough sketches on the board. The exact framing of each shot is discussed as it is set up.

As well as modelling the outcome and the ways of thinking involved, making a film as a whole class demonstrates technical processes. We use basic DV cameras mounted on cheap tripods, and don't ask students to use their manual functions (such as manual focus), but they need to know how to load and eject the DV tapes, how to set up and position a tripod and how to use the zoom when setting up (but never when taking) shots. The exercise also models the disciplined process of taking the shots in sequence. First, a very rough storyboard is drawn up. Then, the first shot is carefully set and rehearsed: the pressing of the record and pause button is practised, along with the action, and seconds are counted: '3, 2, 1, press ... 1 second, 2 seconds, 3 seconds, press'. This may be repeated two or three times, before the actual shot is taken: it is very hard to rewind the tape and take a shot again if it goes wrong. Continuity has to be monitored. For example, if it will be necessary to return to a particular angle, it may be helpful to sketch the way the first shot is framed. In the demonstration, the whole class can do this; in a small group, this might be the responsibility of one student.

Groups spend about half of one 50-minute lesson planning their film – discussing ideas, deciding on a location, sketching a rough storyboard, allocating roles. They then have a lesson (or, if possible a double lesson) to shoot their film. The way in which small groups are allowed to work outside the classroom will depend on the culture of a school, and the character of a class. However, at Parkside small groups are usually trusted to work unsupervised around the school, and the very occasional disruption or damage to equipment that results is accepted as a worthwhile cost; arguably, the risks involved are essential to aspects of the learning, as students develop autonomy and responsibility. Of course, there are very clear ground-rules for where and how groups can work. Teaching assistants are carefully allocated to groups. And the teacher will tend to visit each group during a session. We have experimented with both carefully constructed groups (mixing aptitudes and behavioural traits) and friendship groups. The latter seem to work well, perhaps because – for this age group – the success of the film-*making* is so driven by content. The best films are often dramatisations of specific peer-cultural concerns: teenage risktaking, bullying, conflict between factions, rebellious behaviour and so on. The less successful films are often more straightforward 'accidents' – tripping on stairs, picking up a faulty appliance. Friends are more likely to enact what preoccupies them (Figure 4.2).

> The narrative was based around the action that led up to someone injuring themselves due to a fall. The incident started with someone (me) getting into an argument and pushing the other person (Richard) over. Richard got really angry and decided he wanted to get me back; when I ran away he chased me but I was too quick for him and when I jumped over the pond he tripped and fell, banging his head in the process. (Roger)

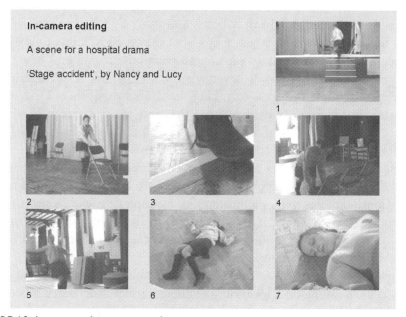

In-camera editing

A scene for a hospital drama

'Stage accident', by Nancy and Lucy

FIGURE 4.2 *In-camera editing: stage accident*

As we have suggested in other chapters, whatever the representational focus of the piece in question (in this case, accidents and hospitals), media productions in schools are always, in a sense, forms of self-representation, in which students explore their own preoccupations, such as friendship, emotion, teenage identity, growing up, curiosity about the adult world. Teachers need to be sensitive to such identity work – it may be, for many students, a more important aspect of the activity than the ostensible topic in the scheme of work. We have suggested in Chapter 1 that such self-representation is a central part of the cultural function of media literacy; and have also noted in Chapter 3 that it is seen as a crucial element of the creative imagination: creativity transforms the creator.

However, Roger's account also reveals a complex set of decisions which form part of the representational system of his group's film: the system of dramatic action. The film does not only consist of the technology of digital filming and the continuity conventions of shot framing and sequencing; it consists also of gesture, facial expression, dramatic movement and speech. These uses of the body as the medium for representation will include the two boys' improvisation of the argument, their use of language, vocal timbre and patterns of intonation to suggest escalating conflict, Richard's representation of anger in facial expression and voice, and dramatic action simulating and emphasising the accident. In drama lessons, the pedagogic tradition of educational drama has its own conceptual frameworks and metalanguages to make these kinds of representation explicit. Similarly, of course, directors of television and film drama will have their own ways to focus on the nuances of dramatic action and speech. These aspects of the multimodal nature of moving image work have, however, been largely absent from formal structures and traditional pedagogies of media studies.

In respect of the filming process, groups' first attempts are not very successful – the process is hard, because of the need for first-time precision. Writing about the process, Will comments:

> At first I thought that in-camera editing would be quite easy, but when I looked at our film my thoughts were different. I realised that people always seem to jump from one place to another and that you see them move forwards and then jump backwards and move forwards again.

This critical reflection is an essential part of the process. Students view their films and consider how they could be improved, either as a class or in groups. The latter is possible on the cameras' flip-out screens, but it is better if the footage can be quickly uploaded to a computer as a movie-file. In this format, it is much easier for a group to view the sequence critically, moving backwards and forwards fluently to analyse edits and to check continuity. Groups' second attempts are invariably much better – more precisely edited and better constructed for meaning, although one student comments revealingly on a tension between the satisfaction of being able to 'do it properly' and the 'excitement' of the first attempt:

> I think our second attempt was much more enjoyable, but it had lost the spontaneity and excitement of the first one, that not knowing how to do it properly had created. (Jack)

We have observed in Chapter 3 how creativity is often perceived as spontaneous and free, but is in fact also structured and rational. This activity, like the structures of improvised drama, suggests that creativity is also about planning, rehearsal, revision and a grasp of the rules of the medium, as the evaluation of the BECTa Digital Video pilot suggested (Reid et al., 2002). However, filming is not exactly like writing – it is a physical activity, and the camera-operator is in some ways like a silent participant in the drama, as well as a proxy for the future spectator, as we have found in previous research on video production at Parkside (Burn and Parker, 2003). In these senses, the creative work here is a judicious mix of risky, improvisatory exploration of spaces, conventions, technologies and a more considered, iterative process of reframing, replanning, refining, revising. We should think, not just of analogies with the writing process (editing is more like writing), but of similarities to drama or dance. Here, then, the digital medium allows for more immediacy in the process, through access to rapid feedback, one of the key affordances of digital video (de Block et al., 2005; Burn, 2007).

The process of revision provides a context for reflective talk and writing like this, in which students can focus their understandings. Students comment on technical and practical difficulties:

> The first attempt the actors stopped but they were not out of the shot. (Jenny)
> Continuity was hard to achieve, but in the second film it flowed more easily ... Some of the voice recording was too quiet to be heard. (Kirsty)
> I found the most difficult sequence was the running, in fact it didn't work the first time as me and Richard were running at different speeds and weren't too sure when to stop. Jumping over the pond was hard too for Richard as he had to slow down to show his foot tripping. In the second filming we managed to improve the running by not starting and stopping too much. (Roger)

Essential to the whole exercise, of course, is students' developing sense of the grammar of moving image sequences.

> ... we used more inventive angles and distances. (Jenny)
> ... we added an extra close-up ... (Ellen)

The process prompts sophisticated thinking about the way sequenced camera shots tell story, create mood and control tension:

> At the end of our sequence, instead of focusing on the injured, we had a close-up of feet from the side running up stairs and a close-up of a face recoiling in shock. We did this to show something had happened, but the suspense came from the fact that you didn't know exactly what. (Lisa)
> We started filming from quite a close distance, and used a POV shot when Richard was angry, by filming over his shoulder to see my scared expression. We also chose to show how Richard had fallen by using a close-up of his foot tripping up. We also used a close-up to show that he had seriously been injured because there was blood on his head. (Roger)

This kind of reflective writing uses language which suggests conscious author-ial intent: 'to show', 'we used', 'chose'. It also shows the beginnings of an awareness of dramatic modes of signification in the multimodal mix: 'a face recoiling in shock', 'my scared expression'.

In-camera editing foregrounds the concept of pace, which is very easy to get wrong: it is easy to linger indulgently over carefully constructed shots, when they need only a moment to convey their meaning.

> In our first attempt, the continuity was not bad but the pace wasn't too good. Some of the shots were too long and other shots went by too quickly ... (Xiumei)
>
> The shot where the person walked to get to the bag was too long, so we had to change it the second time we filmed it. (Jenny)

Of course some 'shots' have more impact when they are left out altogether:

> In the first version the sequence then closed on Gregor's comatose form, but in the second version I decided it was better if we never see Gregor. (Jack)
>
> We used an over-the-shoulder shot of Ella from behind the bamboo. We don't see her face, which implies her loss of importance. We don't see the bag because we only see what she is seeing: she has forgotten the bag. (Jenny)

These comments reflect how some students' analytical thinking is pushed to a high level. But it is the process of making the films which generates the learning. Any work with cameras, rather than just storyboarding, deepens learning about how camera shots relate to each other in sequence, and key ideas, such as conti-nuity and pace. This is to do with the realisation of ideas as actual moving images, and the processes of experimenting, revising and deciding. And it is also to do with the way getting the grammar 'right' is motivated by aesthetic pleas-ures and satisfactions, which some comments eloquently suggest:

> ... we added the bit in the corridors and quad in the end to make it more complete and satisfying overall. (Barney)

In-camera editing seems to promote these understandings particularly effec-tively. This may be because it promotes imaginative ownership of editing decisions. Each one has to be fully realised mentally before the 'Record' button is pressed; and each one has to be explained clearly and unambigu-ously within the group, articulated without the aid of a visual timeline to point to, or to demonstrate on.

Of course, the exacting demands of the process also develop technical skills: they enforce care and precision, and a disciplined approach. While post-production editing allows for errors, in-camera editing has to be right. It is a good example of how production work in media is always about social and problem-solving skills,

placing considerable demands on the ability of small groups to cooperate and negotiate. Roger, a boy with serious behavioural difficulties, reflects:

> The advice I would give to someone about the process is to have patience
> as you are working with other people and having to coordinate all the
> actions and foresee how they will come out. (Roger)

The following transcript of Helen directing a small group shows a student
learning fast to manage other people. As she manages their different *personali-
ties*, she also manages the *process*, keeping it disciplined and purposeful. She
makes her direction authoritative through decisive language, and through providing reasons for her decisions:

> Jack ... JACK!
> Yeah, but you need to walk in quicker, because Chris can't wait on the
> stairs for you to come, so you have to walk in straight away. Chris, step
> up on the next step. Yeah, that's it ... stay there. OK, Jack you have to
> come in straight away. OK. Ready? 1, 2, 3 ... Go!

She reinforces instructions through repetition. She insists on the discipline of
rehearsal. She balances admonitions with praise. And she juggles this leadership role with a creative one, inventing and revising as she goes along:

> Abby, where were you? You were meant to be in that. Yeah, I know, when
> you hear that you can come running, going 'Oh!' Yeah, come running in
> when you hear the crash. OK. We're going to do a real one now. No,
> we're going to do one more practice then we're going to do a real one,
> OK? Chris, step on ... that was really good. OK, so Abby, when you
> hear the crash you come running.
> JACK! Get up!

This sort of talk is familiar to teachers of Drama. As we have pointed out,
acting is as much a part of the multimodal language of film as camera work.
An exercise like this is an excellent context for exploring this with students.
The exacting process demands focused, rehearsed performance, as well as
focused, rehearsed camera work. Subtle and slight actions and expressions
contribute to tension or narrative as much as a well-chosen angle. After all,
the activity is part of a course on hospital *drama*.

However, if dramatic action and language is part of the multimodal ensemble of
signifying systems that make up film, then students and teachers need to find some
way to talk and write about this. The metalanguage of filming is a clear focus of
this project, and the extracts of students' writing shown above include references
to shot types and camera angles which are clear evidence of their conceptual
grasp of how filming creates meaning. But they also refer to dramatic forms of
signification – the 'pro-filmic' modes we referred to earlier in this chapter.

CONCLUSION

This project illustrates all aspects of our model of media literacy, though our focus here is on its critical dimension. We will consider this dimension in other ways in following chapters. An interesting feature of this project, perhaps, is that it does not immediately look like a 'critical' project. It emphasises creative practical work, and is permeated by a sense of students' pleasure in soap operas, serial narratives and television drama generally. In this sense, it is what David Buckingham has called 'television literacy' (1993) – it is infused with the understandings, pleasures and cultural allegiances of television viewers, at a historical moment when television is still the principal medium of choice for teenagers in the West.

Nevertheless, it develops aspects of critical literacy. It encourages students to consider the relationship between media institutions and their audiences. It aims to help them to conceptualise more general aspects of media texts such as genre and narrative. Finally, it helps them to develop a conceptual apparatus and metalanguage to think about, analyse and describe what they are doing. As we have suggested, this is a developing field, and while some modes, such as filming and editing, have relatively settled 'languages', others may need more general everyday terms. We will return to ways of thinking beyond the conventional grammar of film and television in the next chapter.

While it is important to consider *what* we think we are teaching, however, it is just as important to consider *how* we teach it, the pedagogy of media education. Here, two points can be made about what has proven to be effective. First, the process of filming is deliberately broken down into careful stages which emphasise planning, shot construction and the importance of quality, first by modelling the process with the whole class, then by providing a clear structure for the groups to follow. Second, although the emphasis is apparently on *filming*, in fact the whole project teaches the importance of the principles of *editing*, in a series of reiterations. The construction of narrative through editing is viewed and reflected on in extracts from hospital soaps, explored though the card-sequencing activity, conceptualised in class discussion, written about, analysed in work by previous classes, explored by taking sequences apart using editing software, and finally carried over into practice through storyboarding and shooting. Clearly, then, the pedagogy here is to revisit the principles of shooting and editing many times, using different media to anatomise the process – literally, break it down into component parts – in different ways. In this way, understanding of principles and practice grows incrementally with each iteration, each transformation of the same principles into different media. Being critical here, then, means having a secure, grounded grasp of concept and practice together; and having a clear idea of how to produce a high-quality piece of film.

Finally, this project anticipates the theme of Chapter 9. This project only really makes full sense if it is seen as part of a progression of media learning. It builds on earlier work with still images and storyboarding. It deliberately focuses on filming, knowing that these students will move on to editing work later, and will see that editing depends on the framing work of filming, and that filming anticipates the sequencing work of editing. This kind of progression suggests that traditional models of Media Studies, and their sense of what kinds of understanding and production students can be expected to achieve at 16, will need to change in the future. If students can develop these understandings at the age of 12 and 13, our expectations of 16-year-olds and 18-year-olds will need to be dramatically revised.

TEACHING HORROR: INTERPRETATION AS DIGITAL ANATOMY

This chapter looks at two examples of teaching film in the secondary classroom, from courses in horror film at Parkside over the past 15 years.

Teaching film in schools should be uncontroversial: it is, after all, one of the great art forms of the twentieth century, and has been with us for over a hundred years. In fact, it has only secured a place as a university degree subject relatively recently; it has never gained a secure footing in schools in the UK, and is effectively an optional extra in English even now. In recent years in the UK the case for teaching film, as well as the moving image more broadly, has been repeatedly made by the British Film Institute (BFI), with some success in terms of both policy and practice, influencing the inclusion of the moving image in the statutory curriculum for English. In many ways, we concur with their view of the importance of film and the moving image, as well as the way in which they have collaborated with other groups to situate moving image work in schools within a broader model of media education (Bazalgette et al., 2000). The BFI has also made efforts to imagine a moving image curriculum across the age-range of compulsory schooling (FEWG, 1999), and our own account of progression in Chapter 9 picks up this theme. There are two questions in particular the BFI has left unanswered, partly because it has no permanent base in schools to test out its model over time, partly because its brief restricts it to the moving image. One of these is to do with how the study of the moving image might sit alongside the study of other media forms, distinct in some respects, integrated in others. The other is how its proposals for progression might work in practice; although it has directed a teachers' action research project looking at progression in moving image teaching. We were partners in this project, and it has informed our thinking in Chapter 9.

With regard to our model of media literacy, two considerations seem to us the most important. First, that we make room for and respect the *cultural* experiences of film children bring to the classroom. These experiences will be different, and we need to allow space for discussion and comparison of preferences and experiences. Our own research shows that children will passionately debate the virtues (and vices!) of horror, relating them to their own viewing experiences. We interviewed two girls, for instance, whose favourite film was *The Silence of the Lambs* (Demme, 1991). Part of their enjoyment of it was related to the viewing of it on video during a sleep-over, a typical kind of enjoyment in which the forbidden thrills of the horror film become implicated in the night-time excitement of the sleep-over ritual and its place in the social development of teenage girls. Part of it was a specific instance, in which boys from the village in which they lived were knocking on the window, so that the thrill of the unknown as Agent Starling is stalked by the murderer in the film is dramatically connected with the social games played in the girls' home. While these cultural experiences relate to a textual notion of culture – and the gradual accretion of favourable cultural commentary around a film like *The Silence of the Lambs* – they relate more immediately to the 'lived culture' identified by Raymond Williams, which we have described briefly in Chapter 1.

The second consideration, in relation to our notion of the critical function of media literacy, is the idea of cultural value. We have suggested in Chapter 1 that the process by which some texts become culturally valued is a historical process of competing commentary, in which media classrooms can take part through debate and negotiation in the classroom, with teacher and student both learning more about each other's cultural worlds – where they meet or overlap, where they differ or vividly contrast.

Within this context, the focus of this chapter will be on how students develop a critical grasp of aspects of film, expressed in a metalanguage developed in courses of this kind. What do we mean here by 'critical'? What kind of learning does it imply? And how does critical interpretation relate to creativity and production?

TEACHING HORROR: PITFALLS AND PENDULUMS

Horror films are troubling for education. They are often symptoms of profound social concerns themselves: the Toho studio's *Godzilla* expressed Japanese post-war agonies about the nuclear age; the alien invasion movies of the 1950s dealt in metaphors of the communist 'threat'; the AIP studio's *I Was a Teenage Werewolf* presented the novel figure of the American teenager (in the figure of Michael Landon) as both darkly attractive and as violent and transgressive. More recently, horror films have been unjustifiably blamed for tragic events such as child murders (Buckingham, 1996). Obscure and disturbing contemporary fears seem like dangerous stuff for the classroom, and parents, teachers and governors are all likely, at some point, to ask questions about their 'appropriateness' as objects of study.

Behind anxieties about content are a range of other concerns triggered by this particular cultural form: that horror films provoke violent or immoral behaviour, that they are aesthetically debased, that they are inappropriate for young people and in need of regulation, even censorship.

Our view has always been that some of these concerns are ill-founded, while others are precisely what makes horror films attractive to work on with teenagers. Our rationale can be summarised as five points:

- Horror films are of particular interest to young people because some of their key themes – transformation and coming to terms with nameless fears – are precisely what adolescents are preoccupied with.
- Horror films are widely appealing to young people, and are seen as a kind of rite of passage to adulthood: for both boys and girls (though in different ways), enjoying and coping with the pleasurable fear is part of growing up (Buckingham, 1996).
- Horror films are risky texts. Some people do get very scared, though most young people see them as slightly dangerous territory (depending on the perceived fright level, or regulatory certificate). However, we believe this risk is slight – in fact, the only child either of us has taught who has actually fainted in front of a screen was reacting to a television adaptation of Benjamin Britten's War Requiem! More positively, we believe that it is the duty of education to take considered risks: to explore social fears, and the risks of drugs, sex and certain life choices with young people from a safe vantage point, rather than to maintain a censorious silence which in the end defeats its purpose by provoking even greater curiosity.
- The ambivalent aesthetic status of horror makes it an effective challenge to settled notions of cultural value. Is horror really 'inferior' aesthetically to art-house film (or the mainstream novel)? Or is it, like many popular forms, vibrant, dynamic and responsive to the interests, concerns and pleasures of ordinary people? And in any case, are these categories of taste rather than inherent value – and how are these tastes developed, constructed, policed? Finally, as Carol Clover argues (1993), the aesthetic categories which once located horror firmly in the B-movie slot are no longer so clear-cut – films like *The Silence of the Lambs* (Demme, 1991), or *Bram Stoker's Dracula* (Coppola, 1992), are as much art films as popular classics; while earlier shockers like *Psycho* (Hitchcock, 1960) are now acknowledged auteurist masterpieces.
- As with other popular cultural forms, teachers of horror films have the great advantage that students bring a vast fund of knowledge into the classroom. They can make fine distinctions between subgenres; they have a lot to say about the characteristic thrill of horror, the nature of victims, monsters and hero/heroines; and they know a good deal about the social behaviour of horror audiences.

These arguments are not plucked out of thin air. They have been developed over many years. Like other arguments in this book, they are informed by research, in this case in approaches to horror texts in Film Studies, literary studies and game studies; and in research with young viewers of horror films, including our own work (Burn, 1996, 1999, 2000; Burn and Reed, 1999). But they are also informed by debates with students, parents, governors and other teachers. Parents have sometimes singled out this course, for instance, and voiced concerns that their child will find it disturbing. We have always taken time to talk these concerns through. Behind some of them we have found religious objections to representations of the supernatural that we have simply had to disagree with. Behind others we have found worries about what images frighten children. These fears can be real; though we have found that children can also be frightened by fairytales, bible stories and news programmes. All of these present disturbing images of the world; and our argument is that we should explore such representations with children in the safety of the classroom. Perhaps our best vindication came from a mother of a shy, studious boy, who thanked us for introducing an element of risk into her son's otherwise rather protected world.

In the remainder of this chapter, we will describe two approaches we have used to teach about Hitchcock's Psycho, analysing examples of students' work.

DIGITAL ANATOMIES: EDITING AS ANALYSIS

The first example is from a Year 9 course. Hitchcock's *Psycho* effectively began a subgenre of horror, the slasher movie, which provided a powerful metaphor for a complex of fears in post-war small-town America about the possible dangers lurking beneath its apparently placid and sane surface. This general social anxiety was intensified by the real-life case of the multiple murderer Ed Gein, whose story partly inspired *Psycho*, and later slasher films, including *The Silence of the Lambs*. The subgenre evolves into an increasingly self-reflexive, knowing and ironic form, culminating in Wes Craven's *Scream* trilogy. This history connects the generation of students we worked with on the film with their parents and grandparents, who have lived through different moments in the subgenre's journey from *Psycho* to *Scream*. On the one hand, then, it evokes a genre with which they are closely familiar; on the other hand, it distances them, making them think about horror, and the peculiar thrill it provokes in a way which recognises something of its cultural history.

In respect of media literacy, then, the course taps into a current of interest in teenage media cultures in the slasher subgenre, the pleasurable fears it offers, the forms of ironic reflection on the genre and on teenage life and sexuality it provides, and the productive ground for debate about aesthetic merit it allows. However, it also specifically aims to develop a set of conceptual understandings about the 'language' of the moving image, and specifically the conventions of filming and editing.

This raises questions about the critical function of such work, which we outlined in Chapter 1, where we identified two kinds of critical reading, one *rhetorical*, the other *aesthetic*. Though the two can and should be productively combined, the emphasis in this course is on the latter. Its explicit focus is on the visceral effects created by horror: its characteristic affective charge, neatly encapsulated by Buckingham as 'Distress and Delight' (1996).

If this is the critical function, however, there remains the question about the semiotic process through which it is possible. In our schema, the emphasis here is on interpretation; and on the conceptual apparatus students can develop to make such an interpretation possible. We have suggested in the previous two chapters that there is a certain historical consensus about the 'grammar' of film, developed from the earliest film-makers to the present day, and that this 'grammar' is well represented in academic Film Studies by standard texts such as Bordwell and Thompson's *Film Art* (2003). However, we propose a move beyond this language, as we said in Chapter 1, into a more general social semiotic approach. The 'pro-filmic' modes we identified in Chapter 4, such as set design, script, speech, music, dramatic action and facial expression, costume design, lighting and sound, all have their own ways of signifying, as well as the conventions of filming and editing in which they are incorporated. These modes integrate in various ways, and to be truly 'literate' in film is to have a broad understanding of what these different modes contribute to the whole, the kineikonic mode (Burn and Parker, 2003).

Finally, though the emphasis here may be on interpretation, it is conducted though processes of design and production. Digital media here are used to unpick the filmic text, a process sometimes described as 'reverse engineering': undoing the nuts and bolts of (in this case) the editing process, the better to understand it. This can also be seen as a kind of *digital anatomy*, as we have proposed elsewhere (Burn and Durran, 2006): just as Michelangelo and Leonardo illicitly anatomised corpses to understand their muscular and skeletal structure, so students here explore the structures of the horror film by taking them apart.

The sequence of the course begins with a general exploration of the 'slasher' subgenre, using clips to show how *Psycho* gave rise to a whole tradition which culminates in the ironic parodies of the *Scream* trilogy. It then moves on to a viewing of *Psycho*, followed by whole-class analysis of specific clips, modelling how a multimodal analysis might look at dramatic movement and language, lighting, set design, props, shot framing and camera work, editing and music.

Next, the whole of the film is imported into the editing software Microsoft Moviemaker 2, bundled 'free' with Microsoft's XP operating system. This software has a function devised for people making their own videos: a function called 'clip detection', which splits up the incoming video into clips. What the software designers probably did not imagine was the purpose of this function here: to anatomise the film into its hundreds of component shots.

This practice is, in some ways, a technologised version of the classic method of film analysis – shot segmentation or *découpage*, which traditionally means describing separate shots in order to analyse them. However, it goes further. First, it means that students have a shorthand visual representation of the whole film as a series of keyframes: the first frame of each shot. This is a completely new way of looking at a film, and has the ability to arrest narrative time, as Roland Barthes suggested was the case with cinematic stills (Barthes, 1978), but in a way that represents the whole film. The teacher is then able to ask many kinds of question, and to focus on aspects of the film language. If the students are asked to find examples of close-ups, reaction shots, long shots, cutaways and so on, they can find these at a glance. They can then move them to the timeline, instantly creating a new 'movie' made up of exemplars of a particular aspect of film grammar (Figure 5.1). They can also experiment with ways in which shots are combined, and explore questions of order, duration, sequence and other aspects of narrative. This is a kind of analytical activity; but it is also creative. It allows students to experience the film from the perspective of the editor, considering what difference would be made by various combinations, as this student, Ada, says:

> Seeing the film in little clips makes it seem more like a work in progress
> than a finished film. You feel like you are in the editing studio choosing

FIGURE 5.1 *Reverse-engineering* Psycho

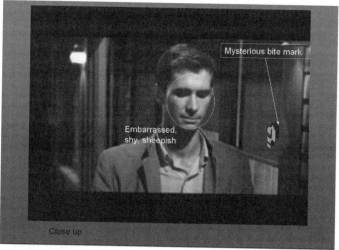

FIGURE 5.2 A *slide from Rosie's PowerPoint*

what clip goes where and analysing what difference things will make. The advantages for this sort of work are that you can experiment many different ways with the clip or frame. You can change the order of sequences or flip the image to see how it would have been done differently. Also you can compare shots, looking at the contrast and similarities between them.

In the next stage of the activity, students export clips and still images from Moviemaker into PowerPoint, to make a presentation about the meanings of *Psycho* and the formal languages that produce these meanings. The focus is on the characteristic affect of the horror film – fear. As the philosopher of film Noel Carroll has pointed out, this genre is perhaps the only one to be named after the emotion it inspires (Carroll, 1990).

If we take one example, a presentation by Rosie (Figure 5.2), we can see what kinds of meanings she analyses. She certainly explores traditional aspects of film language, such as *shot type* (she identifies close-ups and long shots), *camera movement* ('camera goes out with her'), and '*non-diegetic sound*'. However, she arguably pays more attention to dramatic aspects of the shots: 'Her body language is very nervous'; 'Looking around'; 'Closed-off body language'; 'Embarrassed, shy, sheepish'; 'Norman steps back'.

She also looks closely at the significance of lighting: 'Face in shadow'; 'Norman is, quite literally, emerging from the darkness'.

She comments on the significance of aspects of speech in a conversation between Norman and Marion, noting examples of hesitation, changing the subject, and one instance of Norman's identity dissolving into his mother's: 'Norman speaking for mother'.

She analyses the significance of many other aspects of the film: symbolic objects such as stuffed birds, mirrors and curious marks on the wall; set design, such as the Bates house; sound effects and music.

This last category, the music, raises some interesting questions about the language needed to make a better job of exploring this aspect of film with students. Unlike the 'language' of action, where no clear grammar or metalanguage exists, music has, of course, its own formal language, so that the problem becomes one of how technical students need to get to say something about the place of the music in the film.

Here, Rosie makes comments such as:

Non-diegetic sound – strings – T-2 [*Terminator 2*]
The music kicks in as soon as she steps back
The weird T-2-like music fades but doesn't stop

We can say, then, that she is able to connect music with the film action; that she is able to identify details such as the instrumentation; and that she can characterise the effect of the music relevant to the horror text ('weird').

We can also say that she makes sense of the film, as students in this course are encouraged to do, by connecting it with popular horror films in their own experience, in this case, *Terminator 2*.

While this is not conceived as a formal semiotic approach, it does nevertheless move beyond the focus only on filming and editing more typical of conventional forms of film analysis. It begins to recognise the *multimodal* semiotic structure of film: its synthesis of word, image and music.

It also represents ways in which media literacy develops from implicit understandings of, in this case film, to explicit conceptual understandings of a more generalised and abstract nature. Buckingham has employed, in several publications (1993, 1996, 2003) Vygotsky's notion of spontaneous and scientific concepts, suggesting that media education takes informal ideas about the media which children have developed through their experience of media cultures, and develops these into something more abstract and general. However, he has also critiqued Vygotsky's model, suggesting that 'scientific concepts' seem to operate outside the social contexts which are so important for learning in Vygotsky's work generally.

In our own work, we have focused more specifically on Vygotsky's idea of the function of 'semiotic tools' in concept development (Burn and Durran, 2006). We have proposed there that the use of external visual objects in conjunction with terminology in language, reinforced by labels, wordwalls, titling and so on, allow for the gradual development and expansion of conceptual clusters. 'Scientific concepts', while they do possess the key characteristics Vygotsky identified, such as abstraction, generality, systematicity, are by no means neat, hermetically sealed units. Rather, they exist in shades of grey, as patterns and clusters, and as open to contestation and change. These ongoing processes of contestation and change respond to the social environments in which the concepts are developed, tested, amended, reworked. In this way, we can rethink them as part of the social process of learning, in the way Buckingham has argued for.

Rosie's presentation displays, then, the development of particular conceptual groups, associated with forms of language. In some cases, these are ordinary, 'everyday' words which are nevertheless allowing fine distinctions: 'the weird T-2-like music kicks in'. In other cases, what sounds like scientific language has been used: 'Non-diegetic sound'. Of course, it is by no means clear that 'scientific concepts' require 'scientific language' – sometimes, everyday words take on technical meanings in particular academic discourses, such as the meaning of 'fuzzy' in Mathematics. The important thing is that words from different sources are being pressed into service here in the interests of emerging conceptual clusters: how odd music represents fear in horror films; how various kinds of movement represent the 'slasher' character in this kind of film.

There remains a further point about multimodality, however. Rosie's presentation is, in effect, a multimodal essay. It uses moving image, still image, colour, diagrammatic conventions such as arrows, music, sound and written language to present its analysis. This is not the traditional essay of the English curriculum, where print literacy is the only concern and the contribution made by the physical medium is ignored. It also moves beyond the constraints of language as an interpretive medium, which has often been seen as deeply problematic in media education, particularly in the context of Media Studies coursework, which often demands written analysis and commentary. Such work can demand too abrupt a shift from the concrete, visual nature of media texts, or from the practical pleasures of media production work. In Rosie's PowerPoint, by contrast, different modes and media are integrated, and all contribute to the meaning; this is not simply writing about the media, but is a form of media production.

Furthermore, it is not actually writing, or even the PowerPoint file, which is assessed as the outcome of this course, but the oral presentation of the PowerPoint (see the CD-ROM for examples). What is of interest is how the students develop the critical vocabulary central to the course to a level secure enough to be able to improvise orally, while giving some sense of what is culturally interesting for them and their classmates about their analysis. This brief extract from Faiza and Robert's presentation gives some sense of these complex purposes:

FAIZA: Right, here ... if you comp ... If you compare, sorry, compare the scene to the *Gift* scene, you can see that the door opens and the music gradually gets higher and higher until it just blares out and the woman, well, Bates comes from here and attacks him, just as the woman in the bathroom, the music blares out and she turns round.

ROBERT: Erm … the high strings, I think, adds more tension, just as the woman's just about to come out of the door.

FAIZA : OK, *mise-en-scène* very typical – horrible, old kind of doors, and old rugs – gothic rugs …

ROBERT: The door is now fully open, and it makes you really want to know what's behind the door, but you can't tell.

[*They play a short clip, within the PowerPoint presentation. Class laughter. Clip ends. More laughter.*]

FAIZA : Ok, erm, we kind of felt that he's just about to reach the top of the stairs, he's just about to step away from danger, but as he takes that step … something appears.

RICHARD: Erm, the bird's-eye view shot is very good, Hitchcock has used it amazingly well, because you can see Arbogast just getting to the top of the stairs, and you can also see the attacker coming out of the door.

FAIZA : We've highlighted this area because we don't know what it is. It could be something, could it be the attacker, or is it some … freaky … towel-like thing [*Laughter*]…

This begins to give some shape to the social nature of the movement from spontaneous to 'scientific' concepts, then – far from being a move into an abstract realm somehow positioned outside society, it is still firmly attached to the pleasures and discourse of popular viewing; though the readings, language and identities associated with a quasi-academic discourse are also clearly present.

FILM PRODUCTION: MAKING TRAILERS

This example comes from a GCSE Media Studies course. It asks students to make a trailer of *Psycho*, as a way of exploring how films are marketed and distributed.

The students begin by studying existing marketing and distribution materials: posters, press kits, trailers, merchandise. In this sense, then, they are developing a conceptual understanding of the part of the media education framework concerned with media institutions.

They are then specifically required to market *Psycho*: to produce a poster, press kit and trailer for an imaginary re-release of the film. They learn that a film like *Psycho* can be pitched at a target audience, whose interests are addressed in certain ways. This is a complex affair in the case of *Psycho*; for students today, the film can look old and dated, black-and-white films are unusual in today's teenage market, and it is not immediately obvious how the film will be made interesting. But this audience, as a core audience for horror films generally, was included in the brief. The other audience is the older group (the parents and grandparents of these students) who will know the film already, at least by reputation, and maybe in the context of its original screening, and will have a nostalgic interest in its re-release.

Here, then, the critical approach in question is what we have called in Chapter 1 the *rhetorical* one, as distinct from the *aesthetic* one which was emphasised in the Year 9 project described in the first part of this chapter. These simulations of marketing and distribution interrogate the forms of production which lie behind the film, the commercial imperatives which drive it, but also the cultural interests of different audiences, here conceived generationally. This kind of work is very difficult to get right. The work of this group of girls certainly demonstrated an engagement with the marketing and distribution process through the making of press kits that included posters, press releases emphasising the historical importance of Hitchcock, and other materials, some of them adapted from Internet resources. Our interviews suggested, however, that conversations at home had an equal impact on their understanding of how the film was valued by their parents' generation. Here, then, they were participating in a historical process of commentary in which the value of Hitchcock as a cult *auteur* is both developed and challenged. They learnt to look beyond the immediate impression of an 'old black-and-white film'; but at the same time retained their allegiance to the more visceral examples of the slasher subgenre they knew and enjoyed.

The most substantial piece of work in their press kit was the trailer. To make it, they took the whole of *Psycho* and trawled through it, selecting clips through a digital video editing software package (Media 100), and storing them for future use. The editing process went through many stages of selection, ordering, layering and refinement before they were happy with the final version (Figure 5.3)

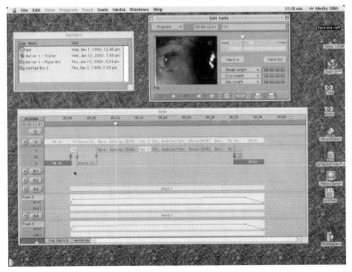

FIGURE 5.3 *Editing a* Psycho *trailer: the* Media 100 *interface*

The students' work, and our follow-up research with one group of girls (Burn and Reed, 1999), showed that they had been very thoughtful about these questions. To begin with, they found that the film did have the power to shock, even though it seemed tame by comparison with more recent films:

> LORRAINE: The fact is, for our generation, it's not, you know, the most terrifying thing, some of the things that are out at the moment –
> GWEN: It's not as graphic –
> ABBY: It is, though – you know the shower scene – doesn't it, like, make you flinch, although it's not [indec.] you actually see the knife going, so …

The girls go on to discuss other films they have watched and enjoyed, including Wes Craven's *Scream* sequence, films based on Stephen King stories – *It* (Wallace, 1990), *The Tommyknockers* (Power, 1993) – the *Nightmare on Elm Street* sequence (Craven, 1984), and the (then) newly re-released *Exorcist* (Friedkin, 1976), which Gwen had just seen. Holly describes how she and Gwen used to get horror videos out every weekend and terrify themselves with them. They make the point that sometimes in these films the frightening thing is not so much explicit images of horror as suggestive, tantalisingly empty images: they mention the blue light of the TV screen in *Poltergeist* (Hooper, 1982) and a 'really scary' green light in *The Tommyknockers*. This discussion shows how interdependent the concepts of the media education framework are. The students are thinking about themselves as an audience, their experiences, tastes, cultural loyalties; but they are also thinking about how a media institution would address such an audience; and they are also considering details of the 'language' of these films which provokes typical responses of pleasurable fear.

These girls bring histories of encounters with popular film that are an important part of their work in Media Studies. Holly and Gwen's account of spending weekends screaming over slasher movies forms an important backdrop to how they have made sense of *Psycho*; indeed, Gwen is now able to explain explicitly how horror movies often play on our society's naive conceptions of childhood and innocence, relating this to the Bulger case (a well-known child murder in the UK); and Holly can make the connections between *Scream* and *Psycho* that appeal to viewers like her:

> There's definitely something intimidating about the young vulnerable woman, because it's part of our culture, that we're more vulnerable than men.

In framing the project as a re-release for a modern audience, the teacher here allows for an exploration of how the selective cultural tradition Raymond Williams identified connects with his notion of the lived culture. While the girls were aware, as we have seen, of the older audience, and in some cases had discussed the film at home with parents, the emphasis in their trailer was, understandably, on the new audience from their own peer group. This interest shows clearly in the trailer they made, and in the evaluative writing they completed afterwards:

> Another successful technique we used to provoke interest or emotion from our target audience was to use text screens bearing captions, as these effectively catch the attention of the audience, who are almost forced to read them. In a sense, these separated different parts of the trailer. The first one, 'WATCH OUT!' (placed after Norman hands the key over to Marion), was designed to put the audience in suspense and obviously hints that Marion will not be safe, whilst not giving too much away. The second, 'SHE'S BACK!', was placed after Norman tells Marion his mother is 'not quite herself' to lead into the horror sequence (a sudden jump from the calmer narrative to fast-moving horror scenes would have looked unnatural and unprofessional) and to arouse the suspicions of the audience, who are likely to guess that 'mother' is the killer. ... The third caption, 'THE MOTHER OF ALL HORROR FILMS', is a clever play on words for anyone who has already seen the film and was placed at the end to draw a close to the action and tell the audience about the film.

The caption technique, and even the wording of it focusing on Norman Bates's mother, recalls marketing approaches for *Aliens* (Cameron, 1986) using the slogan 'The Bitch is Back' to represent the monstrous alien mother. The implications of the 'monstrous feminine' for feminist film theory have been explored in relation to *Aliens* by Barbara Creed (1986); but here we can make the simpler point that this group of girls are more interested in the idea of a female monster than in the figure of Norman himself; theirs is a gendered reading of the film.

While much of the emphasis of this project is on the rhetorical form of critical understanding, an exploration of the film industry and its audiences, students also learn through this kind of production activity a number of important features of the moving image: that narrative is constructed by juxtaposition and implication as well as by straightforward representation of events; that sound and image are independently variable; that pace contributes to suspense, and can be controlled in the editing software – they use 50% slow-motion at one point. They also develop complex understandings of the narrative of a horror film, its dependence on suspense and its interplay between explicitly horrific images and more suggestive ones:

> In our main trailer, we decided to convey more of the narrative to both of the target audiences by building up the thriller element of the film, alongside the horror element. ... we re-structured the trailer on our timeline so that it was segmented, starting with an exposition of the narrative, in which shots of Janet Leigh travelling to the Bates motel, along with shots of Anthony Perkins giving her the key were shown.

In terms of the conceptual framework of media education, then, we can say that these students have developed understandings of institutions (marketing and distribution), audiences (an exploration of their own experiences, pleasures and tastes) and texts (the structure of a trailer).

However, there is more to it than this. Teachers who have worked with students to make short film forms like this – trailers, adverts, pop videos – will often say that the students' work is more than an exercise or simulation; indeed, that it exceeds the genre it imitates, almost becoming a genre of its own. What seems to happen in these projects is that students begin to feel like film-makers, with some of the artistic and aesthetic motivation which this implies. Creativity here seems to involve the opportunity to represent the students' own interests, in the female monster and in their own histories of horror viewing. It also involves an excitement about becoming competent with the artistic medium – the editing software:

> ABBY: Like, normally staying in school till six would be just your nightmare but we actually really got into it last night, and like HEH HEH HEH! [exaggerated triumphant laugh] and we walked out, like, with a smile on our face, as we were so satisfied it had worked!
> HOLLY: We did, we talked about it on the street, 'cos it was so satisfactory.

Creativity here serves a double function. The manipulation of what Vygotsky called semiotic tools (in this case digital editing software) allowed for new expressive purposes, but also for the development of new conceptual understandings of aesthetic and representational aspects of film.

CONCLUSION: MOVING IMAGE LITERACY?

To begin with, these projects demonstrate that, for us, the critical function of media literacy is, as we said in Chapter 1, about *aesthetic* as well as *rhetorical* understanding. It is about understanding how horror produces a pleasurable *affect* as well as representing women in particular ways, about understanding how film trailers have their own emotional and aesthetic impact as well as revealing the mechanisms of how the industry addresses its audience, and how that audience responds.

Secondly, they show that the critical interpretation of media texts, institutions and audiences need not be a cold dissection, divorced from pleasurable engagement or creative re-making. Rather, the design and production of media texts can be combined with analytical readings: the process of conceptualising horror uses the same semiotic tools as the process of creative production. Both are intellectual processes, producing new ideas; both are affective, combining the pleasure of viewing horror with the pleasure of creating new moving image texts.

Thirdly, we can argue that moving image literacy can be seen as a subset of media literacy more generally. It has its own coherence, its own century-long debate about how film is or is not like a language, its own close relation with the cultural forms of film and television, its own history of canonical texts, debates about popular culture, patterns of taste, critical response and fan work among its audiences. For all these reasons, some features of film and television are relatively settled. The 'grammar' of filming and editing, as represented by standard academic text-books such as Bordwell and Thompson's *Film Art* (2003), attracts a wide consensus both among the academic and the professional community, as we have noted in Chapter 4.

In terms of media education, these fairly settled ideas of the language of the moving image, the nature of film and television institutions and production regimes, and the behaviours of film audiences, all lend themselves to the conceptual framework in ways that are relatively transparent and straightforward to teach; and we have seen examples of this in the animation project and hospital drama project described in the previous two chapters.

However, we believe that, to make the most of work with the moving image, teachers and researchers need to be alert to three further points.

While conventional 'languages' of the moving image may serve the immediate purpose well, they may not be adequate in the final analysis. If the focus is on dramatic movement, or musical rhythm, or the visual design of the set, or on the meaning of costumes, or on the spoken language of the film, then the conventions of filming and editing do not provide analytical frameworks. Here, we may need to think of the moving image as multimodal, and to help students to develop ways to think of movement, rhythm, sound, language, as Rosie does in her PowerPoint. In practical terms, this is a tall order for English and Media teachers, who may object that they have no specialised knowledge of music, of choreography, of architecture to equip students with analytical tools. Our response is to say that people work with the resources they have. If they are English teachers, they can help students to think how the grammar, syntax, intonation, lexical choice of the spoken language in the film articulate with the spatial and temporal structures of filming and editing. If they happen to play a musical instrument, they will have additional knowledge about music and sound. If they are interested in architecture, they will have some grasp of that mode of design. In the world, domains of design and production are rarely as compartmentalised as in the school curriculum – most of us have a smattering of more general knowledge.

In these respects, the Vygotskyan notion of the 'scientific concept' needs further work. Certainly, the students described in this chapter are working from everyday experiences of film towards more abstract, more systematic ways of thinking about how horror films represent social fears, create the characteristic affect of horror, and use a range of signifying systems to do all this. We can also claim that, by giving them concrete visual and audiovisual production tools, we make it possible for them to deal with these ideas externally, to develop them through collaborative signifying practices – choosing images, moving film clips around in editing softwares, making trailers – so that the conceptual clusters have room to solidify, develop, be tested.

What remains unclear is exactly how teachers can help students to move beyond the constraints of conventional 'grammars' of film. The language the students use exceeds the bounds of such systems; but frameworks based on multimodal semiotics have yet to be devised for schools, and yet to win consensus. We have experimented with how they might be explicitly used with students, and give examples in Chapter 2 (in relation to comicstrip design) and Chapter 9 (in relation to the reading of film), which give some idea of what such semiotic approaches might look like in practice.

Finally, teachers and researchers need to consider the nature of the digital media used in the projects described here. As we have suggested in Chapter 1, digital media here provide new opportunities. In particular, video editing software allows them to anatomise a film and to make their own creative work; PowerPoint allows for dynamic, multimodal 'essays' which integrate image, word, visual design and diagram. In the case of video editing software, the functions of the authoring tool actually replicate the filmic structures the students are learning about, in a kind of literacy that does resemble writing: the construction of a cinematic sentence on a timeline. More generally, both these softwares are used here for the learning value of two affordances we referred to in Chapter 1: *iteration* and *feedback*. The ability to play repeatedly with, continually revise and continuously view sequences of film is precisely what makes these anatomised pieces of video so effective as semiotic tools for learning.

Rather less certainly, we are beginning to grasp, as Manovich suggests (1998), what it means for moving image texts, familiar in so many ways from the hundred-year history of film, to become computable. The students' recursive process of learning, moving from tentative exploration to confident design through the newly malleable material of the moving image, is working not with strips of celluloid or videotape, but with a database of media objects, and learning by manipulating the algorithms which re-order, re-frame, re-connect and filter these. This new understanding of the marriage of computer and 'traditional' media is something we will return to in the final chapter

SELLING CHOCOLATE: RHETORIC, REPRESENTATION AND AGENCY

In the last chapter we emphasised how students' rhetorical study of texts could help them to explain their aesthetic effects. In this chapter we look at the rhetorical strand more broadly, and at how it can account for the kinds of messages conveyed in advertising. As we have seen, Aristotle's model of rhetoric incorporated three elements – *ethos*, *logos* and *pathos* – which can be broadly aligned with conceptions of institutions, texts and audiences in modern rhetorical studies, and media studies in particular.

Again, critical engagement is seen here in tandem with creative production work, rather than opposed to it, as students make their own TV advert. Television advertising is an important area of the media literacy of young people. It is also difficult to account for as a part of their cultures and the economies in which they live: hard to say how important it is, hard to say how much it influences what they buy and aspire to, hard to say what kind of pleasure they take in it as a condensed form which carries, amongst other things, intense miniature narratives, celebrity vehicles and representations of contemporary tastes and lifestyles. One the one hand, television advertising can be viewed by educators as a seductive manifestation of the power of corporate capitalism; at the other extreme, it can be viewed as a contemporary art form, commercial in its primary purpose, but, like its close cousin the music video, an energetic and playful moving image genre.

Consequently, teaching approaches to advertising need to be similarly ambivalent. Young people certainly need to know that advertising exists to sell them both material products and ideas, and to be critically aware of how it does this. However, they also need room to extend and explore the complex ways in which they engage with them as cultural forms. Teachers also need to be aware of the positive aspects of adverts: their value as a part of shared popular culture (think of James Joyce's play on the Guinness slogan in *Finnegans Wake*); their inventiveness as a moving image form with a washback effect in mainstream video, television and film culture (think of Ridley Scott's Hovis advert on UK television in the 1970s); their mediation of stars of popular culture, such as Nike's mini-essays on the images and skills of international footballing heroes.

The project described in this chapter explores advertising addressed at the new ethical consumer through the marketing of a Fair Trade chocolate bar. It raises the important question of how media production projects simulate the work of media industries. Simulation, as Buckingham argues (2003), is a legitimate and frequently practised approach to media production work, and to classroom explorations of the nature of media organisations. However, in the end, there is always something unsatisfying about endless simulations, not just in the context of media education, but in the educational lives of young people generally. Most of what they do in schools is a simulation of the adult world in some form or another: they move from lesson to lesson discarding and assuming roles modelled on the work of adult professionals, trying on the identities of young scientists, actors, mathematicians, designers, authors, chefs, film directors, geographers, academics, musicians, artists. Many teachers work hard to break out of the glass box of school simulation, putting on public art shows, concerts, exhibitions and so on. At Parkside we can recall many examples of this: exhibitions of student pub sign designs in the local pub; an exhibition of model insects made in Biology in a Cambridge University natural history museum; a concert of music played on instruments made with trash metal performed with a famous London orchestra; a documentary by a group of Bengali-speaking children about their lives, broadcast on regional television for the Millennium.

This project was another opportunity for us to develop a media production course that connected with the real world in some way. We were approached by the UK charity organisation Comic Relief, much of whose work is channelled towards aid for Africa and support for sustainable development projects. In this case they wanted to link English schools with schools in Ghana to promote the idea of Fair Trade chocolate production. The chocolate was made by a London company, the Day Chocolate company, a third of which is owned by the Fair Trade cocoa-growers co-operative Kuapa Kokoo in Ghana.

With Parkside's media specialist work in mind, we suggested an additional element to the project: for students to make a television advert for the new chocolate bar the company was launching – Dubble, a Fair Trade chocolate bar marketed for children. Comic Relief agreed, and we worked with the 'product champion' for Dubble at the Day Chocolate company, Kika Dixon, to develop a brief for a television advert. Kika visited the class of the students whose work is analysed later in this chapter, and gave them the brief just as she would to a professional advertising company.

While we developed this work into a media production course for the GCSE Media Studies exam at Parkside, we also invited a number of other specialist media schools to work with us to write a resource pack for teaching advertising through the Dubble project. Jenny Grahame of the English and Media Centre in London supported the project, and helped to develop the resource pack as part of the Centre's media education resource for Key Stage 4, the 14–16 phase of the UK education system (Grahame et al., 2002).

Finally, while the brief for the advert was real, and the product was real, and the Parkside students even met and interviewed a representative from Kuapa Kokoo in Ghana, there remained the question of what would happen to the adverts once they were made. Needless to say, it was impossible to broadcast them on television (and broadcasting time remains the most valuable resource television companies could offer for young people's media production work; and the least commonly available). However, the students' adverts were viewed with interest and appreciation by the project teams from Comic Relief and Day, who fed back comments. In addition, the Parkside adverts were screened by the Arts Picturehouse cinema in Cambridge as part of a Dubble feature during the cinema's Summer Festival season.

We will look now at two aspects of the project: first of all the pedagogy, as represented by the planning of the course; and then at an example of students' adverts, a selection of which are included on the CD-ROM, along with the original brief from the Day product champion, on video. There are, as with all media production work, two key questions here: how can teachers plan for the kind of critical–rhetorical learning which is the focus here; and what kinds of learning will occur in addition to (even in spite of!) such pedagogic structures?

PLANNING THE DUBBLE PROJECT

Institutions

Like any advertising project, this one invites students to imagine they are an advertising agency given a brief to produce an advert for a particular project. However, more important than this simulation is what students learn about Day Chocolate: that a third of it is owned by the Kuapa Kokoo co-operative; that other owners include Body Shop International, Christian Aid and Comic Relief; that Dubble is a Fair Trade bar, providing a guaranteed price to the cocoa-growers.

In what sense can this kind of information be seen as education about media institutions? In the case of Dubble, the political economy which lies behind the Fair Trade movement needs to be understood, at least to some extent, by students. In addition, the ways in which the media function to sell ideas about aid, trade and Africa in particular are the context out of which any advertising for Dubble emerges. Debt cancellation and trade are early twenty-first century political stances, seeking to improve on the charity impulse that determined earlier models of government and NGO intervention in African poverty and famine. This is the bigger institutional context, and its contemporary manifestations in the UK have been represented in UK politics by the 2005 G8 summit and its debt, aid and trade settlements; and in popular media terms by the Live 8 concert and the prolonged engagement of campaigning music celebrities in such political settlements. Of course, such movements are the subject of intense debate, criticism and contestation: the question for the classroom is how to open up such debate to students.

For teenagers of the early twenty-first century, this form of international politics is visible and motivating. The Dubble project has the potential to tap into the latent or actual political engagement of students, to provide contextual information, personal narratives (from Ghanaian farmers and their children) and a connection through chocolate, a consumer product with a powerful historic presence in children's culture, but also a profound economic history redolent of post-colonial relationships and the poverty trap in which developing economies are confined.

The very identity of chocolate producers such as Cadbury Schweppes in the UK speaks of this history. Cadbury is an old Quaker company characterised by a benevolent paternalism towards its workers in the nineteenth century, for whom it built a working village on the outskirts of Birmingham. Now this village functions as a theme park for children to visit; and the 'educational' message of this 'experience', like the website that supports it, revives the narrative of the historical benevolence of Cadbury in the UK, while reducing the narrative of its relations with cocoa-growers in Africa to a mere cartoon sketch (for a comparative analysis of the Dubble and Cadbury educational websites, and their respective representations of Africa, see Burn and Parker, 2003).

However, presenting the political economy of chocolate production and its mediation through advertising is one thing; guaranteeing that students have 'learnt' this in some measurable way is quite different. In this course they were expected to show that they understood the institutional context in the written work which accompanied the production of their advert. Yet the nature of such work has often been questioned (notably by Buckingham et al., 1995): it is too easy for this kind of writing either to fail to produce evidence of learning beyond the superficial, or for it to obediently rehearse the expected information, concealing where the students' interests and motivations really lie.

Nevertheless, language – whether in the form of speech or writing – remains an important mode for the critical interrogation of media texts, not least because it is well adapted to represent abstract concepts. Media teachers need to work with writing, not denying its place in early twenty-first century culture, but campaigning for it to be seen in a wider context of genres (game walkthroughs, comicstrip captions, agony aunt columns, blogs, text-messages), and to be perceived as one among many signifying systems which today's media interweave. In this respect, the written work accompanying advertising production work can simulate the genres of institutional production (memos, pitches, letters, design specifications). It can be a form of roleplay: students can write in role to the Day company, expressing the merits of their advert; and can also reply in role, criticising it. This kind of writing can incorporate: design features (letterheads, logos, slogans); screengrabs of images from the advert; casting notes and photos; storyboard sequences; interviews with audience focus groups. The writing, rather than being at odds with the digital production of video, can be another form of digital production itself.

Text

The intention in this project is for students to learn about three aspects of media texts: genre, representation and a number of features of the grammar of the moving image.

In terms of genre, the Dubble advert is a hybrid. On the one hand, it requires an advert for a consumer product which typically associates that product with a desirable lifestyle. On the other hand, it is a descendant of the 'charity ad' genre, typified by sombre images of the victims of poverty, abuse and neglect, and produced in the UK by charities such as Christian Aid, Oxfam and the Royal Society for the Prevention of Cruelty to Children (see the English and Media Centre's Advertising pack for examples).

This double lineage (to add to the many puns the name of the bar has intentionally spawned) leads to a number of *representational* issues. Since Fair Trade intends to recognise the self-determination of African farmers, the typical charity ad representation of passive victims needs to be avoided: no easy task when children's experience of these images is profoundly rooted in discourses of victimhood and aid. The representation of chocolate is an easier matter, at first glance: it simply needs to be shown in the advert in a positive light, and associated with desirable qualities, lifestyles or consequences. However, the chocolate itself is related to the Fair Trade theme, and this relationship is difficult to convey in an advertisement.

A second representational problem is to do with the nature of metaphor, something more often associated with English classrooms than media ones, perhaps. Students find it easier to design literal meanings than symbolic or metaphorical ones: so it was simpler to imagine a Dubble advert in which a teenager entered a shop, bought a Dubble bar, ate it and found new friends than to associate the bar with fantasy images, or superficially unrelated objects and events.

When it came to representing the Fair Trade message, the task became even more difficult. This was much more distant from the students' lives than the consumption of chocolate, and required them to move beyond their immediate personal and cultural preoccupations, which media work is often able easily to cater for. How to represent Africa, and African cocoa-farmers? Even more difficult, how to represent the rather abstract idea of Fair Trade? For one thing, it does not lend itself easily to visual representation. For another, the whole idea of Fair Trade, while it was interesting for some students, was a little 'worthy' for others, and less immediately motivating than the process of representing themselves, their friends and the chocolate in narratives that might be witty, ironic, amusing and closely associated with their immediate cultural interests.

These problems betray a dilemma at the heart of media education. It is a commonplace observation that working with popular media allows students to explore and further engage with popular media forms and texts they are familiar with, and which give them pleasure. On the other hand, it is a grave mistake to imagine some homogeneous media culture which all young people inhabit: their tastes and experiences are as wide and varied as those of any comparable group of adults. Whichever texts teachers select to focus on, or to require students to make, they will be more familiar, motivating, interesting to some than to others. Furthermore, media courses, while part of their aim will always be to deepen students' understanding of media texts they know well, will also always want to introduce them to texts, genres, forms they have not experienced. This is a difficult balance to achieve, especially for any given individual student; but the principle is clear enough. The Dubble project offers the possibility of such a balance: the pleasurable exploration of consumer advertising in which many children are experts from an early age, coupled with the challenging task of selling a complex abstract message, rooted in a serious political and economic context.

Finally, this task is a moving image task, and requires students to learn (or further develop) their grasp of the 'grammar' of the moving image. Like music videos, title sequences for films or television drama, and film trailers, adverts are perfect short forms for media production work in schools. They offer all the satisfaction of making a complete text, in a genre whose rich cultural history young people know well. They require economical, precise design of shots, and equally precise and economical editing.

However, this is not just a training exercise in shot construction and editing. The point of this grammar is that it is the semiotic realisation of all the questions of politics, representation, agency and culture raised above. The grammar cannot be divorced from the meaning it conveys – the images and sounds of the advert need to be understood in terms of the social meanings they carry. As in any media project, these meanings will be in terms of the stated aims of the project and the content it is attempting to engage with; but they will always also exceed those aims. Short films of this kind made by young people will necessarily carry unpredictable meanings which emerge from their own preoccupations, experiences, tastes, beliefs and interactions with each other. This needs to be planned for – it needs space, slack, resources and, above all, an openness of mind on the part of teachers. We need to understand the emergence of unexpected meanings, and not automatically censor them because they appear at odds with, perhaps even undermine, the 'official' intention of the course.

Audience

As with any kind of simulation of the media industries, this project asks students to imagine an audience for their advert. The audience is specified in the original brief by Kika Dixon: '11–16-year-olds, boys and girls' (see CD-ROM for the video of Kika's brief). The key question here, as in any exploration of audience, is how the students' notion of audience connects with their conception of representation and mode of address. How will their work represent the target group, or their interests, aspirations, preoccupations? How will it construct a mode of address which will be comprehensible, engaging and credible? How will it locate the viewer?

In social semiotic terms, the idea of address is realised as the function of interactivity: how does the text invite readers or spectators to engage with it, through its choice of content, its framing of shots, its camera angles and distances, and so on. The interactive function also includes the idea of *modality*. Modality is the system in semiotics which determines, amongst other things, the truth claim of the text, which relates to longstanding debates about realism in film and television, for instance; but which here is more to do with authenticity and credibility. We will explore below how examples of students' films work to establish modality claims: how to make both the chocolate *and* the Fair Trade idea seem convincing and believable.

Three things remain to be said about audiences. First, students are not simply addressing their film to an imagined audience in a vacuum. This audience shares their world, and the texts made by students will draw on cultures and discourses which they believe their audience will share. This shared world of discourse connects producers and audiences, though not always in transparent or predictable ways. If we were to provisionally name the discourses these films principally engage with, they might be discourses of chocolate, of childhood and youth, and of Africa (through the eyes of the 'developed' world).

Secondly, to approach an audience is, eventually, to extend the life of a text beyond the process of production. The five strata we have incorporated in our model of media literacy lead to this extension: *discourse, design, production, distribution, interpretation.* It is often not possible in school media production work to reach the fourth stratum, distribution. We might simulate it, asking students to construct schedules for when their work might be broadcast, or press kits for distribution of their films. But the distribution stratum is inevitably elusive. In this project we did manage to show the students' work to the Day Chocolate company, and to screen it in a local arts cinema, but not to broadcast it on television.

Thirdly, as Steve Archer has argued, student productions are, in some ways, a genre of their own; and a corollary of this is that, in many ways, students make them for themselves and their friends rather than for an imaginary, unknown audience (Archer, 2007). This is not necessarily a limitation: it may well be that many professional makers of texts do the same thing. Many authors are on record as writing the books they themselves would like to read. Similarly, we encountered, in the course of a recent research project, a game development company who were clearly making a game for young men like themselves. With this broad description of the course in mind, we turn now to an analysis of one of the first outcomes, which can be viewed on the CD-ROM.

THE GRAMMAR OF CHOCOLATE: AGENCY AND MODALITY

This advert is by a group of four boys which has remained quite constant through the two years of the GCSE Media Studies course. They have already made two productions: one of a trailer for the Luc Besson film *The Fifth Element* (1997), the other a short documentary on skateboarding (an analysis of this can be found in Burn and Parker, 2003).

Their advert is a narrative of chocolate-eating, associated with lifestyle qualities (the brief from Day Chocolate wanted messages like 'cool, cheeky, delicious'). The group found this narrative relatively easy and enjoyable to imagine, plan and construct. They decided early on to recruit a friend from their year group as the star of the advert, and adopted an approach which several other groups also used: to show the boy buying the bar from the local corner shop, followed by some kind of transformation of his life.

They found the Fair Trade message much harder to conceive of. They had real difficulty in imagining how the agency of African cocoa-farmers might be represented. For them, as for other groups, part of this difficulty lay in a desire to represent Africa in a literal way. Eventually they asked if they could take their camera out of school to the Botanical Gardens in Cambridge and film lush tropical vegetation which they hoped could represent cocoa plantations. However, they realised that the rather abstract notion of Fair Trade needed more explication than this, and later adopted other strategies.

The challenge of this task for them is, in many ways, to do with the representation of different kinds of agency. Who or what has agency in the narrative sequences they construct? And who is on the receiving end? Their task has been in some ways explicitly constructed along these lines: they know, for instance, that they must try to avoid representing the Ghanaian cocoa-farmers as passive.

The terms social semiotics borrows from functional linguistics for the performer of an action and the recipient of the action are Actor and Goal. There are, arguably, three Actors in their video. There is the boy who buys the chocolate bar, who becomes replicated – two of him on screen, eating the bar – a visual joke derived from the name of the bar, Dubble. The dynamic movement in the ad is vested in the teenage protagonist. He buys the bar, walks out of the shop, holds the bar in his right hand, the lyrics of the accompanying soundtrack singing 'Take a look at your right hand'. He sits down, eats the bar, is amazed by its taste (big close-up on his wide-open left eye) (Figure 6.1). His replica appears on the bench beside him – more amazement. He laughs and jokes with his double.

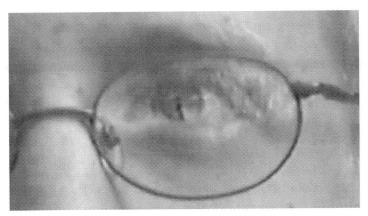

FIGURE 6.1 *Close-up shot of the teenage protagonist of the Dubble advert*

This sequence can be seen as a kind of dramatisation of an idealised everyday life, in which the protagonist represents desirable aspects of the boys' peer group: witty, cool, assured. In their previous video production piece, the skateboarding video, their representational strategy was very similar: they chose to film members of their year group who were accomplished skateboarders. In a sense, both choices were a kind of vicarious construction of teenage cultural identity: they never used themselves as the actors (as other groups commonly did), partly because of a degree of social uncertainty. All three members of the group were relatively retiring boys, and academically successful: the brash, streetwise persona they construct in both videos is an ideal, aspirational fantasy.

These negotiations of identity through clothing, music, consumer choice and engagement with media genres have been theorised in recent youth culture theory as lifestyle rather than as the classic form of youth subculture. In particular, Bennett's account of youth culture as 'glocalisation' (2000), in which global cultural influences become infused with local knowledge, seems an appropriate model to apply to the work of these three boys. Across both videos, the global cultures of skateboarding, hip-hop and associated dress codes are interwoven with the local spaces appropriated by the boys' peer group – a local university forecourt and the corner shop outside their school – as well as local speech forms, interpretations of music genres, and inflections of humour and irony.

In their advert, these qualities are signified in the performance by clothing (hooded jacket, baggy jeans) and comic facial expressions. In the editing it is signified by changes in the speed – slow motion as the boy swaggers into the shop, speeded-up for comic effect as he emerges. It is also signified by the choice of music for the whole piece – a hip-hop song written and recorded by the step-brother of one of the group.

The group has worked to develop the first message of the advert – the desirability of the chocolate bar – and in this respect, the bar itself is constructed as the second protagonist of the video – the 'subject' of the marketing (we are the addressees, in a communicative link between the marketers, the representation of the bar and the target audience). The bar in this respect, is the 'star' of the advert. In the establishing shot, as the boy emerges from the shop, he is seen in long shot; the bar is a mere detail. As he walks towards the camera, though, the bar grows in size in his hand while he moves out of sight to the right of the screen. The grammatical terms, indicated by size and prominence on the screen, are reversed – the bar becomes the Actor, the boy more of an appendage, the Goal of the bar's taste.

In the second shot this reversal is given a new twist. It is a shot from the boy's point of view, looking down at the bar, travelling along in his right hand, the pavement beneath moving along (Figure 6.2).

Again, this strongly suggests the bar as Actor, travelling cheerily along, pulling the boy behind it. The point of view positions the boy with us, observing the bar's antics, being pulled along as well by its insistent message.

Thirdly, there are the cocoa-farmers of Ghana, partners in the Fair Trade enterprise. Not surprisingly, the students in this project found the last idea the hardest to represent, and were obliged to find a range of metaphorical images to suggest the idea of Fair Trade. In this advert, the group film a scene in the Botanical Gardens in Cambridge to represent the cocoa plantations of Ghana (Figure 6.3).

FIGURE 6.2 *The chocolate bar as hero/Actor*

FIGURE 6.3 *The Botanical Gardens, representing the cocoa-growers of Ghana*

However, this sequence is extremely ambiguous. There is little dynamism in this shot: the lush greenery just sits there, as a cascade of coins is poured in the foreground, symbolising the money returning to Africa through the Fair Trade system, while text across the screen hammers the message home. This staticity is a reflection, in the grammar of the image, of the difficulty of conveying this idea. There is an uncertainty in the visual sequence about whom to signal as the Actor, what to signal as the action, what to signal as Goal, bearing in mind that the group don't want to represent the cocoa-farmers as passive beneficiaries.

To push the idea of agency a little further, there are three possibilities.

1 The landscape itself is the Actor, a signifier of the Ghanaian farmers, constructed from a semiotic resource to hand – the Botanical Gardens. If the landscape *is* the Actor, it is, as we have mentioned, notable for its staticity – the image has duration, but no movement, at least as far as the landscape is concerned.

2 The cascade of coins is the Actor. In this reading 'money talks', pouring across the landscape. In fact, of course, this is a signifier where all the key meanings reside in the invisible elements of the image, what is not shown. Somebody must have *poured* the money; somebody must be the *beneficiary*. This is the equivalent of the so-called 'agentless passive' in language, often used to conceal who is responsible for an action (*many people have been injured in the attack*). This leaves unresolved a crucial aspect of Fair Trade. If these students are imagining the invisible agent as a Western group (Comic Relief? Day Chocolate? The Department for International Development?), charitably donating funds to poor African farmers, then they miss the point of Fair Trade, which is to invest in the producers of the raw materials as powerful partners in a fair economic exchange, not passive recipients of charitable handouts. If, on the other hand, the students are imagining the cocoa-farmers co-operative pouring the coins, the picture is quite different. Probably, of course, they don't have a clear image – this area is less clear, less close to them, and the ambiguity of the image reflects this.

3 The Actor is signalled in the written text, which reads: WHEN YOU BUY DUBBLE, MORE MONEY GOES TO THE COCOA-FARMERS AND THEIR FAMILIES IN GHANA. There are two clauses in this sentence, thus two Actors: YOU and MONEY. YOU signals the desire to involve the target audience/market in the Fair Trade partnership, which was one of the key messages in Day's advertising brief. The other Actor – MONEY – suggests the same deleted agency as the visual image. MONEY GOES … but who sends it? The clear inclusion of the cocoa-farmers as the Goal of the clause suggests that the group haven't thought through how the money is produced and by whom, and are thus in danger of reverting to the political 'grammar' of the charity handout.

The grammar of the moving image reveals the ad's ambiguity about agency. In social terms – the meanings these students produce about the world, acting on the world – the advert's grammar is richly suggestive. The bar is humorously personified by the way it is positioned, sized and moved, and by the duration of these shots. The boy toggles between the grammatical function of an Actor in a teenage narrative of cool confidence, on home turf, and that of a Goal, on the receiving end of the delicious and astonishing sensations the bar can deliver. The hardest idea to represent, that of the Fair Trade nature of the bar, remains elusive, its grammar hesitant and uncertain, poised between the imprecision of the exotic foliage and the abstraction of text, and bereft of the movement which is a strong signifier of agency – the boy and the bar are the dynamic elements of the ad – the signifiers of the cocoa-farmers are oddly immobile.

Finally, the pace of the ad is created by its rapid cutting, on the beat of the soundtrack. The music and its lyrics suggest a confident, urban teenage lifestyle, underlining the function of the boy as principal Actor in the piece, the sequence cut to the rhythm of the music which suggests his walk, his dance. This music and its rhythm is possibly stronger than any visual image in the first seconds of the ad, signalling the theme of the whole sequence as teenage identity, and subordinating the bar and the Fair Trade message to this rhythm throughout. Theo van Leeuwen (1999) suggests that measured time in music can represent the concerns of the secular, embodied life, deriving as it does from human footsteps – the walk or the dance. He opposes this to unmeasured time, such as mediaeval plain chant or an eerie soundtrack for a sci fi movie, which might represent eternal time. In this piece, then, the mark of the in-your-face secular can be inferred from the rhythm of the soundtrack, between walk and dance.

This short film works hard to make its messages convincing. The methods it employs can be seen as *modality cues*, the aspects of texts which negotiate with audiences what is credible, authentic, convincing. Just as the group have found it relatively easy to represent the agency of contemporary teenage life in the UK, they find it easy to claim a high modality for these representations. This can be seen in the richness of the multimodal complex employed: so the authenticity of teenage culture is buttressed by mobile camera work, dress, action, gesture, facial expression and music. This complex is assured, confident that its claim to a high degree of credibility is likely to succeed – at least with an audience of its peers.

The modality of the sequence representing Africa is much less assured. It is less dense multimodally, effectively composed of still image and writing. There is an attempt at camera movement, but it lacks the confident sweep of the other sequences. The intermodal links become somewhat incoherent: for instance, the hip-hop music continues from the earlier sequence, though it is arguably less appropriate here. Finally, the modality claim here is not culturally anchored in the secure way typical of the other sequences: the text is abstract and unattributable; the symbolic coins pouring down are also only conceptually related to the other elements of the sequence.

None of this is surprising, and it is not suggested as a criticism of the film. The hybrid modality is a consequence of the difficulty of the task, and the hybrid motivations of the young film-makers. We draw attention to it here partly because, like other aspects of multimodal texts, it is unlikely to be made explicit within existing conventional accounts of media texts in media studies courses.

CONCLUSION

As in the last chapter, this example of media production work suggests that the critical function of media literacy can be most effectively developed through the creative function. In this case, the boys' advert engages critically with the rhetorics of consumer advertising, at one moment ironically emulating the conventions of the genre with exaggerated images of consumer gratification, at another struggling to invert stereotypes of African passivity.

To some extent, this provides evidence of learning in the key concepts of media education. For instance, the advert, along with other work (memos to the director, proposals and storyboards for the advert, letters to the Day Chocolate company, audience surveys carried out in the school), shows that the group have learned something about media organisations and audiences.

Like their earlier projects, this moving image work can also be seen as a minor essay in selfhood. One of its key driving impulses is the desire to explore teenage culture, dress, behaviour, identity; to construct bold, authoritative representations out of the uncertainty of adolescence. This exploration of selfhood, as we have argued in Chapter 2 of the Tiger Woman comicstrip design, is *negotiated* (between the three boys and other members of their peer group who were involved), and *distributed*, in Bruner's terms. The process and product are visible to others for comment and response, both in the local community of the school and in the wider contexts of display and exhibition this work has reached. This aspect of their advert is of importance to them, and is the representational impulse least able to be regulated by the school, and for that reason, most in need of recognition by teachers.

However, the real challenge of this project was to move beyond meanings and representations that are relatively easy to construct – in particular, representations of their own peer group and its culture. The representation of the chocolate bar was more difficult and required the construction of associative meanings that media teachers are used to relating to Roland Barthes's notion of connotation (Barthes, [1957] 1972). But most difficult of all has been the requirement to represent what is, in effect, an example of the 'Other' of contemporary cultural theory, and specifically post-colonial theory. The students have had to imagine a lifestyle and set of economic relations very unfamiliar to them, not least because their prior experience of it exists as a powerful complex of misrepresentations. This struggle to represent the least familiar takes their project to the limits of what they are able to do, to the zone where the greatest learning takes place. This is the place Vygotsky called the 'zone of proximal development', where learners, with the right kind of support at the right time, move into new territory.

GAME LITERACY: LUDIC AND NARRATIVE DESIGN

There are many arguments in circulation at present about the place of computer games in education. They often focus on games as a learning medium: learning through interactive play, through simulation and problem-solving, through the motivating effects of immersion in 3-D worlds. However, these are, in effect, e-learning arguments; they are not media literacy arguments. By contrast, the argument presented in this chapter is about the study of games as a cultural form within a media education programme. In this respect, it considers not only how games might be critically understood by students, but also the making of games as a creative process, just as the making of films, animations and comicstrips have been explored in earlier chapters.

The arguments and examples presented in this chapter emerge from four years of work with computer games at Parkside, and two funded research projects in which Parkside has been involved: 'The Textuality of Videogames' (2001–2003), and 'Making Games' (2002–2006), both at the Centre for the Study of Children, Youth and Media, in the Institute of Education, University of London. The latter project worked with the educational software company Immersive Education to develop MissionMaker, an authoring tool for students to produce their own games.

The particular focus of the chapter will be on how the narrative elements of a game and the ludic (game) elements work together. Can the understanding of these structures be seen as a subset of media literacy which we might call 'game literacy'? Of course, as in all the other projects in this book, such textual understandings cannot be reduced to purely abstract processes of interpretation or design, but need to be seen in the context of the cultural experiences of games which children bring with them. For this reason we will begin with a brief outline of what we found in our research about this context. We will then move to a description of the Year 8 computer games course at Parkside: the scheme of work and examples of students' work can be found on the CD-ROM. In the course of this account, we will analyse a game made by students during the course, using MissionMaker.

The children we worked with had varying experience of games. A minority did not play games or like games particularly, though some who said they did not play (especially girls) later revealed more knowledge and experience than they first claimed. There were widely varying tastes and loyalties to specific genres: some liked first-person shooters, some liked *The Sims*, some enjoyed strategy games and so on. There were some patterns here which, although we cannot claim that they are representative in any way of teenagers, are worth bearing in mind.

To begin with, there were, predictably, gender differences. At first glance it seemed that boys preferred action games, including shoot'em-ups, and girls preferred peaceful constructive games. However, it later transpired that these claims may have had as much to do with children's own construction of themselves through stereotypical images and expectations of gender as with any real preferences (Pelletier, 2005). In fact, some girls did want to play and make 'violent' games, while some boys did play and make 'peaceful' games. This is in accordance with other research into gendered gaming. A study of an Australian High School found that girls enjoyed a much wider variety of game genres than they at first admitted to (Mackereth and Anderson, 2000); while advocates of 'grrl gaming' have proposed that girls can gain pleasure from fantasy roles in games that allow some escape from stereotypical expectations of gendered roles in everyday life (Cassell and Jenkins, 1998). Nevertheless, there was plenty of evidence that this aspect of game-play and design was a valuable context in which to open up discussion of gender and the media with students.

In addition, there were widely varying experiences of games in ways that can be related, on the one hand, to age or maturity, and on the other hand to regulation and censorship. Some children's experience was of games often associated with their age group or even with younger children: *The Sims*, *Crash Bandicoot*, *Harry Potter*. However, a minority had played games with content more often associated with adult audiences, such as the horror games *Silent Hill* and *Resident Evil*, or the controversial *Manhunt*, mentioned by one boy. Two implications follow. First, it seems important to recognise that some children have more adult tastes than others: in a Year 8 discussion about the pleasure of games, for instance, two boys made a series of sophisticated points about the nature of suspense in *Silent Hill*, during a discussion that had begun with Harry Potter. Secondly, controversies about violent content and regulation (*Manhunt* is rated 18 by the BBFC, for instance), are clearly productive topics for discussion or simulation work as part of a consideration of media institutions and audiences. Age is clearly a concern here, but as with other forms of violent content, such as the horror films we discussed in Chapter 5, it may be better to recognise that young people have interests in such content before regulatory authorities permit them to view it legally (indeed, sometimes because of such regulation). The logic is to prepare them, rather than to wait until they have prepared themselves.

Many children had experience of games which had been developed as part of cross-media franchises, such as *James Bond (Goldeneye 007)*, *Lord of the Rings*, *Harry Potter*, *Spiderman* and *Star Wars*. One girl played game spinoffs of film and TV with her father:

> My dad has a different range of like ... Sort of he has like our computer and a playstation and when I'm with my dad I play like ... Usually Lord of the Rings and Harry Potter and sort of known games, like, not sort of ... games that have like got books as well or films or TV programmes that I sort of know.

In some cases, children played the game because of a passionate commitment to the overarching idea, character or narrative, as in the case of a number of ardent Harry Potter fans. There are interesting implications here for how narratives are experienced across literature, film and game, and how they are differently constructed across these media. Such themes can be exploited in the context of literacy work in English or Media Studies, as the work of Catherine Beavis has shown (2001). There are also many questions about the nature of the media industries, and how they organise such franchises, that can be posed in the context of media education. Finally, this kind of cross-media loyalty by fans raises questions about the nature of fandom as an intense form of audience behaviour, again of particular interest to media education.

Finally, the interviews revealed different kinds of critical engagement with games. In some cases, these were forms of appreciation, and expressions of individual taste: children who liked the Harry Potter games, or enjoyed skateboarding games because of the excitement and satisfaction they provided, or enjoyed social aspects of gaming (there were examples of children playing with friends, brothers and sisters, fathers and mothers, and even a grandfather in one case). In other cases, there were very specific kinds of critical comment: on the differences between PC-based and console-based games; on boring aspects of games which were too slow or repetitive; and in one case, a series of critical remarks about the second Harry Potter game, an extract of which opened our discussion of media literacy in Chapter 1 (see Burn, 2004, for a full account). In some respects, then, primarily to do with forms of cultural taste, children and young people may have developed sophisticated forms of critical discourse, which can be further explored in the classroom. There may be other aspects of critical engagement which they are less likely to have considered, however, as we will suggest below.

THE YEAR 8 GAMES COURSE

This course involves designing a game as a class, and making it in pairs using a game-authoring software tool. The course teaches aspects of media industries and audiences, though the focus is on creative production, and the learning of new ways to conceptualise narrative systems and game systems, and how they work together. While some aspects of the course are completely transferable to other classrooms and schools, the making of games using this software is, of course, more problematic. We will consider it closely here, however, as it reveals important principles of game design which students can learn. We will also suggest alternative approaches (and software) which are readily available.

Learning about the games industry

As with the critical–rhetorical aspect of media literacy explored in Chapter 6, students can be expected to learn about the media industries and institutions that lie behind the text. In many ways these are similar to other media industries, and indeed, related to them through multinational corporations. One approach used in the work at Parkside, and easily replicable for teachers in any kind of context, has been to draw attention to the ways in which media industries are represented in the packaging of games. A sequence of activities comparing the book, film and game of *Harry Potter and the Chamber of Secrets*, for example, collected all the logos of companies represented on the covers and boxes of these texts, which included:

- Warner Bros (who own the name of Harry Potter and associated items as trademarks)
- Electronic Arts (who published the game)
- Know Wonder Digital Mediaworks (who developed the game)
- Bloomsbury (who published the book).

In addition, there were the logos of Ford (the texts include a flying Ford Anglia car), Microsoft, *Times Educational Supplement* (who had reviewed the book), Dolby sound (in the film), ELSPA (the European Leisure Software Publishers Association, who had rated the game as appropriate for children of 3-plus.

This kind of investigation makes it very clear how games development and publishing works, but also how cross-media franchises depend on particular economic relations between companies. This kind of work with older students in specialist Media Studies courses would be routine, but it is much less common with students of this age group.

The approach of the course was to simulate aspects of the context of games development: so students were asked to propose names for a game studio, to write proposals for a game for students of their age, to work collaboratively in pairs and as a whole class to design and produce a multi-level game, and to design posters and write press releases and magazine reviews of the game on completion.

Learning about the narrative systems of games

The game was planned as a whole-class activity. After sessions in which students were asked to describe games they had played, both in class discussion and for homework, the work moved on to planning a game. At this stage, central concepts of narrative and game were introduced.

It is helpful, in respect of media education, to think of the textuality of games in two complementary ways, which emerge from a longstanding debate in the fledgling academic field of game studies – the so-called narratology–ludology debate. The origins of this argument are in disputes between academics who believed narrative to be central to many game genres, and that therefore existing theories of narrative could be applied to them, and those who believed that they need to be understood principally as games, and that therefore a new theory of games was needed: *ludology*, from the Latin for game, *ludus* (see, e.g., Frasca, 1999; Carr et al., 2006).

In many ways this debate has been resolved with the agreement that, at least in story-based games, *narrative* and *ludic* systems are *both* important, and how they relate to each other and fuse can often be a marker of how effective the game is. In games where the narrative is a thin and unsatisfactory icing on the cake, there is not much imaginative opportunity for gamers to get involved in characters, events and imaginary worlds. Conversely, games that relentlessly drive a narrative forward at the expense of satisfying game-play (especially games adapted from movies) will frustrate players whose real interest is gaming.

This debate offers a convenient approach for the media classroom. In the Year 8 course, we distinguished between aspects of narrative and aspects of game. In relation to narrative, we found it useful to propose Vladimir Propp's well-known framework of character narrative functions and types ([1928] 1968). Specialist media teachers may well be familiar with this; indeed, sometimes too familiar, as Julian McDougall notes in his criticism of simplistic uses of Propp in media education (2006). However, what is commonplace with older students in specialist Media Studies courses may not be so for younger children; or, indeed, for non-specialist teachers. In addition, Propp's schema can be seen as peculiarly appropriate to computer game narratives. Propp analysed the narrative structures of Russian folktales and discovered a high degree of conformity to a limited number of narrative patterns. These included the narrative functions of certain recurrent character types, such as a hero, a false hero, a villain, a donor, a princess, a father figure, a helper, a dispatcher. This approach is helpful in moving students on from simply thinking about stories as chains of events, and helps them to see characters as functions of narrative rather than thinking of them as real people, somehow independent of the narrative.

Furthermore, Propp's approach suits the formulaic nature of computer game narratives, which resemble folktales and oral formulaic stories more generally. This is partly because they often draw on ancient narrative forms (quest narratives, sagas, romances, epics). As Janet Murray has argued (1998), the characters of games resemble the heroes of oral narrative, such as the Homeric stories, who solve problems through external action rather than the psychologically developed characters of, say, the European novel. Again, then, it is relatively easy for students to imagine Propp's character types in ways which fit the episodic structure of games, and the rewards, challenges, obstacles and so on which also form part of the game structure.

From there, the ways in which characters have specific game functions can also be explored. The protagonist is also the player character, with specific properties which can be managed and designed by the students, such as levels of health, hunger, and so on. All the other characters are NPCs (non-player characters) who have to be designed and programmed to behave or speak in particular ways. Enemies may be inflected as game characters such as end-of-level bosses – especially powerful NPCs who have to be defeated to complete a level (in much the same way as Shelob the spider or Grendel are defeated by Sam Gamgee or Beowulf respectively).

In practical terms, Propp's categories were presented through a Hangman game with the first and last letters filled in. Students were easily able to work out h _ _ o and v _ _ _ _ _ n; and with discussion and a little prompting, were able to complete the rest. As in this kind of gap-filling exercise generally, the process of discussion is the real learning; the categories are not so much guessed as constructed in the process. At the same time, the use of a well-known example, the Star Wars franchise, helped to put flesh on the bones of these categories, as students worked out which characters fitted which categories: Luke Skywalker as hero, Darth Vader as father, Leia as princess, Yoda as dispatcher, Han Solo as helper, Anakin Skywalker as false hero, and so on.

Learning about ludic systems

The next stage was for students to learn about game systems. Two aspects of game texts were explicitly presented to the classes who used *Missionmaker*. First, the idea of *rule*. Many accounts of games define them as rule-based systems (Juul, 2003; Salen and Zimmerman, 2003), and a brief consideration of other kinds of games shows that, indeed, they are based on clearly defined rules: noughts-and-crosses, Monopoly, chess, football.

Students were encouraged to think of examples of rules across many kinds of game. One student, Joe, came up with this list:

Call of Duty – you mustn't shoot your ally
Tennis – the ball mustn't leave the court
Pool – the white ball must not go down any of the pockets
Cards (pontoon) – you must not score more than 21 to win
Cricket – you can't touch the wickets with your bat

Like many other students, he found examples both from computer games (*Call of Duty* is a first-person action game based in a World War Two narrative) as well as from other kinds of game. He also wrote at length about why rules were important, for a homework following a class discussion:

> The reason games have to have rules is because if there wasn't [sic] rules in a game you couldn't have challenges and boundries [sic], limits too, and that would spoil the fun and cause you not to have anything to complete. Rules are needed for objectives because they are almost the same thing because they are both telling you to do or not to do something.

This understanding recognises that rules make a game a different kind of text, as we will argue below: a text largely constructed in the imperative mood, which, rather than simply presenting you with a story, continuously demands that you act within that story.

The discussion also considered the paradox of why we enjoy following rules, which in contexts other than games and play can be oppressive. Again, Joe continues this discussion with himself:

> People enjoy following rules because it creates suspense of trying not to lose the game by breaking the rule, and a lot of people like difficult challenges. For example, on a computer game, trying not to be seen and to sneak somewhere where you are rewarded with a prize ...

Joe's recognition that game rules are related to affective qualities such as suspense, and also to the challenge and level of difficulty posed by the game are sophisticated insights, and prepare the way for his own game design. The notion of constraint related to pleasures of play here can be related to theories of rule-governed, structured play, such as Frasca's use (1999) of Caillois's notion of *ludus* (1979/2001), where a strict rule system is structurally associated with victory or defeat, as in Joe's definition. This is distinct from Caillois's *paidea*, in which less defined rules operate to define pleasurable play not necessarily orientated towards an outcome of quantified gain or loss. The distinction between game and play is an important debate in play theory, and one which students in schools can usefully pick up. Football is obviously a game with clearly defined rules. What about paintballing? What about young children's clapping and skipping games? What about 'I'm the King of the Castle'? Clearly, some kinds of play are also games, with firm rule systems, while others are much less well-defined, much more open, much more improvisatory.

The other key concept of the ludic structures of the game we introduced was the idea of *economies*: quantifiable resources within games, such as health, hunger, power, currency, ammunition, food, healing potions. Again, we began with the common sense notion of economy as a monetary resource. In their written homework, students again developed this idea for themselves, rooting it in their own knowledge of the world and experience of games. Felicity used the example of Ibiza's tourist industry, and the example of *The Sims*:

> Ideas of economy in a game (e.g. *The Sims*) is money as without it your 'sim' will not have a good life and you will find the gameplay much harder and less enjoyable as the sims get mad as they can't have many possessions and sometimes they don't have any food so they are really depressed.

We also explored the idea that economies could be found in stories, and asked students for examples. As an example of a story which used economies, Felicity proposed Hansel and Gretel, the economy being the breadcrumbs Hansel drops to find their way out of the forest.

This work shows that, while children are often familiar with ludic aspects of the text which are explicitly known in popular discourses (in game manuals, magazines, websites, fansites, or within the games themselves), such as NPC, or end-of-level boss, or first-person shooter (FPS), they do not, of course, know unfamiliar terms and concepts which may underlie the ludic structure. The concepts of rule and economy, then, amplify their existing understanding of how games work, make explicit what was previously implicit knowledge, and prepare the way for the use of the tools in the authoring software which allow for the construction of rules and economies. However, it also shows that these concepts are by no means purely abstract: they need to be related back to wider cultural knowledge and experience, both of games and of other relevant experiences which serve as examples and analogies.

Designing a class game

To begin planning the class game, students were asked to write individual proposals: short 'pitches' for a game, which had to include Proppian character types and examples of the rules and economies explored in class. Students' proposals were written for homework, and as many ideas as possible were synthesised by the teacher into a single plan. One girl had suggested a game based on the melting of the polar icecaps due to global warming, as a result of which the protagonist lost his family and had to find and save them. Several others had thriller, assassin or secret agent themes. One girl had subverted the stereotypically female shopping activity in many games by proposing a shoplifting game and so on.

These ideas all became part of the whole game: *Jimmie DeMora and the Dying World* (a title proposed by one of the students), in which secret agent Jimmie DeMora has to find the evil corporation who are causing global flooding through their unscrupulous production of environmentally unfriendly fuels, stopping off for some shopping and saving members of his family along the way. A crucial part of the teacher's role here was mediating the students' proposals, partly by class discussion which opened up contradictions, differences, advantages and disadvantages, and partly by encouraging a consensus which would produce a whole-class design that would be coherent, and to which, as far as possible, everyone in the class had contributed.

Clearly, this game has a central narrative. It also has game structures: levels, obstacles, rewards and clearly defined win–lose states. The player character was named Jimmie DeMora after a proposal by one of the class, who had suggested a gangster-themed game with an assassin as central character (possibly influenced by games such as *Hitman 2: Silent Assassin*). However, as the class game design amalgamated elements from proposals by many members of the class, the character was modified in terms of his mission and narrative background. He was equipped with a gun, but not to assassinate anyone: rather, to rescue members of his family, and to save the world, which was threatened by global warming and evil corporations. If Jimmie was the Proppian hero, then other characters proposed by students fulfilled other functions: his kidnapped daughter was the princess; the evil corporation was the villain; various other characters in other levels helped, donated, misled and so on.

Producing the game

The whole-game design was then divided up by the teacher into 15 levels, one for each pair of students in the class. This allowed each pair to work on their own small game, with its own structure and sense of beginning and end. However, each pair had to constantly negotiate with its adjacent pairs to see how the levels would connect with each other, and with other pairs to achieve other kinds of coherence; for instance, to make sure that NPCs appearing in their level would look, behave and speak in the same way as the same character appearing in another level later or earlier in the game.

A closer look at one of the levels will give some idea of the design processes involved, and how the two students who made this level have considered ludic and narrative elements in their section of the game.

This section is level 6, in which the player, as Jimmie DeMora, enters a secret laboratory where a renewable source of energy is guarded by the evil corporation, so that they can market their own unsustainable energy sources. The students making this level set the initial mission as to find the generator. When the player finds it, they are led through a series of corridors, eventually discovering two guards and a giant 'boss' (Figure 7.4). On killing these characters, the player enters a room containing the 'green gem', which is the renewable energy source. A pop-up tells you to take the green gem back to the generator; when you do, the level is completed.

This level represents a complex series of design processes, in which the narrative system of the whole-class game, as well as the ludic system of this particular level, have been considered by the two students making it.

First, they have had to design a world. Figure 7.1 shows the *tile editor* of this software – a grid onto which pre-designed cells can be dragged, positioned and rotated. From many kinds of available world (Stone Age, sci fi, mediaeval, western, Victorian and so on), the students have chosen one chamber from the Stone Age options, and the rest from a series of blank chambers to represent the sterile world of the laboratory. The Stone Age chamber in which the level begins represents the 'Dying World' of the game's title, with deep pools representing the global flooding which triggers the game's narrative.

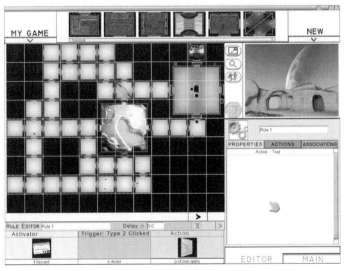

FIGURE 7.1 *The tile editor of Jimmie DeMora and the Dying World*

In terms of media literacy, we can see how the semiotic processes involved here realise the narrative and ludic intentions of the young designers. Sign-making always involves selection and combination. The axis of selection, often referred to in semiotics as the *paradigm*, here involves choosing from a range of genres, as we have seen; and also choosing from a range of shapes of chamber. The chamber which begins the game, then, represents the 'Stone Age' choice and a 'multi-entrance' choice – it has three doors which lead to other chambers. However, these choices from a social semiotic point of view are never simply about selecting a 'ready-made' meaning; they are about transformation, re-purposing cultural resources for particular social purposes. So here, as we have seen, the 'Stone Age' chambers are selected because they are outdoors and because they contain water, which suits the story of global warming already constructed by the class. Similarly, the blank chambers are chosen because their very blankness can be made to suggest a laboratory. In this case, the selected objects are virtually meaningless – literally a blank slate – until they are given narrative meaning by the students.

The axis of combination, usually referred to as the *syntagm*, here involves fitting the chambers together. The Stone Age chamber is where the player's start is positioned, so it is given significance as the beginning of the game, in the dying world. The small square chambers leading off from the starting-point are arranged into corridors forming a maze, which leads in one direction to the chamber containing the generator, and in the other direction, eventually, to the chamber containing the green gem. The maze is a classic ludic formation, and a good example of the ancient lineage of games, if we think of Daedalus's labyrinth in the palace of Minos, with the Minotaur (the original end-of-level boss!) at its heart.

So the tile editor allows for complex selections and combinations, resulting in syntagmatic compositions which imply both *narrative structure* (the journey Jimmie DeMora will have to go through to release the renewable energy) and *ludic structure* (the choices of route offered to the player; the maze which must be negotiated to reach the win-state at the end of the game).

However, although a fictional world is needed for both game and narrative, there is more design work to do, of course, to provide significant objects, events and characters. If the player is the Proppian hero, there will also need to be a villain to combat; and the game will need rules, economies and a win–lose state, as we saw earlier.

Events in the game are designed through another component in the software, the rule editor. Figure 7.2 shows the chamber where the game will end, from the designer's point of view. In the middle of the chamber the students have placed a large generator, which, in the narrative, will be activated by the renewable source of energy. Next to the generator they have placed a large transparent sphere. This is a trigger volume, which defines a space within which an event will be triggered. It will, of course, be invisible to the player. At the bottom of the screen is the rule editor: a three-part box in which the rules which define the game can be composed. In this case, the rule reads: 'If Green Gem/enters Sphere Trigger/My Game is completed'.

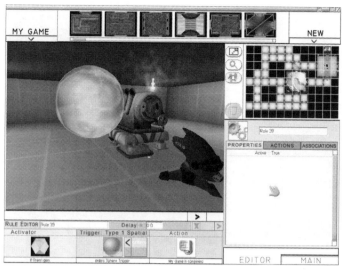

FIGURE 7.2 *The rule editor for level 6 of Jimmie DeMora and the Dying World*

Again, from the media literacy point of view, we can see the rule as a syntagm: elements are chosen from various sets of possibilities defined both by the resources available and by the narrative and ludic intentions of the young designers and their classmates. They are combined in a sequence which reads from activator through trigger to action.

This is a good example of what we meant in Chapter 1 when we said that the idea of literacy in relation to the media was not merely metaphorical, but could be taken quite literally. In semiotic terms, the rule editor is a syntagm, a combination of signs. Specifically, it is also a *linguistic* composition, an *if-clause*. It reveals the foundation of game grammar, in which events are constructed as conditional: *if this, then that*. At the same time, this is the essential language of computer programming, which specifies *if* and *when* conditions for programmed events.

The whole point of conditionality in a game, of course, is that it makes it possible for the player to play: to navigate the ludic possibilities of the game, and to participate in the narrative possibilities. Figure 7.3 shows what the generator chamber looks like from the player's point of view. Here, then, the trigger sphere is invisible. The player knows they have to approach the generator holding the green gem, and when they do, the level is completed in a win-state. It is worth noting here that the rule operating has two faces, so to speak. There is a 'designer' face – the programmed rule, which states that if the green gem enters the sphere trigger the game is over. The 'player' face is necessarily different. The sphere trigger and the programming must be invisible, so that for the player the rule is something like, 'if the green gem is brought to the generator, I will win the game'.

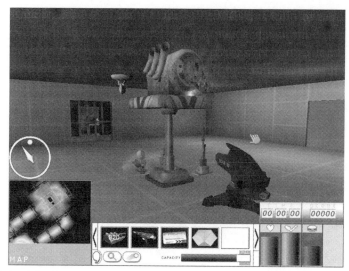

FIGURE 7.3 *Level 6 of* Jimmie DeMora and the Dying World: *the play interface.*

To have reached this point, the player has undergone a series of choices created by the students who made the level. There are many different possible routes through the level, beginning with a choice about which of the three exits to take from the start chamber. At the bottom of Figure 7.3, we can see a map and compass which the students have included in the player's view: they are triggered when the player picks up the keycard in the start chamber. These assets then help the player through the maze, and, having retrieved the green gem (which can be seen in the player's inventory), the map and compass help the player to find the generator chamber again.

As we said in Chapter 1, we might want to examine students' work as semiotic constructs in order to see what it is that they are able to do, just as literacy teachers or researchers might analyse children's writing using a linguistic framework. Here, as we have seen, the students make a rule, which is simple to do in technical terms, though part of the basic literacy of game design in this software. We could see such a rule as a *signifier* – the material part of a sign. However, the point of a signifier is its relation to a *signified*: the meaning it represents. In this case, the rule made by the students has specific narrative and ludic meanings: it enables Jimmie DeMora to take another step towards saving the planet; and it enables the player to finish the level in a win-state. Furthermore, we can say that this is designed, like all ludic signs, as a potential meaning: for the meaning to be realised, the player has to take the necessary action.

From the students' perspective, we can speculate what it might be appropriate or useful for them to learn at a conscious level. It would be unusual for 12- or 13-year-olds to learn the terms syntagm and paradigm, for instance; though students in this age phase in the UK are expected to learn what sentence, clause, phrase and part of speech mean, which are linguistic versions of such concepts. This is a debate for the future, but the need for some framework which will help students to understand how meaning is constructed across and between different semiotic modes seems essential to us.

As we have already outlined, we did explore the ideas of rule and economy. So the rule editor allowed further development of the concept of rule in games more generally, and in relation to the conditional narrative structures of adventure games. Similarly, the design of economies in their game allowed the students to extend their understanding of the idea of economy as quantifiable resource. MissionMaker allows them to allocate defined quantities such as weight, health, hunger, vulnerability, ammunition, game points and so on. Figure 7.4 shows the screen in which the player confronts the giant boss guarding the green gem. The player has been able to pick up a gun early on in the game, and also 1000 rounds of ammunition. The boss's vulnerability has been set quite high; we can see that 28 rounds have been used. However, it is not simply a matter of having enough ammunition to kill the boss; the player's health is also being depleted by the enemy's fire; the bar at the bottom right of the screen shows it reduced by nearly half.

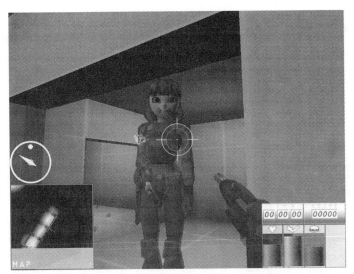

FIGURE 7.4 *The player fights the giant boss character in level 6 of* Jimmie DeMora and the Dying World

This brief analysis shows that even designing one level of the whole-class game is a complex affair. These two students have made a satisfying narrative setting, appropriately 'dressed'; have designed characters to provide narrative opposition to the hero; and have created a sense of quest and of ending. At the same time, they have designed a coherent set of ludic elements: a mission, challenges, obstacles and rewards; rules; the related economies of ammunition and health; and a win–lose state.

'Publishing' the game

When the game of *Jimmie DeMora and the Dying World* was complete, the class were asked to think about the institutional context of game production again: to choose from activities such as making a poster to advertise the game, writing a review for the game magazine *Edge*, or writing a press release for the game's publication, including an imaginary interview with one of the game's designers.

One of the posters gives a good impression of what kinds of knowledge about media institutions are made explicit through these activities (Figure 7.5). The student has created a logo for the imaginary game studio invented by the class: PIG studios (Parkside Interactive Games). He has selected an image to represent the game, a close-up of a hand and rifle, emphasising the 'first-person shooter' genre in which the class's game has been constructed. He has added a strapline: 'Trained to kill … He is the perfect assassin'; which again emphasises the FPS genre.

FIGURE 7.5 *Year 8 Student poster for the class game* Jimmie DeMora and the Dying World

Other posters suggest wider awareness of games development. One uses the PIG games brand again, followed by 'Challenge Everything', the slogan of the game publishers Electronic Arts. Another refers to the game as an 'RPG' (role-playing game), which emphasises the dramatic qualities of the characters rather than the FPS mode emphasised in Figure 7.5. The notion of genre, though in literacy work it is usually treated as a property of texts, is arguably just as well approached through the study of audiences. As in film, where some have argued that genres are constructed and negotiated between the industry and the audiences (Neale, 2000), so in games the industry proposes categories, while audiences may dispute them (Carr et al., 2006).

A review of the class's game, written by a Year 8 girl, suggests other kinds of awareness of the media institutions which surround games development and publication:

> Saturday 25th March, 2006
> Kids Make Their Own Game!
> Students in Year 8 at Parkside Community College in Cambridge have formed a games company named PIG productions, in order to create a spectacular adventure game with an impeccable plot.
> PIG is an acronym for Parkside Interactive Games, and PIG's first game is currently in the making, by the name of Jimmie DeMora and the Dying World. Using MissionMaker and just under 30 creative minds, students work in one of the English rooms at their school to design and make the game. ...
> The game is scheduled for release at all good game stores from May 2006, as the final touches are currently being made to the game. Lucky people who have had the opportunity to preview the game have never given it less than 4 stars, mainly for the plot.
> The game follows secret agent Jimmie DeMora, who is living in a world that is deteriorating thanks to global warming, and is suddenly faced with the kidnapping of his daughter and sister. He has to rescue many prisoners, including much of his family, and seek a holy artefact for renewable energy. Some say the game is a cry for attention to the melting polar ice-caps, some say it's an exaggerated joke.
> Whatever is said, we can't wait to see how the final release is seen by the gaming world!

As well as several references to the work of the game studio, this review refers to the marketing of games, the previewing of games for review purposes and conventions of game journalism, such as the use of star rating systems and the language and style in which the whole piece is written.

These kinds of activity, clearly, are aimed at consciousness-raising: at helping children to begin to recognise the commercial interests behind the production of media texts like computer games. They do not lead here to exhaustive critiques of global capitalism, or to analyses of the ideological effects of such corporate interests. But they do begin the process which at a later stage could address such questions more critically, in the context, for instance, of A Level Media Studies.

Other approaches

It is important to say that schools without access to software of this kind can produce plenty of 'proto-design' work. In the first year of this research project we explored such activities before the software was developed. Ideas here included:

- Proposing amendments for existing games (like Snakes and Ladders) in which the rules were changed.
- Making boardgames of favourite books and films (one student produced an elaborate Harry Potter boardgame).
- Designing game characters, labelled with their functions, but emphasising the cultural importance of concept art in game design.
- Writing game outlines, including both narrative and ludic aspects.
- Drawing screen shots for their game, of the kind used in publicity materials, but to show a concrete realisation of what their game might look like as it was played.
- Developing drama pieces based on moments in their game proposals, such as the player's first meeting with an NPC.
- Writing walkthroughs for their game, giving players instructions on how to progress successfully through the game sequence.
- Writing game proposals to game publishers such as EA.
- Designing posters and boxes for their own games.

In addition, in earlier years of the project, before the MissionMaker software became available, we used cheap commercial software packages which made a degree of game design possible. One of these, though it does not provide all the design opportunities of MissionMaker, did allow for a wide range of productive work. It is called The 3-D Game maker, and was available cheaply online at the time of writing. It allows students to design game-worlds in a wide range of settings (horror, racing, adventure, sci fi and so on), simply by clicking on a menu; or, more challengingly, by using a tile editor – a grid onto which component elements of the environment such as corridors and chambers can be dragged. This element is similar to one included within MissionMaker. In addition, users can choose different player characters, weapons, obstacles, bosses and so on. This can all be done very rapidly (in a matter of minutes), producing a simple but satisfying game with very little design effort. Alternatively, the software allows for many more design decisions, such as varying the potency of characters, weapons and other assets, or importing graphic designs and music.

With this kind of readily available software, the principles of ludic and narrative design outlined above can be easily explored, and all of the simulation activities related to commercial design, marketing and publicity can be carried out. In addition, several of the aspects of game design learnt by students using MissionMaker can also be learnt with packages such as The 3-D Gamemaker.

CONCLUSION: TOWARDS A MODEL OF GAME LITERACY

We proposed in Chapter 1 that media literacy can be defined both at a generic level and at the level of more specific subcategories related to specific media. In Chapter 2 we explored aspects of visual literacy in relation to the visual design of comics; in Chapters 3, 4, 5 and 6, we looked at different ways of approaching moving image literacy through animation, television and film. The games course we have described in this chapter, then, and the research accompanying it, suggest what game literacy might look like. The following list of components include some which are generic to media literacy, and others which are specific to games.

1 It draws on *cultural experience* of games and other media texts.
2 It involves *critical* understanding of the social meanings games can carry; and some grasp of how games are produced and consumed.
3 It requires specific kinds of *operational literacy*: a fluency in aspects of game-play, whether console-based or PC-based; and in the use of the tools for game design provided by the software.
4 It requires an understanding of *key concepts* important to game-texts – in this case, rule and economy; but also principles of narrative composition, such as protagonist, quest, conflict. It recognises how these concepts are elaborated in building the grammar of the game.
5 It is *multimodal* and *multiliterate*. It involves visual design, writing in different genres, sound, music, speech and simple programming within the limits of the rule editor.
6 It is *creative*: it involves the manipulation and transformation of semiotic resources, both memories of game structures previously encountered and the actual physical assets and tools available for design.
7 A wider notion of game literacy will also involve *peripheral literacies*, many of which will involve writing, in genres such as proposals, interpretive and critical writing, walkthroughs, fan fiction, narrative backstories.

Of course, game design of the kind enabled by this software package could easily find a curriculum home in any subject where aesthetic and technological design are of relevance. It would be entirely possible to construct different rationales for game-making in Design and Technology, Art, Music and ICT. The argument in this chapter, however, is that to see game design as a form of writing in relation both to print literacy and to media literacy is to see it as a valuable extension of concepts of narrative, grammar and textuality for learners.

But games also require that literacy and media teachers do some hard thinking about what kinds of narratives they value, and how they conceive them. Characters like Jimmie DeMora, and the protagonists of adventure and role-playing games more generally, stand in a tradition of popular heroic narratives that stretches back through the superheroes of twentieth century comicstrip, film and television; but also much further back in the oral formulaic narratives of Europe, from Robin Hood to Beowulf; and even further back to the Homeric narratives, as we suggested earlier. By contrast, the literacy and literature curricula are more accustomed to privilege the forms of psychological 'realism' typical of the European novel. We need to be wary, then, of simplistic value judgements about formulaic narratives in contemporary media. When conventional evaluations of media texts represent characters like Superman or Spiderman as reductive constructs that value action over psychology compared with the Brothers Karamazov or Jane Eyre, we should ask if such evaluations would make the same judgements about Beowulf, Achilles or Robin Hood, who are just as formulaic as modern comicstrip protagonists. To accommodate game-writing in the literacy and English curriculum, then, productively extends and challenges our ideas of literacy at all levels: cultural, aesthetic, technological, conceptual. In earlier traditions of Cultural Studies – and indeed media education – this kind of widening might have been seen as a battle between popular and elite cultural forms. In our experience, there is little need for such combative stances. The wider the mix of textual forms, the richer and deeper are the possibilities for learning about the fundamental questions of how texts function and how people create, use and engage with them.

THE HORIZONTAL ANGLE: MEDIA LITERACY ACROSS THE CURRICULUM

Arguments for media education across the curriculum have a long pedigree (see Buckingham, 2003: 89–93 for a detailed account). Essentially, the argument has been that all subjects use media of one kind or another, and that a critical and informed understanding of such media makes sense. In the past, this has largely been confined to *understanding* media content, especially in television and film, as it might be used in Science or the Humanities. However, the advent of digital authoring tools, just as it has made possible a shift in emphasis from analysis to production in specialist media education, has also encouraged a similar shift in the use of media across the curriculum. The work of the specialist media schools in the UK incorporates a cross-curricular use of the specialism required by the conditions of designation, so a range of inventive applications in different subjects is beginning to appear. Meanwhile, the British Film Institute, with other partners, has published a pack on the use of moving images across the curriculum, for instance, which includes suggestions about the making of documentary films in History and Science, or films about aspects of the design process in Design and Technology (Bazalgette et al., 2000).

As we began, in 1997, to consider how to develop cross-curricular uses of media education, this emphasis on production work dominated our early experiments. The Humanities departments agreed to explore the making of documentary as a way of investigating evidence and constructing arguments; the Maths department undertook to try animation software to represent mathematical concepts; the Music department decided to develop a Year 9 project on the composition of music for horror films, and so on. In the ensuing years, we realised that there were two related cross-curricular debates.

The first was the issue of literacy across the curriculum, which has been the subject of contentious debate in the UK over recent years. For us, however, both print literacy and media literacy can be seen as subsets of a more general notion of multiliteracy; and the model we have outlined in Chapter 1 can apply to both print and media. As in literacy work across the curriculum, media literacy work can attend both to larger textual dimensions such as genre, text type, or narrative, and smaller units such as individual sentences or words – or syntagms and signs, in semiotic terminology. We will give examples of how teachers and students can work at such a detailed level below.

The second issue is the question of the use of ICT across the curriculum. The danger here for media schools is that 'media across the curriculum' degenerates into 'media *technologies* across the curriculum': that the use of PowerPoint in Science, or digital video to record sports events, is seen as 'media literacy', when in fact it lacks the attention to critical understanding and systems of signification which are central to any model of media literacy. The evaluation of BECTa's digital video pilot project (Reid et al., 2002) found that the use of digital video was most effective where teachers had given explicit attention to the 'language' of the moving image; and argued that there could be no 'transparent' use of the moving image as a vessel to 'contain' subject-specific content. At Parkside we have tried to avoid this by pairing subject specialists with media specialists, and our most successful projects have developed from this kind of team-teaching. We will return in Chapter 10 to the wider question of how media literacy and ICT in education are often confused, but have the potential to connect.

The development of media literacy across the curriculum necessarily relates to the media literacy model we outlined in Chapter 1. We will explore, then, as we consider specific examples of projects at Parkside, how they relate to the cultural, critical and creative aspects of media literacy; and, in some cases, address the semiotic properties of media texts, whether implicitly or explicitly. The examples we consider can all be found on the CD-ROM.

CROSS-CURRICULAR MEDIA PRODUCTION AT PARKSIDE

Over the ten years of the school's media specialism, a wide variety of work in different subject areas has been developed (an early account of which can be found in Burn, 1998). It falls into three main areas: documentary work, mediated performance and animation.

The first of these is a broad category under which we subsume any work which has an informational or explicatory function. An example from the early days of the school's specialist work was a Geography project on coastal erosion, in which Year 10 GCSE students filmed processes of coastal erosion in Norfolk, and interviewed local government officers and members of the public in the seaside town of Cromer. They then edited a documentary film which explored the rhetorics surrounding this topic, from those which represent natural processes to those in which the politics of the local economy are formulated. Other examples took place in History (the filming and editing of a 'dramatic reconstruction' of the Lord of the Manor's visit to a medieval village) and in Classical Studies (the scripting and editing of voice-over commentaries for footage of Pompeii). In the third section of this chapter we will give a more detailed account of films of Science experiments.

Mediated performance represents work in the Arts, which recognises that most experience of the performing arts is now mediated by film or television, as Raymond Williams, in his role as Professor of Drama at Cambridge, once observed of popular experiences of drama (1983). While on the one hand this work challenges teachers of Drama, Music and Dance to think how their respective expressive modes are framed and transformed by the conventions of the moving image and its cultural contexts, they are also a challenge to media specialists. Media educators are comfortable with rhetorics of the technical apparatuses of production, and with the conceptual apparatus of text, institution and audience. They are less certain about the close relationship between media texts and drama. Media theory is not good at explaining how the signifying properties of continuity editing, or computer game narrative, are complemented by the conventions of dramatic action, the human voice, the affective charge of dramatic expression, the rhythmic, melodic and harmonic properties of music, the formalised movement and gesture of dance. Conversely, arts educators are traditionally not good at thinking about the structures of the mass media. We have made this point in previous publications. One of these, co-written with two Drama lecturers, explores how a drama at Parkside made by members of the head injury group Headway represented their experiences through combinations of physical movement and speech with live camera projection and segments of pre-recorded drama (Burn, Franks and Nicholson, 2001).

In addition to the Headway project, which ran over four years, mediated performance at Parkside includes music composed by Year 9 students for horror films, a Year 9 Drama course in acting for film, the filming and editing of performed poetry in English, and the filming and editing of Dance. Examples of the last two will be outlined in more detail in the third section of this chapter.

Our third category, animation, has proved a popular choice for the development and expansion of subject knowledge in several areas. We have given examples in Chapter 2 of how animation can bring together modes of expression in different subject areas such as literacy, Art, Music and ICT. Computer animation has also been extensively used by the Maths department at Parkside, initially to represent concepts of two- and three-dimensional space in their Year 8 programme. This work in many ways adopts a genre common in televised instruction, such as Open University broadcasts in the UK, which would, in Maths and Science programmes, represent abstract notions – or indeed physical processes such as the circulation of the blood – with animated diagrams.

The Maths work produced a number of interesting issues. It was clear from the beginning that the oscillation between highly abstracted conceptions of space governing the area of circles, or the measurement of cubic space, and concrete visual representations of these, such as images of the moon, kites, houses and fantasy machines, was helping the children to grasp the concepts, while at the same time challenging them to re-formulate them. A question here related to what Kress and van Leeuwen call 'naturalistic modality' (1996). The animation displayed a continuum from highly abstract images representing simple geometric shapes (though colour was almost always used), to a comicstrip modality, complete with witty animals such as bees and worms giving a running commentary in speech bubbles. Arguably, the comicstrip style provided a more concrete, reassuring mode, a degree of cultural anchorage in popular media forms; though also, perhaps, an opportunity to gently subvert the seriousness of official discourses of Science and Maths.

Animation has also been used for several years in Design and Technology, in the form of stop-frame 'claymation'. The construction of Plasticine models on aluminium wire armatures, and miniature sets of cardboard and wood, fitted the 'design and build' requirements of this curriculum area, while integrating these with the semiotic notion of design and production we outlined in Chapter 1. Model-building as a creative process was informed by notions of narrative and message (in one version of the project the animations were safety adverts for Design and Technology, for instance); and the filming and editing of the animations took the design and production processes into the specific moving image conventions we have described in Chapter 2. We include below a more detailed account of a Plasticine animation project in Geography.

While the Maths work used computer animation software (first The Complete Animator, then Macromedia's Flash), and Design and Technology used digital video and editing software, a more specialised digital animation package has been used in Modern Foreign Languages, for teaching French to children in partner primary schools. This package, Kar2ouche, is made by the Oxford software company who worked with us to develop the games authoring package described in Chapter 7. The Modern Languages department have, in addition, explored a range of other ways of addressing media literacy, including the viewing and reviewing of popular French cinema, such as *Amélie* (Jeunet, 2001) and *Kirikou* (Ocelot, 1998), the 'grammar' of *bandes dessinées* (comicstrips) in *Tintin* and other French language comics, and the exploitation of popular media crazes such as Harry Potter in French children's media magazines.

Finally, media work in different genres has been developed in extracurricular contexts also. These allow for the representations of intensive experiences, such as films made by students of their Duke of Edinburgh Award trips, in the mode of personal videos combining generic features of video-journals and music video; or music videos made for school rock bands winning a 'Compose a School Anthem' competition. By contrast, they also allow for long-term 'slow-burn' activities, such as the work of an animation group which began in Year 8 making a film about microbes for a national science competition, and ended in Year 11 with a humorous take on the Garden of Eden in claymation form, *The Bare Blob Project*. While such projects offer more expansive recognition of students' lives in school, they also offer ways in which popular media forms can represent formative experiences, extending the social function of the exploration and transformation of self which we described in our media literacy model in Chapter 1.

The final section will provide more detailed examples of media production activities in each of the three categories outlined above.

DOCUMENTARY

Documenting Science

This project began as a primary liaison project, in which Year 6 (aged 10–11) children used digital video cameras to make short films demonstrating a procedure: how to separate rock salt. They did the planning and filming, but had help with the editing. Latterly, the project has taken root in Year 8 (aged 12–13). The students work in small groups of about four. Each group uses a webcam (Figure 8.1) to film a different bench-top procedure from several different angles, and the students then edit the film themselves, using Windows Microsoft Moviemaker 2. They also use the 'Narrate' function in Microsoft Moviemaker 2 to record their own scripted voice-over.

Media literacy: media, society and culture Underlying and essential to students' developing media literacy is their learning about the social and cultural place and function of media texts, about the institutions which produce them and about the ideas and ideologies which they represent. This project offers an opportunity to develop a critical awareness of the role of television in mediating science and scientific ideas – in education, in documentary and in entertainment. And it requires a consideration of the way audiences' perceptions of science might be shaped by media representations.

As they are introduced to the project, the children discuss what they already know about the way science is represented on television and film: where they have seen science, and how it is made to seem; how it is shown in films they know; and what messages about science they are given by the television they watch in school. As they then watch and deconstruct examples of filmed experiments, some discussion focuses on how choices encode attitudes and values surrounding science. Children may decide that in one film the choice of music connotes mystery and suspense, while in another it connotes fun and delight. Meanwhile, cutaway shots of experimenters' faces seem to humanise science; setting an experiment on metals in a shipyard connotes industrial relevance and usefulness; and the consistent presence of both male and female experimenters suggests that science is ungendered.

Such discussion has a clear place in the Science curriculum, developing children's understanding of how science is perceived and valued in society. A question about the role of texts in shaping or reflecting such perceptions is a question about science, as well as the media.

Children learn that representations of Science are just that: representations. They learn that an experiment they see on screen is in fact a sewing together of several, filmed with one camera from different angles and distances. (They can work this out in examples by mapping camera positions, which would be visible in other shots if it had been a single event filmed with multiple cameras.) As they plan how to make their own films, they have to plot deceptions. Continuity is an illusion: the cut to a close-up is actually a cut to a different experiment. Cutaway shots are not filmed in sequence: the image of an experimenter, apparently concentrating on the action in hand, is actually from another session. The passing of time – signified in one of the children's films by hands turning on a toy clock – is a fiction. Smoke apparently being drawn through a tube by convection is actually being blown by a child off-screen; salt crystals triumphantly displayed at the end have really been prepared earlier. On screen, the experiment can only have one, predetermined result. So the science represented in the films is – in a sense – ideal, rather than real.

FIGURE 8.1 *Setting up the filming of a Science experiment*

Media literacy: larger textual structures One aspect of literacy is to recognise and to have expectations of the overall form and structure of texts: of broad genres such as narrative, argument or – in this case – explanation; and of more specific genres, such as – in this case – a filmed scientific demonstration. As experienced readers of media texts, children can already have a strong implicit understanding of such structures, but have not usually articulated or processed this understanding.

So, before they look at examples, the children consider the purpose of filming an experiment, for a given audience – in this case other children. They then consider what such a film should contain, referring both to prior knowledge and to expectations. They then watch a deliberately weak, unclear example, carried out in front of them but seen through a video camera, pointed at the bench and connected to a projector or screen. Enjoying picking it apart, they quickly identify what was lacking: the purpose wasn't apparent; it wasn't obvious what was being used or done; and the outcome, and what it meant, was not clear.

As they list these negatives, and plan positively the content of their own films, children are learning about scientific method, articulating the importance of clear expression of aims, materials, process, observation and conclusions. Learning about science and learning about the medium have converged.

Media literacy: smaller textual structures At a finer scale, children can learn progressively the vocabularies and grammars of different kinds of media text – verbal, visual or audio. Again, much of this learning is the making explicit of what is already implicitly understood.

Before planning their own films, the children analyse examples of filmed experiments for a similar audience, from schools' television. They count shots, they spot camera angles and they discuss the function of different shots and shot types. They see shots presented as a 'moving storyboard' on PowerPoint, and they consider the grammatical principles of how shots of different types can be sequenced. They decide what the function of cutaways might be (smoothing over edits, or providing context or perspective) and they notice how and why the camera moves during shots.

This learning is reinforced as children discuss how to arrange and conduct their own experiments before the camera, as they make specific shot choices and as they plan the use of captions and titles.

Again, learning about the vocabulary and grammar of the moving image converges with learning about science and scientific method. All the time there is reinforcement of the need for clear expression in science; the effectiveness of choices is always defined in terms of how well the science is being communicated. More interestingly, shot types can be related to different levels of precision and to different components of scientific method; and shot choices are often analogous to the conventions of written explanation, which children have to learn. To generalise: wide shots state context and relevance; mid-shots describe process; close-ups describe fine action; extreme close-ups observe and measure. Oblique angles tend to narrate action, while shots directly in front of, or above, a subject suggest observation. A static, presentational shot of materials or the bench is like a subtitle for the next stage of the procedure, or introduces equipment to be used – the latter especially if it is held aloft by a hand, like an instruction: 'Next, take the ...' Panning shots can list materials and equipment, or can describe simultaneous actions; tracking shots narrate complex actions. And zooms, while tightening or broadening the viewer's attention, can describe the significance of an observation or the intricacy of an action. (It can be useful to draw comparisons with the photography in television cookery programmes, which uses a similar visual language to narrate a bench-top procedure.)

Media Literacy: creative production This project presents children with a significant challenge, which they tackle in groups – negotiating, problem-solving and cooperating in sophisticated ways. Collaboratively, they plan and storyboard their films. They use webcams to film the experiment repeatedly, obtaining different camera angles for subsequent editing (Figure 8.2). Groups assign and develop production roles. Some children take responsibility for camera work; some are performers; one member of each group is put in charge of continuity, carefully noting the arrangement of equipment, which hand an object is held in and what clothes the experimenters must remember to wear next week.

It is in the process of production that some of the benefits to children's learning in Science is clearest. Their learning about scientific method, and about the topic in hand, is reinforced, as they rehearse the translation of scientific method into camera shots, explaining visually what they are doing and finding out. The performance element enforces unusual levels of precision and care in the way students conduct experiments. The need to make explicatory captions, labels and titles for an audience reinforces concepts, as does the element of repetition:

> It made me more confident and familiar with convection, because we had to explain it accurately in our narration and watching it again and again makes us know it back to front. (Harriet)

Perhaps most importantly, the process is highly motivating, and developing of different learning styles and intelligences. Students who can be reluctant to engage in 'ordinary' Science lessons and in a writing-based approach, can become intensely thoughtful, and even take a leading role in their group; and students of all abilities and aptitudes comment on the relationship between the practical and fun elements and learning:

FIGURE 8.2 *Positioning the webcam for the Science experiment*

> I think that it was great being able to have a different atmosphere to working out of books and just answering questions. It made me learn a lot because we all had great fun. (Joe)
> I remember more about the experiment through the film, rather than revising out of a notebook. (Matt)
> I realised that there isn't just one way to learn, there are plenty. (Deepa)

Media literacy: working with technology Part of being literate is having control of a range of inscriptional tools. Children are already familiar with using some media technologies, such as word processing, as an everyday resource; such 'democratic' tools as webcams and freely bundled editing software mean that children are on the verge of being able to regard digital video as part of their everyday repertoire of communicative media. For example, when students write up Science experiments, why should they not include appropriately composed and edited moving images? Such combining of communicative modes in children's work through new technology has already begun to be realised, as the innovative use of mobile laptop computers and interactive whiteboards becomes increasingly continuous with traditional classroom activity.

This project models the way that learning to use such media technology can and should be integrated with other aspects of literacy; children can and should have a critical understanding of the forms they are constructing, if they are to control them.

FIGURE 8.3 *Camera's-eye view of the careful performance of the experiment*

Media Literacy: creativity and pleasure To be media-literate is, also, to learn to control the aesthetic, emotional and entertainment value of media texts – just as in art, design or writing. And it is to know and to own the pleasures of reading and producing media texts. In this project, although the aim of the film is to explain, children have opportunities to discuss and explore creative ideas: how a filmed experiment can be made more interesting or more entertaining to watch; what will make the film fluent and lively; the emotive function of music.

Children enjoy inventing ways to lend their films distinctive character – to make their films seem constructed in a way which is stylish, rather than just careful.

> My favourite part is when it finishes with a close-up of the spiral rotating; I felt this was a very effective ending. Almost hypnotic. (Gunnar)

One group decides that only the hands of the two experimenters will show, entering the shot from opposite sides: the device lends a witty poise to the film, and the symmetry is pleasing. (It also asserts the objectivity of science: the experimenters are detached.) Another group begins and ends their film with the careful opening and closing of an exercise book, on the pages of which captions appear. Again, the effect is visually arresting, the framing is pleasing, and there are witty echoes of the book opening at the start of classic Disney films. (It also asserts the authority of science, through – ironically, in this context – the image of written text.)

In terms of learning about science, children are exploring the emotional and aesthetic satisfactions of its disciplines. At times this is knowing – proclaimed in the way their visual accounts are stylised. But it is also evident in the performative care with which materials are handled and actions carried out on camera (Figure 8.3); in the way the camera zooms slowly, to suggest the tension of discovery; or just in the smiles on the experimenters' faces. And it is clear that the performative, aesthetic element gives children a strong sense of ownership not just of their films, but of the science itself; teachers have been struck by how children, in becoming real film-makers seem to become real scientists.

Overall, our film was successful as we got everything done, we got across our scientific point and it flowed well and had good clarity.

MEDIATED PERFORMANCE

Filming Dance

Recently, James Durran was talking to a group of subject leaders about using moving image in their teaching. A Dance teacher suggested that there was little relevance to her subject, which is all about live performance. This seems an odd assertion, when most of the dance experienced by children is viewed on television or film, seen not from a fixed point as in a theatre, but mediated through a camera lens, and through the decisions of an editor. Indeed, at GCSE Dance students are often required to study 'dance on film', but not necessarily to produce their own. At Parkside, however, all GCSE Dance students do make dance films, as part of a course. Each film is a complex, multimodal text, in which the choreography, dance, camera work and editing are all the students' own: only the music track is 'borrowed'.

Having looked at examples of dance choreographed specifically for film, they work in small groups to choreograph a piece for camera. At all times they are considering the responses of an audience for whom the dance will be mediated by a lens. Considering the particular possibilities for communicating through film, they create patterns and moves which anticipate camera shots – close-ups of detailed hand gestures, or high angle shots of floor work, for example. The design of the dance and the design of the film are inseparable.

They then use digital video cameras to film the dance several times from different angles, and from different distances. They also film in different locations – in the studio, outside, in a corridor and so on; they may even change costume for different locations. To film the whole group, they set the camera going on a tripod; at other times, they take it in turns to film each other in close-up, and with camera movements.

Finally, they edit their different takes into a seamless whole, using editing software. Some editing decisions are suggested by the choreography: particular moves are designed for particular angles or distances, and the pace of the edits may be determined by the pace of the music. But this is also a highly creative stage, at which the affordances of the editing software offer new layers of meaning and effect. For example, students can choose from a range of transitions beyond simple fades and cuts; they can superimpose simultaneous shots on each other – such as a detailed close-up on a long shot – and they can stylise the dance with colour, motion and other effects (Figure 8.4):

FIGURE 8.4 *A slow dissolve transition in the students' Dance video*

> We used many different editing techniques to represent our dance on film.
> Using a cross-dissolve in between shots helped to bring fluency to the
> film, and using transparency meant that we could show several aspects
> of the a moment of the dance at once. We tried to cut from one shot to
> another on the beat of the music, which helped to bring focus to the
> rhythm of the dance. (Hannah)

This comment indicates how decisions made at the editing stage affect how
the dance is itself represented. This student also shows an explicit understanding
of how the dance on film has its own aesthetic integrity; of how film adds
elements unavailable in a live performance, such as superimposition; and of
how the moving image can enhance and reinforce familiar elements of performance
such as rhythm.

This student's group also used the editing of the film to change the intended
choreography of the dance, by re-sequencing moves:

> One of the good things about putting our dance into film was that we
> could change the order and the timing of the choreography for the
> best effect. (Hannah)

The Dance teacher's annotated response to this written comment by Hannah
reflects an emphasis in the course on seeing filmed dance as a distinct art form:

> Yes, a new kind of choreography.

The films are exhibited alongside staged dances at the school dance show, on a
large screen, as an alternative kind of formal performance. As such, they are,

quite explicitly, given similar status to live performances. The screen is on the stage and the same captive audience watches them. However, the films are also exhibited informally, cycling round on a small screen in the school's reception area, for example, watched by whoever happens to be passing or waiting there. The films, along with many other moving image texts created by children, become part of the school's cultural backdrop in ways which live performances cannot.

Filming performed poems

Six years ago Andrew Burn worked with a Year 11 English group on the poem 'Search for My Tongue' by Sujata Bhatt. (The poem was part of an anthology of set texts for GCSE English. It evokes narratives of bilingualism, diaspora, the loss and rediscovery of mother tongue and the way identity is not only expressed in language but is made out of the stuff of language amongst other things. It is also a poem about the body – specifically, about the organs of speech. It operates organic metaphors of plant life to signify the decay and regrowth of Gujarati in the mouth of the speaker – her tongue, literally and figuratively.

The poem proved difficult for the class to engage with. It seemed remote from the experience of many of them. So we got together five bilingual students in the year group (in Cantonese, Vietnamese, Bengali and French) and asked them to write, perform and film poems modelled on Sujata Bhatt's. We gave them a day off timetable to make short films of their poems with a media specialist, Kate Reed. Two further signifying systems came into play. First, performance – they had to perform their poem to the camera. Second, the signifying affordances of camera and editing software – they had to do the filming and editing (on the digital video editing system Media 100). The films were later incorporated into an online multimedia resource for English, created by a team led by Jenny Leach of the Open University (www. open.ac.uk/movingwords). They can also to be found on the CD-ROM.

These short films combine a variety of signifying modes – speech, facial expression, posture and gesture, the built environment, music – and the two representational systems which together make up the mode of the moving image – filming and editing. In a small way, these are dramatic texts, though the students wouldn't have thought of it in that way. But they are dramatising something specific – the bilingual identities of the young poets. It is identity across languages, cultures, countries and communities which is represented in the central metaphors of Sujata Bhatt's poem, and of these teenage responses to it. These performances, then, are what the sociologist Erving Goffman called, in his classic study, 'the presentation of self in everyday life' (1959). But they are more than the daily enactment of bilingualism in the home and school – they are self-consciously artistic expressions of these selves. The performance of selfhood is not only of someone who is bilingual, but someone who is a poet, a film-maker, an exam candidate, a school student. All of these selves and their respective social motivations inform the construction, performance and reworking of these pieces.

The central paradox the poems deal with is the schism and the unity of bilingualism – how it makes a whole person in whom the two languages are harmoniously united, but at the same time is an effect of cultural difference. Fatima says:

> My life is split into two pieces
> Like a fruit that has been cut into two halves.

For her, the difference between Bengali and English is a marked thing: the voices jostle for control, like disobedient children, emphasising the split between worlds and cultures which bilingualism entails. She is also cannily aware of the confusion and difficulty of language, how it can trip you up as well as bravely represent your dual identity:

> Voices can make a fool out of you.

She chooses to perform against a stark brick wall, whose uncompromising materiality carries messages of its own. She decides to film it from two different angles, so that she is shown in three-quarter profile, from one side for the English parts, from the other for the Bengali. This strong device is a visual transformation of the first lines of her poem, but says something different from the fruit simile – something more like 'I am a speaker who faces in two directions'. The distinction between the languages is sharply marked by the transition between the alternating shots, which is always a cut.

FIGURE 8.5 *Fatima's poem: left-facing close-up*

She also chooses different framings, which change the meaning of the lines. A command to one of the voices cited above to be quiet, is a good example. The English version – 'Quiet!' – shows a head-and-shoulders close up, facing left (Figure 8.5); the Bengali version – 'Chup thako!' – is an extreme close-up of her mouth. The second shot associates the spoken Bengali more emphatically with the organ of speech, representing this language more intimately.

Nayana's poem 'Brothers and Flowers' (also in Bengali and English), uses an editing technique to distinguish between the two languages. She makes the English sections black and white, and the Bengali sections sepia, which suggests a kind of starkness across the whole poem, but one tinged with nostalgia for the Bengali shots. She speaks with a serious, musing tone of voice – the paradox here seems more to do with the way bilingualism is for her a completely everyday fact, but at the same time a fascinating mystery:

> Everybody says that it is amazing.
> I never saw anything great about it.
> It's just me, a part of me, the way that I always have been.
> ...
>
> Two tongues – a strange thought.
> I look in the mirror – I open my mouth.
> Go cross-eyed in the attempt to focus
> On the pink muscle that is the source of this mystery,
> The solution to which remains
> Forever elusive.

Where Fatima has used a constant camera distance and frame (a head-and-shoulders close-up), Nayana uses in the first three shots a long shot with a slow zoom in to close-up, situating her in a wider outdoor landscape with trees, houses, roads, before emphasising her speaking presence. She also locates herself in different positions – against a tree, walking from an open background, sitting on a park bench. The effect, in combination with the words, is to suggest both an exploration of a self constantly on the move but also to suggest a self-confidence – the positions are controlled and calm, and the camera angle is often low.

These films, though they include the traditional genre of poetry, raise all kinds of problems for the conventional structures and assessment mechanisms of English. Should they be assessed, for instance, as Reading or Writing (two separately assessed areas of the UK curriculum)? How do we assess their nature as an oral performance? The 'Speaking and Listening' part of the curriculum is more to do with debate and chairing meetings than about the finer points of spoken language and its performance. And as for the moving image – this is consigned, as we saw in Chapter 1, to the 'Reading' section of the curriculum in the UK, so you get no marks for being able to 'write' it. In short, these are complex multimodal texts to which a monomodal curriculum and assessment model is completely unable to do justice.

But they raise problems for media teachers too. They require a view of representation as social performance, in which the signifying properties of faces, hands, mouths, voices, integrate with those of the new media, in multimodal combinations which demand an expanded vocabulary from us if we are to describe them adequately. And, by the same token, we need this expanded vocabulary if we are not to develop for our students metalanguages which distort and limit their understandings of what they can do with this mix of bodies, voices and digital resources.

ANIMATION

Animating volcanoes

In this project, Year 7 students make animations of volcanic processes. Previously, classes have made *papier-mâché* models of volcanoes; animation, however, offers a way actually to *show* geomorphological processes happening in compressed time, rather than just implying them from a static representation. And perhaps animation's intricate, stepped form promotes an equally intricate, stepped analysis of how the Earth has been formed.

In the past, animating required expensive equipment, and was usually attempted with small numbers of students. But just as developments in digital video have democratised video-making in the classroom, so developments in ICT have made it possible for a whole class of children to make animations. At Parkside, children use the software Stop Motion Pro on laptop computers, with ordinary, focusing webcams. The software allows them to capture single frames, 15 per second; to review captured frames running as a film, at any point; and to delete unwanted frames as often as necessary. The webcams do not offer the picture quality of a digital video camera, but are affordable, very easy to use and take up little space on desktops.

Before beginning to make their volcano animations, students practise positioning and focusing the webcams, which are attached to laboratory clamp-stands and focused vertically onto the desktop. They practise lighting this surface with table lamps, and they practise animating small pieces of Plasticine, with which they 'paint' on a flat surface, aiming to create smooth, measured movement, such as they will need to animate lava and ash.

As with any production process, students learn a series of protocols for working with the equipment and with each other. The webcams have to be secured carefully, so that they are held firmly, but are not broken; then they have to be focused using a hard-edged object, such a ruler. The Plasticine is manipulated on a mini-whiteboard, which has to be fastened down using Blu-tack®. To avoid accidentally capturing fingers, the students moving the Plasticine use an agreed signal to tell the student operating the laptop to capture a frame. And so on (Figure 8.6).

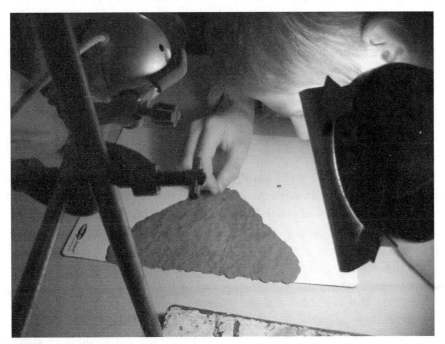

FIGURE 8.6 Animating the Plasticine volcano

Once they have a good sense of the affordances and limitations of the medium, they plan their animations. Each group of three students works on a different aspect of volcanic activity – composite cone formation, plate tectonic movement, the creation of ash layers and so on. They work to a given 'script', which they time and visualise as a moving image, sketching 'key' frames for the start, for the end and for one interim point in their animation. At this point the convergence of disciplines is particularly apparent: the consideration of image and representation is inseparable from the consideration of geomorphological processes. Compromises have to be teased out: how to simplify the real world for diagrammatic clarity, or how to compress geological time. Specialist verbal language, such as 'pyroclastic' or 'transverse', has to be translated into an accessible visual language. And more everyday terms, such as 'flow', 'eruption' or 'cone', have to be represented in their specialist meanings.

Team-teaching Geography and Media teachers play out this collision of conceptual disciplines, often referring on students' questions: 'Check that with ...', 'You'd better ask ...'. In so doing, they underline the breadth of expertise expected of the students.

When their plans are approved, the students begin to make their animations. To make a film of about 30 seconds can easily take two or three hours, yet the process is satisfyingly absorbing, even for more easily distracted students, especially if working in small groups of about three. There is, of course, an element of trial and error involved, but the software – unlike film – allows frames and chunks to be deleted and inserted immediately. When their sequences are completed, the students record their voice-overs. These and the completed sequences are then edited together into one film.

In a sense, this seems much less to do with media literacy, or the concerns of media education than, say, the animations described in Chapter 2, in which children engage with narrative, shot types, the grammar of sequences and so on. After all, children are just making a moving model. Is it, perhaps, just a technical feat, not a creative or 'literate' one?

However, we would argue that the project is very much about media literacy. First of all, it is to do with the struggle to *represent* – to mediate. They are not just reproducing what they have been taught, they are seeking a way to make the idea clear to a new audience. In this striving to represent an idea – in this case a complex physical process – in a symbolic form, students engage analytically and imaginatively with concepts, becoming responsible for them, owning them. But they also become owners of the medium, of the form. They are becoming 'literate' film-makers, addressing and considering an audience. They are making creative decisions, as film-makers, about colour, shape and scale, about pace, repetition and duration, which are not to do with geomorphology but with addressing that audience.

Students also reflect explicitly on the nature of 'animation', and they discuss the reasons for using it as a medium to represent the volcanic processes about which they have been learning in Geography. They look at paintings, photographs and schematic diagrams of volcanoes, and think about what these forms offer; then they consider the particular affordances of animation: perhaps coupling the symbolic nature of diagrams with movement and fluid change. And they consider the logic of using stop-motion animation, which runs together multiple stepped images, for representing processes through time.

Of course, such an approach is much more time-consuming than a lesson in which students draw diagrams, and then move on. But the subject teachers would argue that the investment of time is worthwhile – that learning is deepened by the activity, for familiar and established reasons. It is, for a start, highly pleasurable, and therefore motivating, engaging and memorable. The process is intensely social, and requires precise negotiation and articulation of ideas within groups. It makes reference to cultural forms (television, animated films) of which students have extensive experience. It involves a real audience (other students; public exhibition on screens around the school). It may emancipate reluctant or unconfident writers from the confines of the exercise book.

Then there are the broader learning objectives, to do not with Geography but with students' personal development. Animation is a challenging activity, which demands a sustained, high level of cognitive activity, intense cooperation, considerable patience and precision, fine motor skills, confidence and fluency with ICT, and a lot of problem-solving.

Of course, like any chosen classroom approach, film-making suits some children – some learning styles – more than others. These different preferences can emerge strongly in students' comments, as in the following extracts from a discussion between a small group and a trainee teacher.

All the students are eager to identify pleasure in the activity; interestingly (and typically) they define this pleasure in terms of difference from conventional classroom activity, and from what 'learning' is expected to be like:

> *How does this activity compare with other classroom activities that you might do?*
> ALL: It was fun.
> TIM: Yeah, it was much better than Maths.
> ELENA: It wasn't just fun though because it did make me learn as well.
> ANDREW: We had fun, it was better than written work.

But to some students the conventional approach would have been as effective on its own:

> *Do you think the work we have done in class will help you remember about the Geography more?*
> SITARAM: Yeah, yeah, you were explaining it and we were looking in the books and everything … … don't get me wrong, I did like doing the animations, but it didn't help me.

However, others insist that making the animations has helped to fix or consolidate concepts for them (Figure 8.7):

> ELENA: Yeah, but I think I will remember it because it was more fun than normal lessons, and I learnt more as well, I will remember more.
> INDIA: I learnt more, like those shield volcanoes, I thought every volcano was just like a volcano … I will remember loads … shield volcanoes, destructive boundaries, constructive boundaries, tectonic plates … I'll remember it.

This approach is not, then, an answer in itself; it is just part of a necessarily broad repertoire of approaches, addressing the range of students' preferred ways of learning.

Shield volcano

FIGURE 8.7 *Concept as word and image*

CONCLUSION

As we suggested in the introduction to this chapter, there may be one dominant principle in the development of media literacy across the curriculum: that such work should not regard media texts and technologies as 'transparent'. Films, games, documentary, animation are all forms that have rich cultural histories, and well-developed theories of signification, which children need some understanding of. They cannot simply 'contain' information, like transparent glass jars: they will always, by their nature, mediate such information; and this mediation, whether through argument, narrative, or appeal to emotion, constitutes the rhetorics of the media as they might be used in Science or History.

Culturally, the media often operate as the site in which children's interest in and commitment to different domains of human knowledge is negotiated. Here, culture needs to be understood in its widest sense, as in Raymond Williams's notion of a 'whole way of life', which we cited in Chapter 1. A child's viewing of a documentary about the Romans on the Discovery Channel may be an example; but so might the chemistry set they are given for their eleventh birthday; or their participation in a local children's drama group; or what they pick up about the Hittite empire from playing Microsoft's *Age of Empires* computer game. It is all too easy for school culture to become hermetically sealed against these popular cultural worlds. For media literacy to flourish across the curriculum, our classrooms and curriculum structures need to become more porous.

Media literacy across the curriculum is, then, not at all the same thing as 'e-learning'. It involves learning *about* media as well as learning *through* media. We will consider in Chapter 10 what this distinction means, both for ICT in education and for media teachers.

THE VERTICAL ANGLE: PROGRESSION
IN MEDIA LITERACY

Furthermore, in both drama and media study, insufficient attention is given to progression, with students doing similar activities and demonstrating similar skills from year to year, such as 'freeze-frames' and 'hot-seating' in drama, and simple storyboards or advertisements in media work. It remains rare for secondary schools, either individually or working with their primary feeder schools, to consider in any detail how students' media literacy is developed through the English or wider curriculum. (OFSTED, 2004)

This judgement by the UK's education watchdog is a fair reflection of the fragmentary nature of media education in this country, and of the lack of any real sense of progression as a consequence. This book is an attempt to demonstrate how the media specialist schools in particular have begun to provide more of a continuous experience of media education throughout the secondary phase. Until now, the substantial tradition of media work in the UK has mainly been in the public examination courses in Media Studies, which have been the engines of curricular development, the providers of much of the in-service training and the innovators with production technologies.

Nevertheless, while practice remains fragmentary, the question of how progression in media literacy might be planned into the curriculum has been an issue for some time. One context which has produced a model of progression has been the introduction of a statutory National Curriculum in 1988. Like curricula elsewhere in the Anglophone world, the UK associated media literacy primarily with the English curriculum; though unlike some, such as Ontario, where the production of media texts is required, it situated its requirements for the study of the media within the Reading section of the curriculum, as we have noted in previous chapters. In the UK, then, school students are required by mandate to read and interpret media texts, but not to make their own. For us, this has always represented only one side of the literacy coin.

What the curriculum in England and Wales currently requires is essentially a critical understanding of media texts, constructed within the 'ages and stages' model of the National Curriculum. However, while other aspects of literacy become progressively more complex and sophisticated, the minimal representation of media literacy fails to indicate progression. There is no provision at all for the primary school stages; and the provision for Key Stage 3 (11–14) and Key Stage 4 (14–16) remains unchanged across the two stages:

Media and moving image texts

5) Students should be taught:
   a. how meaning is conveyed in texts that include print, images and sometimes sounds
   b. how choice of form, layout and presentation contribute to effect (for example, font, caption, illustration in printed text, sequencing, framing, soundtrack in moving image text)
   c. how the nature and purpose of media products influence content and meaning (for example, selection of stories for a front page or news broadcast)
   d. how audiences and readers choose and respond to media.

While this represents some improvement over previous curriculum models, in that it makes specific mention of the moving image, it cannot be said to offer an adequate model of progression.

Institutions which specialise in media education in the UK have made their own suggestions. The British Film Institute has proposed a model which lays out stages that roughly correspond to the five key stages of the National Curriculum, though they are careful to emphasise that these are not necessarily age-specific (FEWG, 1999). While this model has been a valuable contribution to the debate about progression, it is limited by its focus on 'cine-literacy', and by its assumption that specific knowledge and concepts can be assigned to specific stages of development. So, for example, students at Stage 1 would learn about 'long shot' and 'close-up', while those at Stage 2 would learn about 'angle' and 'frame'. While the idea that conceptual understandings of the media will become increasingly sophisticated is obviously desirable, it is hard to see how this kind of staged progression would work. However, the bfi has also initiated teacher action research projects looking at progression, and our partnership in these projects has informed our thoughts in this chapter.

Perhaps the most detailed picture of how progression might take place is represented by the English and Media Centre's resource packs. *The Media Book* provides resources and guidance linked to the National Curriculum for 11 to 14 and *The Media Pack* (Grahame, 2002) contains five units of work for GCSE English or Media Studies, one of which is the project we describe in Chapter 6.

Our own work has evolved rather than being neatly planned from the outset. Like many of the early media arts colleges, we began with a focus on the specialist media studies courses already established at 14–16, and with projects for primary schools, which were required by the conditions of designation. Only later did the gap in the lower secondary years begin to be filled, at least in terms of production work: we already had other media projects established within English. In the remainder of this chapter, we will give an idea of what progression at Parkside looks like at the time of writing. The emphasis is very much on provision – on a rich and varied series of experiences which take in different media, different cultural references and contexts, and different production technologies.

MEDIA LITERACY PROGRESSION – A RECURSIVE MODEL

Throughout our ten years of specialist media work, we have become convinced that the best model for progression is a recursive model. It is impossible for us to say that we will artificially withhold knowledge of how to edit sequences of film, or how to frame a shot, or how to write a script, in our work with 7-year-olds. In a general sense, a production project with young children is the same as such a project with 16-year-olds, and might involve the full array of signifying practices with the moving image. The shape of progression is, then, the repetition of such work over and over again, just as English always involves reading literature and writing stories. Whatever it is that changes as students move through the years can be better seen as expansion rather than addition: expansion of concepts, of metalanguage, of media forms, of cultural purposes and cultural horizons.

We have seen in Chapter 3, for instance, how the 7-year-olds' animation process is much the same as the process undertaken by the 11-year-olds. Both groups script, storyboard, animate, record vocal performances and edit. Both learn about shot types and narrative. Both learn through the playful manipulation of semiotic tools. What is different is an expansion of the abstract ideas of moving image semiotics; the same concepts are there, but they are dwelt on at greater length, followed through from storyboard to production more insistently.

Recursivity, a familiar notion in literacy learning generally, can be seen in terms of our three-part model of media literacy, and it is this alignment that we propose.

First, then, progression in cultural development. Needless to say, this cannot be constrained by ages and stages. Nevertheless, there will be development. The social interests of 8–12-year-old girls, for instance, are often characterised as aspirational, motivated by an interest in the obscure attractions of adolescence, the changing nature of gendered identity, and beyond, the forbidden fruits of adolescence (Richards, 1995; Willett, 2006). We have indicated in Chapter 2 how these kinds of changing cultural interest can find expression in the popular media of comicstrips; the same applies to the way teenagers might learn about sexuality from magazines and soap operas (Buckingham and Bragg, 2003).

Also, we know that children and young people develop certain aspects of media literacy through their own engagement with the media outside school; and we have shown how such experience will inform their understanding of animation (Chapter 3), horror films (Chapter 5), or computer games (Chapter 7). In a recent debate about media literacy, part of the Digital Generations international conference (Institute of Education, 2004), the media researcher Mimi Ito represented this aspect of media literacy succinctly:

> Now the second point that I want to bring up is that this fluency that kids are exhibiting, it's an extremely high level form of literacy, not necessarily the kind of content that educators are interested in, but it happens in a natural social ecology, much like kids learn spoken language. So the analogue is closer to learning spoken language than written language, Math or Science. So kids can master highly ... complex content within peer-to-peer social ecologies and I think that an important lesson from an educational perspective is that media literacies perhaps are learned most effectively in the naturally occurring peer-to-peer social ecologies.

This kind of fluency, which we have also compared to the fluidity of oracy in Chapter 1 and other chapters, is something we need to meet halfway, and recognise as far as we can. And, like any other aspect of literacy, it is everchanging, quite regardless of what we do in schools. Children will at some point acquire a mobile phone, a playstation console, a computer in their bedroom; they will develop specific tastes in different media forms and genres; they will negotiate the regulatory regimes that seek to protect them from certain kinds of content.

At the same time, this kind of development and expansion will meet the school culture of media literacy, if it is there to be met, in what Gutierrez et al. call 'the third space', where the cultural worlds of student and teacher come into contact (1995). Ideally, this is a kind of dialogue between cultures. We have proposed in our model that, while the lived culture of media pleasures should be central to our work, we also have a role in deepening historical understanding of media cultures, and in introducing students to the kinds of evaluative commentary which surround culturally valued texts. The work on *Psycho* in Chapter 5, for instance, while it begins with an exploration of students' immediate experiences of horror films, and sustains that context throughout the project, also introduces a film with a particular cultural history, and a particular cultural status.

Secondly, progression will be critical. It is easy enough to imagine that children might arrive in the classroom completely un-critical, and that education will furnish them with the necessary critical skills. Indeed, this has often been a dominant rationale for media education, and remains so in some respects.

Furthermore, there is a good deal of truth in this assumption. Recent research shows, for instance, that young people find certain aspects of the Internet confusing – how search engines work, or what the legal status of downloadable music might be (Cranmer, 2006; de Smedt et al., 2006). Similarly, we have argued in Chapter 6 that young people may not be aware of some aspects of the rhetorics of advertising – in this case, the representation of Africa as passive in charity ads.

However, this is not to say that children do arrive in classrooms in some state of ideal critical 'innocence'. Indeed, they may have well-developed critical senses in some respects. As Buckingham argues (2003), by secondary age they are likely to be well aware that advertising functions to sell them products and ideas, that media fictions are constructions rather than realities and that the value of media texts is at least partly a matter of taste. However, the movement from more subjective engagement with media cultures to a more objective critical understanding is by no means linear, or entirely predictable. We have seen that it can only take place in the meeting-place between the students' cultures and the teachers'; but of course the students' cultural experiences are themselves heterogeneous. If a progression of critical understanding depends partly on understanding how other people interpret and value different media texts and cultures, then, as Engeström argues (1999), this kind of expansive learning must be horizontal as well as vertical – to progress, it must look across cultural divisions in its own community.

Thirdly, progression can be seen as creative. We have argued throughout this book that conceptual development in media literacy needs to happen through production work, not just as an adjunct to it. The obvious way in which this might happen is to imagine that practical work rehearses and consolidates abstract conceptual ideas; and in some ways, this is what we believe is happening. It is difficult for children to really understand what it means for their work to address an audience unless they repeatedly have the experience of seeing people view their films in a local cinema, or respond to their game designs on the Internet. It is difficult to grasp what a media institution might be like without imaginatively inhabiting it through simulation or roleplay. It is, arguably, impossible to conceptualise the structures of media texts without some opportunity to manipulate them.

However, a more startling view of how such progression might work is Engeström's notion of 'the dialectics of ascending from the abstract to the concrete'. Contrary to the conventional assumption (and the Piagetian model of conceptual development), this argument proposes that the cycle of learning might begin with a simple abstract idea and progress, through the manipulation of semiotic tools and the creation of artefacts which is central to Vygotsky's notion of development, to more complex and sophisticated ideas. We provided an example of this in Chapter 3. In the Red Riding Hood animation made by the Year 4 children, the concepts introduced to them of shot type, while in one sense new and challenging, were also abstract and partial. Only when the specific images of the wolf's rotating head and rumbling stomach were introduced by the children did the notion of how form and content meet to produce rich and complex representations become evident. What we have called an 'oscillation' between internal imaginative and conceptual work and external production continues, then, throughout the span of children's educational lives, as long, that is, as there are sufficient opportunities for it to grow.

SEMIOTIC PROGRESSION

In our model of media literacy, we have also emphasised the semiotic dimension. What might progression mean, then, in relation to media texts as systems of signification? On the one hand, we might expect the texts made by students to become semiotically more complex in various ways. On the other hand, we have raised the question in Chapter 1 of how students might gain an explicit grasp of semiotic principles, just as in English they might learn about the grammar of language. While no clear consensus exists about what the 'languages' of the media might be, our research has explored the social semiotic approach we have cited throughout this book. The best chance for a coherent approach to media texts lies in some kind of mediated version of this approach, we suggest. In our own teaching, we have incorporated aspects of social semiotics and multimodal theory: it is explicitly used in the analysis of comicstrip front covers in the Year 8 project described in Chapter 2, for instance.

In terms of progression, we would expect an increasingly sophisticated grasp of such as system. However, we envisage this not as an empty, decontextualised rote-learning, but a provisional analytical structure repeatedly tested against the concrete contexts of the texts themselves, the social meanings they represent and the students' relations to these social meanings. As an example, here is an account of a project with Year 10 students (14–15), working on an analysis of *In the Heat of the Night* (Jewison, 1967), as the media element within a GCSE English course. The students' task, as a GCSE oral assignment, is to analyse still images from the film, both to explain how they carry the narratives and social messages of the movie, and also how they do this using particular filmic conventions, including those described by a social semiotic grammar of the visual, derived from Kress and van Leeuwen (1996).

A member of the class, Megan, is analysing two images from early on in the film, where the black detective Virgil Tibbs has been wrongly arrested by the local police of Sparta, Mississippi, unaware of his identity as a police officer. The images show a close-up of the face of the officer, Sam Woods, who has arrested Tibbs and is guarding him and then the reverse shot of Tibbs, seated facing the officer.

Megan, correctly applying the terms she has been taught, identifies Sam as the *Actor* and Tibbs as the *Goal*. These terms, derived directly from functional linguistics, denote processes of social action – who's doing what to whom. The power relations of the grammatical construction are, in this case, directly linked to the central themes of race and civil rights with which the film is concerned, as Megan makes clear.

Megan's next concern is to describe the *process* taking place – the action; in traditional language grammar this would be the verb. This process is constructed by the juxtaposition of the two shots in her sequence (or montage, in the more familiar film term). Megan decides that the action is *thinking* – Sam is thinking that Tibbs is guilty. He performs the thought; Tibbs is the Goal, on the receiving end.

She goes on to explore the second metafunction, the *interpersonal metafunction*. This is to do with how texts function to construct relationships between text and audience. In the case of these the camera angle is low in the first shot, high in the second, thus placing Tibbs in a weaker position relative both to Sam and to us. Megan develops this, suggesting that this encourages sympathy in the spectator.

At this point, an interesting argument develops, as a boy in the group, Rupert, disputes Megan's interpretation of Tibbs's low physical position. Rupert points out that, later in the film, when Tibbs is questioned by the sheriff, Gillespie, the shot showing Gillespie has him seated at his desk, and uses a high camera angle, showing him from the point of view of Tibbs, who is standing in front of the desk. Rupert argues that, despite the high camera angle, Gillespie is undoubtedly represented as powerful in this shot.

Though they never quite resolve the argument, both of them are right. In the case of the Gillespie shot, two signifiers of power are at work. One is the filmic signifier of the camera angle, lending some power to Tibbs (and us) – appropriately enough, since Tibbs, as the film goes on to show, is equal in power to Gillespie, even superior in certain ways – and he is the character who attracts the weight of audience sympathy, as Megan suggests. The other signifier of power is what we have referred to in earlier chapters as pro-filmic. It is a dramatic signifier – an expressive use of the human body conjoined with a dramatic prop. This is Gillespie's casual sprawl, legs up on the desk, allied to another signifier of power – Gillespie's hand, gently caressing one of the rifles in a rack of guns behind him.

This can be seen as another example of Engeström's (1999) 'abstract into concrete' dialectic. Megan has successfully learnt the general abstract principles of the 'visual grammar' here. However, as soon as this account connects with an image from the film on the one hand, and (an example of the

Engeström's (1999) horizontal expansion) with the different interpretations of other members of the group, these abstract principles immediately appear too simple, too reductive and need to develop into something more complex, more nuanced, more responsive to the concrete detail of the text and the experience of the audience.

EXPANDING OPPORTUNITIES

The planning of media literacy progression as expansion also needs, in our experience, to cover two further dimensions: range of media, and increasing diversity of location in the curriculum.

In respect of the first, there is a real logistical problem for media educators. If, as we argued in Chapter 1, media literacy subsumes a set of subliteracies specific to different media, how are these to be covered in the time available; and even more problematically, how are they all to be revisited in the recursive model we have proposed in this chapter?

This is a matter of emphasis and judgement for individual schools. Parkside is a Media Arts college and as we have pointed out in the preface, this has led us to an emphasis on the media arts, so that journalistic media, for instance, has not been such an evident part of our work. Our choices have been made partly because of the cultural dominance of media forms such as film, television, comics and games; partly because these forms have relatively long histories which can be 'mined' in the classroom; and partly because they are demonstrably important aspects of children's cultural lives. In these respects, the moving image forms the most substantial part of Parkside's work at present. Students are given opportunities for moving image production work in every year, from Year 6 to Year 11. The 'recursive spiral' most obvious, then, is the revisiting of the principles and practice of filming and editing, in widely varying contexts, as we have seen in Chapters 3, 4, 5 and 6. In addition, it takes into account the cross-curricular contexts in which such work is developed, as we have described in Chapter 8.

In respect of the second form of expansion, increasingly diverse locations in the curriculum, opportunities develop as students move through their lives at Parkside. In particular, the 14–16 stage opens up a range of specialist courses tied to national forms of accreditation. All students take GCSE Media Studies, in a course integrated with English and English Literature. There are also options to take the first part of an advanced AS-Level course in Film Studies, and also an entirely practical (non-accredited) course in video production.

In some ways the conceptual apparatus of media education becomes more specialised and compartmentalised at this stage: Media Studies and Film

Studies have their own quite specific versions of the conceptual and semiotic aspects of media literacy. However, in other ways the increasing familiarity of media concepts becomes transferred to other curriculum areas. This may be by deliberate planning, as in the Dance project described in the previous chapter. However, it might also be serendipitous: we have noticed students in English, for instance, referring to the 'representation' of trench warfare in poetry of the First World War. 'Representation' is a concept they have learnt in Media Studies, not English. Although it certainly should be a central idea in all textual study, it is not to be found in conventional English Literature syllabuses.

ASSESSMENT AND EVALUATION

Media education has an ambivalent relationship with practices of assessment. Media educators have pointed to the paralysing effect of assessment practices on students' reflective work (Buckingham et al., 2000). More generally, arts educators have found attempts to quantify achievement inimical to the creative process (Sefton-Green and Sinker, 2000). On the other hand, without any system of evaluation it is impossible to judge whether learners are getting any better at what they do; or whether what they have done is as good as we might expect it to be at any given age. A review of media production projects in the informal sector, for instance, observed that there was no consensus across the UK about how to evaluate the work produced, and called for the development of an 'evaluative matrix' against which such projects could judge their outcomes (Harvey et al., 2002).

Our view is similarly ambivalent. However, not to assess media work is, in any educational system that assesses what it judges to be most important, to allow such work to drift to the margins of the curriculum. A central place demands assessment. Furthermore, we do consider it important to judge what has been achieved and learnt, where it is possible and practicable to do so. Parkside's approach is to use, therefore, an adapted version of the levels for Reading and Writing in the English National Curriculum. This practice recognises the importance of creative production work as well as interpretation and analysis, and allows for a charting of progression in media literacy to run parallel to judgements about students' development in the field of print literacy.

As shown in Table 19.1, in examples from Levels 5 and 7, these are written in the second-person, reflecting an emphasis on formative dialogue and self-assessment.

Comparing the Level 5 and 7 descriptors, English teachers will recognise the elements of differentiation. Level 7 Reading requires more confidence, more secure awareness of authorial intent, more rigour in analysis and a more evaluative response. Meanwhile, Level 7 Production emphasises originality and

TABLE 9.1 Parkside sample level descriptors for media texts

Level 5 Reading media texts	Level 7 Reading media texts
• You read *further* under the surface of media texts. (For example, how is a viewer meant to feel, and why? What does a detail in a picture suggest? How are particular types of people represented in a film or a TV programme?) • You can refer to more detailed evidence to support your ideas. • You use technical terms to describe media texts.	• You write and talk confidently about meanings and ideas in media texts – about what the producers of media texts are saying, and about how they are telling stories, or expressing ideas or feelings, or persuading. • You always refer to well-chosen details, to support your ideas. • You can also explain the techniques that the makers of media texts are using to do these things. • You always use technical terms to describe the way they are structured. • You can show that you have your own views on media texts, and that these views are based on thoughtful reading. • You can evaluate media texts – judge how effective they are, and back this up with reasons and references to details.
Level 5 Production	**Level 7 Production**
• You are careful and thoughtful when producing texts. • You use what you have seen and discussed to make media texts interesting, or effective. You are starting to imitate the methods that professionals use. • You show that you are aware of the audience and the purpose of a media text. You understand what genre it is, and so what conventions or style you need to use.	• You work hard to make texts as professional as possible. • You use a wide range of techniques that you have seen in professionally produced media texts, but in a way that is original, and that makes them your own. • You use techniques confidently and interestingly, in a way that shows clear awareness of audience and purpose. • You always make your media texts thoughtfully organised, and carefully structured.

ownership, a clear relation of chosen techniques to audience and purpose and high levels of organisation. It also uses the notion of 'professionalism', suggesting an element of aspiration, in students' work, to the standards of media texts with which they are familiar.

We would not pretend this framework is ideal, future-proof or suited to everybody. It would have been easier to omit any consideration of assessment. We present it here, then, in a spirit of experimentation and provisionality; our hope is that, if media education in the UK below the age of 14 can expand beyond the current reductive model, adequate assessment systems will follow. In the meantime, those who elect to develop routes of progression through the secondary age range will rely, as we have done, on home-made frameworks, though these are beginning to be discussed and shared among the community of specialist media schools in England.

A FINAL WORD: BEYOND SCHOOL AND ASSESSMENT

As we have indicated already, progression in media literacy is an unpredictable and leaky process. The cultural worlds of the media leak in where they are least expected; children's developing tastes, pleasures and subversive intentions conspire to rock any neat programme schools might try to set up. Progression is 50 per cent opportunity planned by us, and 50 per cent improvisation: indeed, it is likely that the key guarantor of effective progression is skilful improvisation by teachers attentive to children's experience and interests, with suitably catholic tastes in media themselves.

To cite Engeström one last time:

> the key feature of expansive cycles is that they are definitely not predetermined courses of one-dimensional development. What is more advanced, 'which way is up', cannot be decided using externally given fixed yardsticks. Those decisions are made locally, within the expansive cycles themselves, under conditions of uncertainty and intensive search. (1999: 2)

Furthermore, while our model of media literacy is, in Engeström's sense, a model of progression through expansive cycles, it also recognises that many purposes of creative work in media education are not principally oriented to future goals, competences or identities, but to the expressive needs of the moment. In this sense, children's uses of media literacy are exactly like those of adults. They are more interested in the job in hand, in what they can say now with the tools available. Conversely, we may be caught up in learning and progression in ways we often do not realize: it may be us, the teachers, parents and researchers, who need to continue learning as much as the students. In this sense, progression can be seen beyond the age of compulsory schooling as a lifelong social project, in which the growth of the younger age group is bound up with the growth of their parents and teachers.

We will end with Henry Jenkins, professor of Comparative Media at MIT, who recently enunciated a series of reasons why adults are more in need of media literacy than children. His remarks, while they apply in specific ways to the USA, can also be applied to the state of affairs internationally:

> Well first of all let me briefly answer the question, 'Media Literacy, who needs it?' First of all I think teachers, secondly parents, government officials, industry leaders. In other words, grown-ups are one of the groups that need Media Literacy. . . Media Literacy begins at home with parents and pre-schoolers, they've got to deal with media the same way they deal with books. You know, it's got to include the teachers who need to be re-told and re-taught. And if we don't do that then the real risk is that

Media Literacy as it happened in the American context will be held hostage by a variety of ideologues and moral reformers and what you get is anti-media education rather than Media Literacy education which I think has been one of the dangers of the American context. (Media Literacy debate, Digital Generations International conference, Institute of Education, 2004)

BACK TO THE FUTURE: POSSIBILITIES AND PITFALLS FOR MEDIA LITERACY

In many ways attention to media literacy seems to have a bright future, in education and in wider society, in the UK and in the world at large. In Chapter 1 we cited the emphatic endorsement of the importance of media literacy by the then UK Culture Secretary, Tessa Jowell. In the UK education system the number of specialist media colleges has grown from 1997, when Parkside was the only one, to a current community of more than fifty schools. A new media education association has been formed, to develop collaboration between media educators (www.mediaedassociation.org.uk). Internationally, media literacy is a live issue in the European Union, with specialist research commissioned by the EC, media literacy experts recommending future policy and media educators signing up to the media literacy charter. Media education is well-established in Canada, Australia and New Zealand (though the picture in the USA continues to be fragmentary, as Henry Jenkins points out in the remarks we have quoted at the end of Chapter 9). Meanwhile, there is evidence of the development of media literacy policy and research in Taiwan, Korea, Japan and China.

For all these reasons, we remain broadly optimistic. What we are able to do at Parkside now with media texts and technologies has grown beyond our wildest dreams over a decade or so. Further developments seem now both possible and urgent. We will briefly consider three questions for the future which seem to us interesting and important: the recognition of media literacy in relation to school curricula (especially literacy curricula); the scope and content of future media education; and the question of new media.

MEDIA LITERACY AND THE LITERACY CURRICULUM

As we have seen, conventional models of print-based literacy often seem determined to resist expansion. In the UK, while the Department for Culture, Media and Sport is busily promoting media literacy, the Department for Education and Skills is doggedly preserving an English curriculum where the

practices and values of print literacy and of literary studies keep media education and multiliteracies strategically confined. There is, however, plenty of
room to work within these constraints: to worry away at the loopholes, grow
media literacy in the gaps, graft popular cultural forms and new semiotic
approaches onto the sparse twigs of the literacy curriculum as it stands.
Andrew Goodwyn gives a detailed account, for instance, of how moving
image media can be used in English (Goodwyn, 2004); while Kirwan et al.
(2003) provide a comprehensive picture of media literacy work in the UK
both in relation to specialist media courses and in relation to English. Where
all this might go in the future is hard to predict, though there is no shortage of
models which would address the problems we identify. We referred earlier to
the changing approach to media education which Buckingham and Sefton-
Green tentatively labelled Cultural Studies over a decade ago (1994). Julian
McDougall, in his wide-ranging account of media education practices (2006),
imagines an ideal model of Textual Studies which would subsume both
English and media education. Gunther Kress, in a recent government-spon-
sored 'conversation' about the future of English (2005), argued for a shift
from a linguistic to a semiotic model of English. All of these suggestions have
merit, and they are in our view compatible in many respects. The relationship
between English and Media Studies, always close, but always fraught with
contradictions and beset by confusions, would become more coherent within
any of these models. To return to the example of the Harry Potter franchise
we used at the beginning of Chapter 1, a semiotic or textual model, with a
sustained attention to popular culture, would allow teachers of English and
Media to make sense of a literacy which spans book, film and computer game.

However, for a shift towards an expanded, semiotic conception of literacy
and meaning-making in the curriculum, there needs to be enough of a consensus in the teaching profession and the research community for such an
expansion to be understood, accepted and adopted across the educational
sphere. For English teachers, this would involve recognising that modes of signification other than language also have 'grammars', that fundamental
semiotic principles governing how representations are framed and composed,
and orientated towards audiences, can be applied across media. The research
community has for some years now explored how social semiotic and multimodal approaches to literacy can make possible an understanding of how
children interpret and make images as well as linguistic text (Bearne, 2003);
how they make sense of the moving image (Burn and Durran, 2006); and how
they engage with digital media (Jewitt, 2005). There is, however, a long way
to go before such findings can build a substantial consensus among the teaching profession, and become part of its stock repertoire.

For Media teachers, we envisage a parallel but rather different debate about
how media education might deal with the 'languages' of the media. Unlike

English, Media has always had a kind of semiotic model at its heart, as we suggested in Chapter 1. The problem we identified there is that, while Cultural Studies produced new ways of thinking about media audiences, it retreated from textual analysis, and generated no new ways of thinking about texts. At the same time, the conceptual framework of media education, as we argued in Chapter 1, was continually obliged to fall back on fragments of older semiological and narratological approaches. So, while Buckingham and Sefton-Green (2004) were undoubtedly right to call for something like Cultural Studies in media education, which would establish a dialogue with the lived cultures of young people, such a model needs to be supplemented with new ways to think about texts.

Our proposal of a social semiotic and multimodal approach to this issue will continue in our own work and research, and we hope to continue this debate both with the UK and the international communities of media educators. At the same time, social semiotics and multimodality theory will need development and adaptation: to meet with the familiar semiotic models which Media teachers still find useful; and to connect with research into the cultural practices of young people and the media. We hope to have given some idea, if only fleeting, of how these theories can help us to analyse what young people do when they make media texts; and also how they can be adapted to be accessible to students as they engage in critical reflection about how texts work.

Finally, however, we should recognise a tension between models of media literacy and media education historically associated with English, language and the literacy curriculum, and models which pull towards other areas of the curriculum. Although our own history is as English teachers, and this context remains important to us, we are also both Drama teachers, and aware of the very different context of Arts education. At the same time, the Arts umbrella under which the specialist media schools in the UK are situated has led to closer links with Art, Music, Dance and Drama, aspects of which we have illustrated in this book. This fluidity is part of a wider picture, of course. In the UK, it is associated with government policy interests in the development of the economic sphere, of which the creative industries form a part. In Europe, it is possible to see a wide variety of models and locations of media education, with concomitant rationales based in different notions of media literacy. For some countries, national film heritages are important; for others, media literacy is closely associated with mother tongue teaching; for others, it is seen as part of the fine arts; for others again, it is a kind of curriculum supplement, permitted only in voluntary after-school provision or 'flexible zone' time.

The conception of media literacy, and its relation to other literacies, will depend, then, on differing national and local contexts, and on national and international activity among practitioners, researchers, lobbyists and policy-makers. It is clear, on the one hand, that sufficient flexibility is needed to respond to the particular circumstances and histories of different contexts. At the same time, there is a danger that too much diversity will render international consensus meaningless, and will fail to respond to global aspects of youth culture and its engagement with popular media and the digital era.

THE SCOPE OF MEDIA EDUCATION AND MEDIA LITERACY

We expect there to be certain predictable shifts over the next decade or so. Although Buckingham and Sefton-Green anticipated the importance of computer games and hypertextual media in *Cultural Studies Goes to School* (1994), it is still true that media teachers in the UK in general favour the old certainties of film, television and the print media over the rather less certain territory of computer games and the Internet. In consequence, the medium of choice for production projects is still digital video. There is a long way to go with this medium, which has only been available affordably for ten years at the most. The expressive and critical possibilities of this access to the powerful moving image culture of the last century have, perhaps, barely been probed yet, though its rich potential is signalled in accounts of practical production (e.g. Frazer and Oram, 2003). It may be too early to be hurrying Media teachers away from the moving image to games and the Internet. Many schools have only recently worked out how to approach video and animation; many others have not yet begun such work in earnest.

At the same time, it is clear that games, in particular, are rapidly gaining ground as an important cultural form of the late-twentieth and early twenty-first century. Their importance is attested to in many ways familiar from older histories of other media: they cause agitated cultural comment; they provoke new uncertainties and possibilities about how technologies represent and mediate 'reality'; they are surrounded by 'moral panics' of the kind which have erupted over other troubling media in the past, from the perceived moral threat of romantic fiction to the young women of nineteenth-century Europe to the horror comic and video-nasty of mid-twentieth century America and Britain. These anxieties are currently being played out in public discourses about violence, addiction and the cultural value of games. More positively, however, games are being taken seriously in the 'quality' press review sections, and in policy, research and development in the arts, commercial and educational sectors. The industry, anxious to be perceived positively, is taking its duty of self-regulation seriously, building relationships with the research community, and beginning to consider the place of games in education.

In this context, and the context of young people's media cultures, in which games play a significant role, it is clearly incumbent upon media educators to recognise and incorporate games into media curricula. The obligation here is to the interests of the students, not the comfort zone of the teachers. In this respect, getting to grips with games is perhaps no different from taking on other unfamiliar content in Media or English teaching, such as sports television, or Augustan poetry.

Perhaps the biggest shift in computer games in recent years has been the growth of online gaming. The vast populations of players who meet each other in MMORPGs (Massively Multiplayer Online Roleplaying Games) like the currently popular *World of Warcraft* are experiencing aspects of gaming quite different from those offered by offline games – most importantly, the opportunities to meet, roleplay, fight and otherwise engage with other players in the guise of avatars. These differences, along with the new experiences provided by vast virtual worlds that can be explored endlessly, provide new kinds of text and player engagement for media classrooms to explore, new kinds of play to understand, new kinds of narrative to conceptualise (Carr et al., 2006: Ch. 8).

In relation to the range of media encompassed in this book – print media, film, television, animation and computer games – the future also demands attention to new forms of authorship and exhibition, which are much less predictable than the growth of computer games. New forms of social networking and the generation and sharing of content by users have certainly made the transformation of 'audiences' into 'producers' a kind of reality, though whether this will really shift relations of power in the production and consumption of media texts remains to be seen. The DIY ethic and aesthetic of *MySpace*, *YouTube* and *Flickr* promise for the first time that work on the Internet will reach an audience with some kind of cultural substance; though the nature, durability and purposes of these communities is not well understood at present. Nevertheless, these shifts in agency and function in the Internet carry forward some of the possibilities envisaged in the traditional broadcast media's notion of 'user-generated content', and without the paternalism and practical limitations that this can sometimes seem to carry.

These developments will require changes throughout the customary objects of rhetorical inquiry for media education. The media industries here become, in some cases, harder to distinguish from audiences; indeed, movements like the Wiki ethic remain committed to the agency of user-groups. On the other hand, it is also apparent that sites aiming to democratise the creation and sharing of media representations can be rapidly assimilated into traditional corporate forms of ownership and control, as *MySpace* has been by Rupert Murdoch's News Corporation, and *You Tube* by Google. Nevertheless, while the nature of the media industries remains ambiguous here, it is clear that mass groups of users whom it has only been possible, historically, to regard as audiences, can now be seen, studied, analysed and conceptualised as media producers, publishers and exhibitors.

Finally, it may be worth trying to distinguish what in the world of new media might fall within the remit of media education and media studies, and what might not. It is not clear, for instance, that talking to or texting a friend using a mobile phone, or indeed using instant messaging software, is any more of interest to media education than using an analogue telephone was previously. Such technologies of communication, while they do represent important kinds of social change, are certainly of interest to researchers in the fields of sociology, Cultural Studies and Communication Studies; but this is not to say that they are a part of media literacy or media education. The critical distinguishing factor, perhaps, is the distinction between functions of communication and representation in new technologies. All utterances will, of course, perform both functions; but the interest of media education has traditionally been primarily in representation. 'Communication' is not usually seen as a 'key concept' in media education; 'representation' most certainly is. Buckingham, for instance, argues for four key concepts: *production, language, representation*, and *audience* (2003: 53). While aspects of communication play a part in how 'languages' are conceived, certainly, it is the representational aspect of media texts which is important: how they construct the world. Therefore, the use of a mobile phone to talk to a friend seems not to be a part of media literacy (and requires no real intervention from media education to develop competence of critical understanding). The use of the same phone to take photos or videos of an event, and the subsequent use of such material as part of a website, or an act of 'citizen journalism', clearly do involve complex, sustained acts of representation directed at wider audiences, and as such clearly do invite critical consideration, and can thus be seen within the concept of media literacy as we have developed it in this book. The alternative would be for media education to reconsider how it constructs 'communication' as part of its conceptual field and at the same time to move beyond text-focused models of media literacy to include something like 'media oracy', perhaps.

DIGITAL TECHNOLOGIES: REVOLUTION OR EVOLUTION?

In our model of media literacy, we identified production as one of our semiotic processes. This provides, we think, the right context in which to consider the significance of digital technologies. They are new tools with which young people can accomplish their expressive and critical purposes. They do not displace the old tools; indeed, in Chapter 3 we explored a media form which depends on old-fashioned drawing. They do represent a kind of revolution, as the mass media have been said to do more generally and, as McLuhan argued, the Gutenberg revolution similarly did half a millennium ago (McLuhan, 1962). They do make new things possible. However, we wish to resist a particular rhetoric which pervades discussions of new media, whether among teachers, academics, policymakers or the public at large, which we have termed the *rhetoric of rupture* (Burn and Durran, 2006). This rhetoric encourages us to think that the digital world is newly forged and completely different from what went before. Children's brains are literally changing, being 'rewired' (Tapscott, 1988; Prensky, 2001). Digital media present magical solutions to an array of social problems, and in particular have the capacity to transform learning (Gee, 2003).

Our position is more cautious. Our own research in digital authorship suggests that the work of the teacher is at least as important as the technology (Reid et al., 2002). It also suggests that children cannot be assumed to be 'digital natives' (Prensky, 2001), who spontaneously know how to use digital technologies. Indeed, the research suggests that they learn very quickly how to use forms of digital *communication* such as instant messaging, which is now almost universally used by young people in Europe; but are much less likely to use authoring softwares to make their own websites, edit their own videos, compose and edit their own music (de Smedt et al., 2006). In a prescient essay of the early 1980s, Raymond Williams argued that the technologies of media production were likely to become much more widely distributed, and would, like telephones and tape-recorders, teach their users how to use them; and this would lead to profound social change in forms of representation and power (Williams, 1989). In fact, it seems as if the proportion of the population who actually use digital authoring tools in any developed way are a self-selected (and often self-taught) minority, the digital successors to the minority who, in the twentieth century, would have had their own darkrooms rather than just taking snapshots. The power (and exclusiveness) of auto-didacticism and peer pedagogy are factors Williams failed to predict.

Our argument is that this (admittedly substantial) minority group currently occupies a critical space between the professional and the domestic spheres; and that this is exactly the space in which media education should locate itself, offering the experience of the few to the many, levelling the playing-field.

Perhaps the biggest impact digital tchnologies have made on media education over the past ten years is simply bringing creative production work within the reach of all schools. The advent of i-movie bundled with Macs provided the first 'free' editing software, leading to initiatives in the UK such as BECTa's Digital Video pilot project, in which 50 schools were given an i-mac and a digital camcorder, to see what kind of creative uses they would make of digital video filming and editing (Reid et al., 2002). The problem posed by the Mac platform for the majority of schools committed to PCs was subsequently solved by the arrival of Microsoft Moviemaker 2, which, while far from perfect, now allows 'free', intuitive editing for all schools.

In some ways, then, Williams's vision is proving prophetic. For media education, the centre of gravity is shifting from the analysis of media texts to the production of them. As Buckingham and Sefton-Green argued in 1994, and we continue to argue in this book, the development of a critical grasp of the systems of meaning-making which operate in media texts is best achieved by making them.

If the most significant impact of digital authoring tools is their wide distribution, it is also true that they change the processes of authorship in specific ways which are beneficial to learning. We have explored in the chapters where they are most directly relevant certain specific affordances of the digital medium, such as iteration, feedback, convergence and distribution. These affordances are important, and change what can be done in specific ways. However, there are larger questions about what has happened over the past decade, as representational media such as photography, film and television have converged with computers. The media have changed in profound ways and so must our understanding of the function of computers, not least their cultural function. Lev Manovich (1988), in his wide-ranging account of digital media, *The Language of New Media*, relates two parallel narratives, both beginning in the 1830s. One is of Babbage's Analytical Engine, the precursor to the modern computer, which sets off a story of the computer as information-processor. The other is of Daguerre's Daguerrotype, the precursor to the camera, which initiates a history of technologies of representation, from photography through cinema to television. Manovich's point is that in recent years these two histories have converged in what we call 'new media', so that they are composed, in Manovich's terms, of the 'cultural layer' and the 'computer layer'.

From the perspective of media educators and schools, we suggest that this story is particularly pertinent. Schools can be said to have inherited the computer as information-processor, as we suggested above, with no sense of wider cultural functions. In this respect, the ICT 'revolution' in schools does not know what to make of its technology: or more particularly, of the cultural and semiotic aspects of it. When ICT handled spreadsheets, databases and control systems it knew what it was doing, and how it was acting upon a part of the wider world, how it was located within a domain of educational knowledge and practice, and how this related to domains of professional knowledge and practice in the adult world. Now that it can do what Disney, the BBC, Eisenstein and even Shigeru Miyamoto of Nintendo do (and formerly did exclusively), it has no obvious way to make sense of these new cultural functions, not having the years of puzzling over narrative structure, aesthetic functions, cultural politics and audience behaviours which are the inheritance of media educators. As evidence that the ICT curriculum has failed to grasp the new functions its technology performs, we need only glance at the official national prescription in England and Wales. The word *culture* predictably does not appear in the ICT programme of study for 11–14-year-olds. Rather more surprisingly, neither does the word *communication*, although this curriculum domain is named as Information and Communication Technology. By contrast, the word 'information' occurs 17 times.

Copyright © 2002 Photographica, Ake Borgstrom, www.photographica.nu/219.htm. Reproduced with permission.

FIGURE 10.1 *Babbage's Analytical Engine, brass Daguerrotype lens, and the Acorn Archimedes: the first multimedia computer to arrive in Parkside in 1988.*

At the same time, the image of computer as information-processor may have done damage to our understanding of the relationship between culture and mind. Bruner argues that the metaphor of mind as computational machine typical of the 'cognitive revolution' in psychology interrupted the development of cultural models of mind of the kind he proposes (Bruner, 1990). So, while ICT in education may suffer from an inadequate notion of the computer's cultural functions, it may similarly suffer from inadequate cognitive models of what kinds of learning and development can benefit from digital technologies.

On the other hand, media educators, who in the UK have a long if fragmented history of interpreting the cultural attributes and representational
functions of photography, film and television, have no obvious way to understand the profound implications of these cultural practices becoming
computable. Early research in the use of digital video in schools has managed
to identify particular affordances of the medium, but not in the depth that
Manovich proposes. Indeed, it is often hard to identify the specific benefits of
the digital medium in much of this research, as opposed to the benefits simply
of making video with school students. Within a Cultural Studies approach
such as the one suggested by Buckingham and Sefton-Green (1994), it is certainly possible to delineate how uses of digital media in schools can take
account of newly emergent digital cultures in young people's lives. However,
they also suggest that the whole attitude of media education to notions such
as 'text' and 'audience' might have to change dramatically; and it is changes in
the textual structures of new media that Manovich proposes.

If the problem here were only an issue of lack of mutual incomprehension
between media and ICT specialists, it would be bad enough, given that they
use the same technologies, and that in spite of what they do children and
young people will increasingly make creative use of these media in their own
lives in ways which respect no such boundaries. However, there is a further
problem for media educators, which is a blurring of boundaries between
rhetorics of media literacy and of e-learning in the public and educational
domains. There is no room to document this exhaustively here, but the principle is clear enough. A confusion between the two suggests that all uses of
digital media in education count as media literacy and, conversely, that media
literacy is only about *digital* media.

In the coming years we anticipate an urgent need to oppose this kind of
blurring. The use of digital media across the curriculum may be termed e-learning: that is for others to decide. It is certainly not media literacy, however: it has
no clear relation with the critical or cultural aspects of media literacy, and,
despite frequent claims to creativity, it is not at all clear that creativity means the
same thing here as it does for us in this book. Furthermore, media literacy is not
confined to digital technologies: the work on comicstrips we described in
Chapter 2 was confined to pencil crayons and felt-tip pens; and the filming of
hospital dramas we described in Chapter 5, although it used digital cameras, did
not exploit any affordances that were specifically digital.

To simplify the argument: as David Buckingham has often asserted, learning *through* the media (of which e-learning is a subset) is not the same thing as
learning *about* the media. E-learning is *not* media literacy.

We hope the approaches we have borrowed from Cultural Studies, Social
Semiotics and cultural psychology avoid these pitfalls and confusions, and
offer some way forward. At the same time, as we have argued, we as media

educators need to learn to understand these newly computable media forms. If the media literacy of the children we teach increasingly contains views of the world in which narratives are formed of numerical representations, montage is to be found in the interactive loops of game sequences as well as the familiar juxtapositions of film shots, and characters behave as programmed modules as well as narrative entities, then our familiar conceptual apparatus will need amending. However, the lesson of Manovich is that, while the future demands change, history is equally important. We need an eye on the exciting possibilities of new media, and the changing social practices which accompany them; but we should keep the other eye on the rich cultural and semiotic histories of the 'old media' which are still with us.

CONCLUSION: MEDIA LITERACY IN PRACTICE

Jack was a student at Parkside some years ago. He struggled with print-based literacies, and the motivation needed to complete exam assignments. His strengths were in music, dance and media. He played drums in a school rock band, and edited the band's video on the school editing software. After his exams, he came back to compere demonstration break dance sessions in school assemblies during an arts week, when most of his peers were enjoying post-exam holidays. His music video, for the band's college anthem 'Ride', can be seen on the CD-ROM.

One of his GCSE media coursework projects was an advert for an imaginary trainer, which he and his partner called 'Odin: footwear of the Gods'. The advert showed a slow-motion basketball slam-dunk sequence, followed by a partly choreographed, partly improvised celebratory dance, featuring close-ups of the feet shod in the divine shoes. The percussive nature of the soundtrack underlines the aggression of the slam-dunk; the rise and fall of the melody echoes the leap of the player and the arc of the ball; the cultural references of the musical genre amplify the cultural tastes encoded in the piece, and the social identities bound up in it.

Sport becomes dance; dance becomes sport. Digital music is recruited by a boy experienced in DJ technologies to supplement the bodily rhythms of basketball and dance. Aspiration, pleasure and peer group allegiance are signified through a digital bricolage which is partly made up of informally acquired skills and cultural experiences, partly of formally taught techniques and knowledge.

Jack's advert and music video exemplify most of the elements of what we call media literacy. They show how creative media production for teenagers can work as a focal point for many parts of their cultural lives; indeed, it can articulate what Williams called relations between elements in a whole way of life (1961). These films hover productively on the borderline between the commercial discourses of media texts and their status as art forms. They emerge from the contexts of the classroom and informal after-school education yet they exceed their well-regulated boundaries. They are made with the digital tools of contemporary media production but they also incorporate the expressive work of the body, the physical materiality of a drum-kit and the culturally salient locations of the schoolyard. They take the global discourses of hip-hop, music video and sportswear ads, and infuse them with local meanings, enthusiasms and imagery.

Parkside's efforts to realise what media literacy might be in the twenty-first century, and how it might be developed, have partly been the efforts of curriculum design, theoretical modelling, research and pedagogic experiment. We hope we have given some idea, in this book, of what these processes might look like. However, the real payoff is in what happens when these rational but necessarily partial procedures meet up with students like Jack. This meeting, with all its contingent messiness, patient negotiations and cultural complexity is media literacy in practice.

REFERENCES

Andrews, R. and Haythornthwaite, C. (2007) 'Introducing e-learning research', in R. Andrews and C. Haythornthwaite (eds), *Handbook of e-Learning Research*. London: Sage.

Andrews, R., Torgerson, C., Beverton, S., Locke, T., Low, G., Robinson, A. and Zhu, D. (2004) 'The effect of grammar teaching (syntax) in English on 5 to 16 year olds' accuracy and quality in written composition', in *Research Evidence in Education Library*. London: EPPI Centre, Social Science Research Unit, Institute of Education (http://eppi.ioe.ac.uk/reel).

Archer, S. (2007) 'Media education, music video and glocalisation', in A. Burn and C. Durrant (eds), *Media Teaching*. Norwood SA: AATE, NATE and Wakefield Press.

Aufderheide, P. (1997) 'Media literacy: from a report of the national leadership conference on media literacy', pp. 79–86 in R. Kubey (ed.), *Media Literacy in the Information Age*. New Brunswick, NJ: Transaction Books.

Bakhtin, M.M. (1968) *Rabelais and His World*, trans. H. Islowsky. Cambridge, MA: MIT Press.

Baker, M. (1984) *A Haunt of Fears: The Strange History of the British Horror Comics Campaign*. London: Pluto.

Banaji, S. and Burn, A. (2006) *Rhetorics of Creativity*. London: Creative Partnership.

Barthes, R. ([1957] 1972) *Mythologies*, trans. A. Lavers. New York: Hill & Wang.

Barthes, R. (1978) 'The Third Meaning', in *Image–Music-Text*, trans. S. Heath. New York: Hill & Wang.

Bazalgette, C., Earle, W., Grahame, J., Poppy, J., Reid, M. and West, A. (eds) (2000) *Moving Images in the Classroom*. London: British Film Institute.

Bearne, E. (2003) 'Rethinking literacy: communication, representation and text', *Literacy*, 37 (3): 98.

Beavis, C. (2001) 'Digital culture, digital literacies: expanding the notions of text', pp. 145–161 in C. Beavis and C. Durrant (eds), *P(ICT)ures of English: Teachers, Learners and Technology*. Adelaide: Wakefield Press.

Bennett, A. (2000) *Popular Music and Youth Culture*. Basingstoke: Palgrave Macmillan.

Bigum, C., Durrant, C., Green, B., Honan, E., Lankshear, C., Morgan, W., Murray, J., Snyder, I. and Wild, M. (1998) *Digital Rhetorics: Literacies and Technologies in Education – Current Practices and Future Direction*. Canberra: DEETYA.

Boden, M. (1990) *The Creative Mind: Myths and Mechanisms*. London: Weidenfeld & Nicolson.

Bordwell, D. and Thompson, K. (2003) *Film Art: An Introduction*, 7th edn. New York: McGraw-Hill.

Bourdieu, P. (1984) *Distinction: A Social Critique of the Judgement of Taste*. London: Routledge.

Bruner, J. (1990) *Acts of Meaning*. Cambridge, MA: Harvard University Press.

Buckingham, D. (1993) *Children Talking Television: The Making of Television Literacy*. London: Falmer.

Buckingham, D. (1996) *Moving Images: Understanding Children's Emotional Responses to Television*. Manchester: Manchester University Press.

Buckingham, D. (2003) *Media Education: Literacy, Learning and Contemporary Culture*. Cambridge: Polity Press.

Buckingham, D. and Bragg, S. (2003) *Young People, Sex and the Media: The Facts of Life?* London: Palgrave Macmillan.

Buckingham, D. and Jones, K. (2001) 'New Labour's cultural turn: some tensions in contemporary educational and cultural policy', *Journal of Educational Policy*, 16 (1): 1–14.

Buckingham, D. and Sefton-Green, J. (1994) *Cultural Studies Goes to School*. London: Taylor & Francis.

Buckingham, D. and Sefton-Green, J. (2004) 'Gotta catch 'em all: structure, agency or pedagogy in children's media culture', in J. Tobin (ed.), *Nintentionality: Pikachu's Global Adventure*. Durham, NC: Duke University Press.

Buckingham, D., Grahame, J. and Sefton-Green, J. (1995) *Making Media*. London: English and Media Centre.

Buckingham, D., Harvey, I. and Sefton-Green, J. (1999) 'The difference is digital? Digital technology and student media production', *Convergence*, 5: 4.

Buckingham, D., Sefton-Green, J. and Fraser, P. (2000) 'Making the grade: evaluating student production in Media Studies', pp. 129–153 in J. Sefton-Green and R. Sinker (eds), *Evaluating Creativity: Making and Learning by Young People*. London and New York: Routledge.

Burn, A. (1996) 'Spiders, werewolves and bad girls: children reading horror', *Changing English*, October.

Burn, A. (1998) 'The robot in the cornfield: visual media across the curriculum', *The English Magazine*, 39 (Autumn), pp. 27–32.

Burn, A. (1999) 'Grabbing the werewolf: digital freezeframes, the cinematic still and technologies of the social', *Convergence*, 3 (4): 80-101.

Burn, A. (2000) 'Repackaging the slasher movie: the digital unwriting of film in the secondary classroom', *English in Australia*, Spring, pp. 24–34.

Burn, A. (2004) 'Potter-Literacy – from book to game and back again; literature, film, game and cross-media literacy', *Papers: Explorations into Children's Literature*, 14 (2): 5–17, reprinted in *Contemporary Literary Criticism*, Vol. 217, April 2006.

Burn, A. (2007) 'Making the moving image: literacies, communities, digital technologies', in R. Andrews and C. Haythornthwaite (eds), *Handbook of E-learning Research*. London: Sage.

Burn, A. (forthcoming) 'Writing computer games: game-literacy and new-old narratives', *L1: Educational Studies in Language and Literature*, 6 (2).

Burn, A. and Durran, J. (2006) 'Digital anatomies: analysis as production in media education', in D. Buckingham and R. Willett (eds), *Digital Generations*. New York: Lawrence Erlbaum.

Burn, A. and Durrant, C. (2007) *Media Teaching*. Norwood, SA: AATE, NATE and Wakefield Press.

Burn, A. and Leach, J. (2004) 'ICT and the moving image', in R. Andrews (ed.), *The Impact of ICT on Literacy Education*. London: Routledge-Falmer.

Burn, A. and Parker, D. (2003a) 'Tiger's Big Plan: multimodality and the moving image', in G. Kress and C. Jewitt (eds), *Multimodal Literacy*. New York: Peter Lang.

Burn, A. and Parker, D. (2003b) *Analysing Media Texts*. London: Continuum.

Burn, A. and Reed, K. (1999) 'Digiteens: media literacies and digital technologies in the secondary classroom', *English in Education*, 33 (3): 5–20.

Burn, A., Franks, A. and Nicholson, H. (2001) 'Looking for fruit in the jungle: head injury, multimodal theatre, and the politics of visibility', *RIDE* (Research in Drama Education), 6 (2): 161–77.

Burn, A., Brindley, S., Reid, M. et al. (2001) 'The rush of images: a research report on a study of digital editing and the moving image', *English in Education*, 35 (2): 34–47.

Caillois, R. (2001) *Man, Play and Games*, trans. Meyer Barash. Chicago, IL: University of Illinois Press.

Carr, D., Buckingham, D., Burn, A. and Schott, G. (2006) *Computer Games: Text, Narrative, Play*. Cambridge: Polity Press.

Carroll, N. (1990) *The Philosophy of Horror: Or, Paradoxes of the Heart*. New York: Routledge.

Carter, A. (1991) *The Virago Book of Fairy Tales*. London: Virago.

Cassell, J. and Jenkins, H. (1998) *From Barbie to Mortal Kombat: Gender and Computer Games*. Cambridge, MA: MIT Press.

Clarke, J., Hall, S., Jefferson, T. and Roberts, B. (1976) 'Subcultures, cultures and class', in S. Hall and T. Jefferson (eds), *Resistance through Rituals*. London: Routledge.

Clover, C. (1993) *Men, Women and Chainsaws*. London: British Film Institute.

Connor, S. (1990) *Postmodernism – An Introduction to Theories of the Contemporary*. Oxford: Blackwell.

Cope, B. and Kalantzis, M. (eds) (2000) *Multiliteracies: Literacy Learning and the Design of Social Futures*. London: Routledge.

Cranmer, S.J. (2006) *Families' Uses of the Internet*. PhD thesis, Institute of Education, University of London.

Creed, B. (1986) 'Horror and the monstrous feminine: an imaginary abjection', *Screen*, 27, 44–70.

De Block, L., Buckingham, D. and Banaji, S. (2005) *Children in Communication about Migration* (CHICAM). Final Report of an EC-funded project, at www.childrenyouthandmediacentre.co.uk; project website: www.chicam.net.

De Smedt, T., Verniers, P. and Bevort, E. (2006) *Mediappro: Final Report*. Available at: www.mediappro.org.

DES (Department of Education and Science) (1988) *English for Ages 5 to 11* (The Cox Report). London: HMSO.

Engeström, Y. (1999) *Lernen durch Expansion*. Marburg: BdWi-Verlag; trans. Falk Seeger (Introduction to the German edition of *Learning by Expanding*)

Fairclough, N. (1989) *Language and Power*. London: Longman.

FEWG (1999) *Making Movies Matter*. London: British Film Institute.

Foucault, M. (1976) *The History of Sexuality*, Vol. I. Harmondsworth: Penguin.

Frasca, G. (1999) 'Ludology meets narratology: similitude and differences between (video) games and narrative'. Available at: www.ludology.org/ (accessed 2 February 2007). Finnish version originally published in *Parnasso*, No. 3, Helsinki.

Fraser, P. and Oram, B. (2003) *Teaching Digital Production*. London: British Film Institute.

Gee, J. (2003) *What Video Games Have to Teach Us about Learning and Literacy*. Basingstoke: Palgrave.

Gibson, M. (2000) 'Memories of reading: British girls and their comics', in N. Moody (ed.), *Consuming for Pleasure*. Liverpool: John Moores Press.

Goffman, E. (1959) *The Presentation of Self in Everyday Life*. New York: Anchor Books.

Goodwyn, A. (2004) *English Teaching and the Moving Image*. London: RoutledgeFalmer.

Grahame, J. (2002) *The Key Stage 4 Media Pack*. London: English and Media Centre.

Green, B. (1988) 'Subject-specific literacy and school learning: a focus on writing'. *Australian Journal of Education*, 32 (2): 156–79.

Gutierrez, K., Rymes, B. and Larson, J. (1995) 'Script, counterscript, and underlife in the classroom – James Brown versus *Brown* v. *Board of Education*', *Harvard Educational Review*, 65: 445–71.

Haas Dyson, A. (1997) *Writing Superheroes: Contemporary Childhood, Popular Culture, and Classroom Literacy*. New York: Teachers College Press.

Halliday, M.A.K. (1985) *An Introduction to Functional Grammar*. London: Arnold.

Halliday, M.A.K. (1989) *Spoken and Written Language*. Oxford: Oxford University Press.

Harvey, I., Parker, D. and Skinner, M. (2002) *Being Seen, Being Heard*. London: Youth Work Press.

Hodge, R. and Kress, K. (1988) *Social Semiotics*. Cambridge: Polity Press.

Hodge, R. and Tripp, D. (1986) *Children and Television*. Cambridge: Polity Press.

Holbrook, D. (1961/1967) *English for Maturity*. Cambridge: Cambridge University Press.

Jenkins, H. (1992) *Textual Poachers: Television Fans and Participatory Culture*. New York: Routledge.

Jewitt, C. (2005) 'Multimodality, "reading", and "writing" for the 21st century', *Discourse*, 26 (3): 315–31.

Juul, J. (2003) 'The game, the player, the world: looking for a heart of gameness', in M. Copier and J. Raessens (eds), *Level Up*. Digital Games Research conference proceedings, University of Utrecht, 4–6 November.

Kirwan, T., Learmonth, J., Sayer, M. and Williams, R. (2003) *Mapping Media Literacy*. London: British Film Institute/Independent Television.

Kress, G. (2003) *Literacy in the New Media Age*. New York: Routledge.

Kress, G. (2005) 'Communication now and in the future', *English*, 21, retrieved 16 May 2005 from www.qca.org.uk/12292.html.

Kress, G. and van Leeuwen, T. (2001) *Multimodal Discourse: The Modes and Media of Contemporary Communication*. London: Arnold.

Kress, G., Jewitt, C., Ogborn, J. and Tsatsarelis, C. (2001). *Multimodal Teaching and Learning. The Rhetorics of the Science Classroom*. London: Continuum.

Kress, K. and van Leeuwen, T. (1996) *Reading Images: The Grammar of Visual Design*. London: Routledge.

Lanham, R. (1993) *The Electronic Word: Democracy, Technology, and the Arts*. Chicago: University of Chicago Press.

Leadbeater, C. (2000). *Living on Thin Air: The New Economy with a Blueprint for the 21st Century*. London: Penguin.

Leavis, F.R. (1948) *The Great Tradition*. London: Chatto & Windus.

Leavis, F. and Thompson, D. (1933) *Culture and Environment*. London: Chatto & Windus.

Lunzer, E. and Gardiner, K. (eds) (1979) *The Effective Use of Reading*. London: Heinemann.

McDougall, J. (2006) *The Media Teacher's Book*. London: Hodder Education.

Mackereth, M. and Anderson, J. (2000) 'Computers, video games, and literacy: what do girls think?', *Australian Journal of Language and Literacy*, 23 (3): 184–95.

McLuhan, M. (1962) *The Gutenberg Galaxy: The Making of Typographic Man*. Toronto: University of Toronto Press.

McRobbie, A. (1978) *Jackie: An Ideology of Adolescent Femininity*, Occasional Paper. Birmingham Centre for Contemporary Cultural Studies.

McRobbie, A. (1991) *Feminism and Youth Culture: From Jackie to Just 17*. London: Macmillan.

Manovich, L. (1998) *The Language of New Media*. Cambridge, MA: MIT Press.

Messaris, P. (1994) *Visual Literacy: Image, Mind and Reality*. Oxford: Westview Press.

Metz, C. (1974) *Film Language*. Chicago, IL: Chicago University Press.

Millard, E. (1997) *Differently Literate: Boys, Girls and the Schooling of Literacy*. London: Falmer Press.

Morgan, W. (1997) *Critical Literacy in the Classroom: The Art of the Possible*. London: Routledge

Moseley, D., Higgins, S., Bramald, R., Hardman, F., Miller, J., Mroz, M., Tse, H., Newton, D., Thompson, I., Williamson, J., Halligan, J., Bramald, S., Newton, L., Tymms, P., Henderson, B. and Stout, J. (1999) *Ways Forward with ICT: Effective Pedagogy using Information and Communications Technology for Literacy and Numeracy in Primary Schools*. Newcastle: University of Newcastle.

Murray, J. (1998) *Hamlet on the Holodeck*. Cambridge, MA: MIT Press.

Neale, S. (1980) *Genre*. London: British Film Institute.

Neale, S. (2000) *Genre and Hollywood*. London: Routledge.

OFCOM (2005) 'What is media literacy?' Available at www.ofcom.org.uk/advice/media_literacy/of_med_lit/whatis/ (accessed 30 November 2006).

OFSTED (2000) *Section 10 Inspection Report on Parkside Community Collage*, May 2000.

OFSTED (2004) *English in Secondary Schools*. February 2004.

Ong, W. (1982) *Orality and Literacy: The Technologizing of the Word*. London: Methuen.

Opie, I. and Opie, P. (1959/2001) *The Lore and Language of Schoolchildren*. New York: New York Review of Books.

Parker, D. (1999) 'You've read the book, now make the film: moving image media, print literacy and narrative', *English in Education*, 33: 24–35.

Pelletier, C. (2005) 'The uses of literacy in studying computer games: comparing students' oral and visual representations of games', *ETPC*, 4 (1): 40–59.

Perrault, C. (1991) 'Little Red Riding Hood' (trans. A. Carter), in A. Carter, *The Virago Book of Fairy Tales*. London: Virago.

Prensky, M. (2001) 'Digital natives, digital immigrants'. Available at www.marcprensky.com (accessed 2 February 2007).

Propp, V. ([1928] 1968) *Morphology of the Folktale*, 2nd edn, trans. Lawrence Scott. Austin, TX: University of Texas.

Pullman, P. (1995–2000) *His Dark Materials (Northern Lights, 1995; The Subtle Knife, 1997; The Amber Spyglass, 2000)*. London: Scholastic.

QCA (2005a) *English 21/Playback: A National Conversation on the Future of English*. London: Qualifications and Curriculum Authority.

QCA (2005b) *Media Matters: A Review of Media Studies in Schools and Colleges*. London: Qualifications and Curriculum Authority.

Reid, M., Burn, A. and Parker, D. (2002) Evaluation Report of the BECTa Digital Video Pilot Project. Available at www.becta.org.uk/page_documents/research/dvreport_241002.pdf (accessed 2 February 2007).

Richards, C. (1995) 'Room to dance: girls' play and The Little Mermaid', pp. 141–150 in C. Bazalgette and D. Buckingham (eds), *In Front of the Children: Screen Entertainment and Young Audiences*. London: British Film Institute.

Robinson, K. (1999) *All Our Futures: Creativity, Culture and Education*. Sudbury, Suffolk: DfEE publications/National Advisory Committee on Creative and Cultural Education.

Rowling, J.K. (1998) *Harry Potter and the Chamber of Secrets*. London: Bloomsbury.

Salen, K. and Zimmerman, E. (2003) 'This is not a game: play in cultural environments', in M. Copier and J. Raessens (eds), *Level Up*. Digital Games Research conference proceedings, University of Utrecht, 4–6 November.

Saussure, F. de (1983) *Course in General Linguistics*, trans. Roy Harris. London: Duckworth.

Scruton, R. (1987) '"Expressionist education"', *Oxford Review of Education*, 13 (1): 39–44.

Sefton-Green, J. (ed.) (1999) *Digital Diversions*. London: UCL.

Sefton-Green, J. and Parker, D. (2000) *Edit-Play*. London: British Film Institute.

Sefton-Green, J. and Sinker, R. (eds) (2000) *Evaluating Creativity: Making and Learning by Young People*. London and New York: Routledge.

Seltzer, K. and Bentley T. (1999). *The Creative Age: Knowledge and Skills for the New Economy*. London: DEMOS.

Styles, M. and Watson, V. (1996) *Talking Pictures: Pictorial Texts and Young Readers*. London: Hodder & Stoughton.

Sutton-Smith, B. (2001) *The Ambiguity of Play*. Cambridge, MA: Harvard University Press.

Tapscott, D. (1998) *Growing Up Digital: The Rise of the Net Generation*. New York: McGraw Hill.

Thornton, S. (1995) *Club Cultures: Music, Media and Subcultural Capital*. Wesleyan University Press, distributed by University Press of New England. Middleton, CT.

Todorov, T. (1981) *Introduction to Poetics*, trans. Richard Howard. Minneapolis, MN: University of Minnesota Press.

Tyner, K. (1998) *Literacy in a Digital World: Teaching and Learning in the Age of Information*. New York: Lawrence Erlbaum Associates.

Van Leeuwen, T. (1999) *Speech, Music, Sound*. London: Macmillan.

Van Leeuwen, T. (2005) *Social Semiotics: An Introductory Textbook*. London: Routledge.

Vygotsky, L.S. ([1931] 1998) 'Imagination and creativity in the adolescent', pp. 151–66 in R. W. Rieber and A. S. Carton (eds), *The Collected works of L.S. Vygotsky*, Vol. 5. New York: Plenum Press.

Vygotsky, L.S. (1978) *Mind in Society*. Cambridge, MA: Harvard University Press.

Walker, M. ([1980] 2000) *The Lexicon of Comicana*. Available from Backinprint.com.

Walkerdine, V. (1997) *Daddy's Girl: Young Girls and Popular Culture*. London: Macmillan.

Willett, R. (2006) 'Constructing the digital tween: market discourse and girls' interests', pp. 278–93 in C. Mitchell and J. Reid Walsh (eds), *Seven Going on Seventeen: Tween Culture in Girlhood Studies*. Oxford: Peter Lang.

Williams, R. (1961) *The Long Revolution*. London: Chatto & Windus.

Williams, R. (1983) 'Drama in a dramatized society', pp. 11–21 in *Writing in Society*. London: Verso.

Williams, R. (1989) *What I Came to Say*. London: Hutchinson.

Willis, P. (1977) *Learning to Labour*. Aldershot: Ashgate.

Willis, P. (1990) *Common Culture*. Buckingham: Open University Press.

Zipes, J. (1982) *The Trials and Tribulations of Little Red Riding Hood: Versions of the Tale in Socio-Cultural Context*. London: Heinemann.

Zipes, J. (1983) *Fairy Tales and the Art of Subversion*. New York: Routledge.

FILM AND TV REFERENCES

Adamson, A. (2001) *Shrek*. USA: Dreamworks.

Altieri, K. (1992-95) *Batman: The Animated Series*. USA: Warner.

Besson, L. (1997) *The Fifth Element*. France: Société des Etablissements L. Gaumont.

Bird, B. (2004) *The Incredibles*. USA: Pixar/Disney.

Brock, J. and Unwin, P. (1986) *Casualty*. UK: BBC.

Burton, T. (1990) *Batman*. USA: Warner.

Cameron, J (1986) *Aliens*, USA, Fox.

Cameron, J. (1991) *Terminator 2: Judgment Day*. France/USA: Le Studio Canal+.

Clements, R. and Musker, J. (1989) *The Little Mermaid*. USA: Disney.

Columbus, C. (2002) *Harry Potter and the Chamber of Secrets*. USA: Warner.

Coppola, F.F. (1992) *Bram Stoker's Dracula*. USA: American Zoetrope.

Craven, W. (1984) *Nightmare on Elm Street*. USA: The Elm Street Venture.

Craven, W. (1996) *Scream*. USA: Dimension.

Crichton, M. (1994) *ER*. USA: Constant C Productions and others/Warner Television.

Demme, J. (1991) *The Silence of the Lambs*. USA: Orion Pictures.

Fowler, G. Jr (1957) *I Was a Teenage Werewolf*. USA: American International Pictures.

Groening, M. (1989) *The Simpsons*. USA: Fox.

Hay, A. and Bridgeman-Williams, E. (1999) *Holby City*. UK: BBC.

Hitchcock, A. (1960) *Psycho*. USA: Universal.

Honda, I. (1956) *Godzilla, King of the Monsters!* Japan: Toho Company.

Hooper, T. (1982) *Poltergeist*. USA: MGM.

Jeunet, J.-P. (2001) *Le Fabuleux destin d'Amélie Poulain*. France: Claudie Ossard Productions.

Jewison, N. (1967) *In the Heat of the Night*. USA: UA/Mirisch.

Lasseter, J. and Stanton, A. (1998) *A Bug's Life*. USA: Pixar/Disney.

Ocelot, M. (1998) *Kirikou et la sorcière*. France: Exposure.

Park, N. (1989) *A Grand Day Out with Wallace and Gromit*. UK: Aardman.

Power, J. (1993) *The Tommyknockers*. USA: Konigsberg/Sanitsky.

Radomski, E. and Timm, B. (1993) *Batman and the Mask of the Phantasm*. USA: Warner.

Raimi, S. (1995–2001) *Xena, Warrior Princess*. USA: Renaissance Pictures Universal Television.

Raimi, S. (2002) *Spiderman*. USA: Warner.

Redmond, P. (1978) *Grange Hill*. UK: BBC/Mersey Television.

Rose, A. (1989) *Byker Grove*. UK: BBC/Zenith Entertainment.

Russell, C. (1994) *The Mask*. USA: Dark Horse Entertainment.

Scott, R. (1979) *Alien*. UK: Fox/Brandywine Productions.

Scott, R. (2000) *Gladiator*. UK/USA: Dreamworks/Universal.

Wallace, T.L. (1990) *Stephen King's It*. USA: Green-Epstein.

Whedon, I. (1997–2003) *Buffy the Vampire Slayer*. USA: Mutant Enemy 20th Century Fox Television.

Who Wants to be a Millionaire? UK: Celador.

GAME REFERENCES

Age of Empires (1997) Ensemble/Microsoft.

Call of Duty (2003) Infinity Ward/Activision.

Crash Bandicoot (1996) Naughty Dog/Sony.

Goldeneye 007 (1997) Rare/Nintendo.

Harry Potter and the Chamber of Secrets (2002) Knowwonder/Electronic Arts.

Hitman 2: Silent Assassin (2002) IO Interactive/Eidos.

Lord of the Rings: The Return of the King (2003) Hypnos: EA.

Manhunt (2003) Rockstar/Rockstar.

Resident Evil 2 (1998) Capcom/Capcom.

Silent Hill (1999) Konami/Konami.

Spiderman (2002) LTI Gray matter/Activision.

The Sims (2000) Maxis/Electronic Arts.

Tomb Raider 4: The Last Revelation (1999) Core/Eidos.

INDEX